THE FIRST WORLD WAR
IN 100 OBJECTS

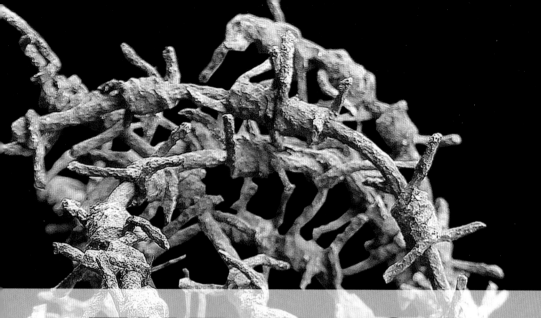

THE FIRST
WORLD WAR
IN 100 OBJECTS

PETER DOYLE

The History Press

To those who served with integrity: on land, at sea,
in the air and at home

First published 2014

The History Press
The Mill, Brimscombe Port
Stroud, Gloucestershire, GL5 2QG
www.thehistorypress.co.uk

British Library Cataloguing in Publication Data.
A catalogue record for this book is available from the British Library.

ISBN 978 0 7524 8811 0

Typesetting and origination by The History Press

Printed in India

Contents

100 Objects

THE OUTCOME OF the Great War of 1914–18 has shaped the world we live in, yet it is difficult to understand. One hundred years after this cataclysmic episode erupted from the confines of 'a little problem in the Balkans', it continues to both shock and fascinate in equal measure. The war that followed it, ignited from its dying embers – though both complex and grandiose in scale – can at least be reduced and distilled into a crusade against evil, of the rights of human beings to escape bondage and repression. These concepts are more complex in the Great War, discussion of which still promotes argument and dissent.

For example, while most of us are at ease with the idea of an armada of landing craft dispatching its living cargo onto the beaches of Normandy on D-Day, 6 June 1944, few of us really understand the motivations behind the landings at Gallipoli on 25 April 1915. And it is difficult for us to escape from the present and consider the past with a wholly objective viewpoint; typically, we have difficulty coming to terms with the sheer number of casualties from this terrible war. So while the Allied dead from El Alamein are around 2,350, those from the first day of the Somme are 19,240. The reason why the scale of suffering on the battlefield should be so high is still something with which people have difficulty coming to terms.

British recruiting posters issued as cigarette cards.

7

At a personal level, one of the advantages we have in considering the Second World War is that we perhaps have more sympathy with the time frame. Things seem reasonably familiar to us. With the creation of the jazz age came the development of modernism – houses were sleeker, their contents functional, their residents' lives not a million miles away from our own. Images of London high streets in 1940 differ dramatically from those of 1910; there are fewer horses, a greater number of motor vehicles, more garish shop signs and less uniform people. And it helps that we have a direct connection with people who lived through rationing, the formation of the welfare state, the era of make do and mend and the chirpy voices of chipper radio comedians and music hall stars. But peering at films of the imperial powers in the run-up to the Great War, it is difficult for us to make a direct comparison of our lives with those of our forebears. The everyday life of the average citizen seems so different, with its class structures and food and clothing that are so different to our own; the average person in the street seems so remote to us. And our direct connection with those who lived during the Great War is very nearly extinguished – the few people still around who were alive at the time were too young to understand its significance and are now perhaps too old to recall with understanding that life, so remote 100 years on.

But the Great War has left us with a rich legacy of writing, art, music and poetry. This legacy allows us to perceive what life was like during the period. By their nature, many of these records present a very particular view of the war, one informed by the natural anti-war reaction of that generation. Much of the writing from participants in the Great War that appeared in the fertile ten-year period after the war is disillusioned with it, distanced from its purpose, disassociated with the ideals that led people to join the forces and serve their country.

For many today, jaundiced with conflict and high ideals, the idea of mass recruitment to fight 'for King and Country' seems alien. Seeking to understand the lives of our families, to connect with their experiences, is how many people now connect with the past that is the First

World War. In many cases, their starting points are the creased photographs, the fading postcards and the tarnished medals. In the United Kingdom, soldiers, sailors and airmen were awarded campaign medals that, fortunately, were named. This act of naming allows the narrative of both the medal group and the person who was awarded it to be interpreted and read. Each campaign medal is essentially the same yet ultimately different. Coupled with the availability of records through archives and the Internet, family historians are able to unlock the stories of their objects and the actions of their forebears.

As one writer has put it, 'Objects hold within themselves the worlds of their creators'. They represent a time capsule, a direct link with the time in which they were made. But they are also mute witnesses to events, recording devices that might allow a clearer understanding of a time or event – if only we can read them. Each object has a story, a unique narrative that is there to be interpreted, to be read. For many of the objects associated with war, that narrative is plain to see: machine guns were intended to kill, gas masks to protect. But like any story, there are subtexts – the suitability of these objects for the job at hand and the value that was placed on them by their user or captor. While objects in a pristine state might tell of storage and disengagement, others with wear relate to us that they were there – soldiers' equipment with regimental numbers, spoons sharpened to take on more than one role, abandoned and excavated objects found on the battlefield. Each of these allows us to explore a narrative of their creation but also of their subsequent use.

As Nick Saunders and Paul Cornish have put it, 'The objects of the Great War have a curious and unique character. More than any other kind of matter they seem to exist in a seemingly infinite number of [...] worlds simultaneously, and so can appear as worthless trash, cherished heirloom, historical artefact, memory item or commercially valuable souvenir.' The objects selected for this book fall into one or all of these categories.

The basis for the book is an examination of surviving objects and the interpretation of their individual narratives. The number of objects selected – 100 – is an arbitrary one and constraining; there are so many objects to chose from, each of which would add to the patchwork of our understanding. The objects had to be extant: on public display, in a national museum or local collection or dug from the ground from an archaeo-logical investigation. They had to be individual – in my view, it was not good enough to be generic – as each individual object has its own story to relate. Scale and rarity were not significant factors. While some, like the Douaumont Ossuary or the Loos football, are unique, others, such as the Adrian helmet or Mills grenade, are common. But the discussion relates directly to the object illustrated.

Can an exploration of 100 objects be sufficient to bind together a coherent story of the tumultuous episodes of 1914 to 1918? It is a hard task, and the selection of the objects was difficult (though guided by the principles set out above). I had to cover the many fronts, nations and phases of the war, the war on land and in the air, the war on the home front. But what can be achieved is an examination of the high points, of way markers that allow us to connect directly with the events and times of this war. And that is why this book is set out in the manner it is.

The book opens with 'Nations to War', the descent of the European nations into war, and examining rival-ries, arms races, Imperial ambitions. With almost 10 million military deaths and 21 million wounded, the next section deals with 'The Soldier', followed later by 'War at Sea, in the Air'. 'First Moves 1914' examines the developing war in northern Europe in the last quar-ter of 1914, and considers the descent into the static warfare that typifies the Great War. The next section, 'Developing Trench Warfare', examines the peculiar-ity of the war in the trenches. 'The War Deepens and Expands' and 'Plumbing New Depths' both consider the phenomenon of industrial slaughter on the Great War battlefield, and the means by which the trench deadlock was broken. The war on the Home Front, and the after-math of the conflict, are examined in 'At Home'.

Nations to War

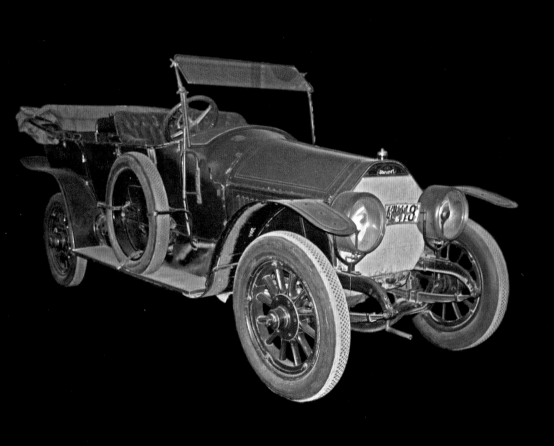

I

Archduke Franz Ferdinand's car

IN 1914, THE world descended into a war that would see over 16 million people killed and would be fought on four continents. Yet, when war came, it was perhaps expected. Since the later part of the nineteenth century, the relationship between the most powerful nations of continental Europe – France and Germany – had been a difficult one. The Franco-Prussian War of 1870–71 had ended with France roundly beaten by the Prussians and had precipitated the end of the rule of Napoleon III and the proclamation of the Third Republic. With the termination of this war came the unification of the German states and the loss of the provinces of Alsace and Lorraine, a loss that would be viewed with great bitterness by the French. Elsewhere in Europe, old empires were crumbling and contracting.

Country of origin:
Austria-Hungary

Date of construction:
1911

Location:
Heeresgeschichtliches Museum,
Vienna, Austria

In the Balkans, the complex ethnicity of the region led to tensions and the creation of the 'Balkan Powder Keg' in the wake of the slowly crumbling integrities of the Hapsburg and Ottoman empires. The disintegration of these edifices had created new states – Serbia, Montenegro, Bulgaria and Greece among them – each jockeying, aggressively, for position in the new world order. And it was the tension created by the Austro-Hungarian annexation of the former Ottoman province of Bosnia-Herzegovina in 1908 that created the tensions between Serbia and Austria-Hungary that would violently erupt into world war after the assassination of Archduke Franz Ferdinand, heir presumptive to the Austro-Hungarian imperial throne, in Sarajevo on 28 June 1914.

Franz Ferdinand was shot with his wife, Sophie, on the streets of Sarajevo while travelling in this 1911 Gräff and Stift Double Phaeton open car, today preserved in the *Heeresgeschichtliches* Museum in Vienna. Car manufacturers Gräff and Stift had been in business since 1904 and had made a name for themselves as the manufacturers of luxurious models; but with the killing of Franz Ferdinand, their most notable vehicle instantly became one of the most infamous in history. This impressive four-cylinder 32hp black car, the property of Lieutenant Colonel Count Franz von Harrach, the archduke's bodyguard, had been deemed a suitable vehicle for members of the Hapsburg imperial family to be seen in. Today, it remains one of the most important artefacts of the war, representative of both the opulence of antebellum imperial Europe and the tragedy of the spark that ignited the powder keg of world conflict. Its single bullet hole, to the rear of the car, was the first of many bullets to be fired over the next four years. Yet the event could have been so very different.

Death notice of the assassination of Archduke Franz Ferdinand.

With orders to travel to Bosnia at the command of Emperor Franz Josef, the archduke was to review the military manoeuvres and visit the city of Sarajevo to open the State Museum with his wife, Sophie. Neither was to know that the 'Black Hand', a group committed to freeing Bosnia from Hapsburg rule and joining with Serbia, had targeted them for assassination. Arriving at Sarajevo on the morning of 28 June 1914, the royal couple transferred to the open-topped Double Phaeton car. Travelling as part of a motorcade of six, the third car was the archduke's; the first car, due to a misunderstanding, was carrying the security officers. Only Colonel Harrach was there to secure the safety of the archduke and his wife. Inspecting the military barracks early on in the day, Franz Ferdinand was en route to the town hall when, at 10.10 a.m., the Black Hand threw a bomb at the car. It bounced off and rolled under the vehicle behind, disabling it and wounding its occupants. Severely shaken, the archduke and his wife went on to the town hall to attend a brief reception; after just over thirty minutes, they left to visit those wounded in the earlier attack. This proved to be a deadly mistake.

In a state of confusion, the driver of the archduke's car took a wrong turn into Franz Josef Street. Reversing, he stalled the car. Gavrilo Princip, a 19-year-old member of the Black Hand, grasped his opportunity, firing his pistol twice. The first bullet mortally wounded Archduke Ferdinand in the jugular vein; the second hit Duchess Sophie in the stomach. Driven to the governor's residence, and nearing the point of death, Franz Ferdinand's thoughts were for his wife and children and for the perhaps millions of men who would be killed as a consequence. Princip was captured, tried and sentenced to twenty years in prison. He died in captivity.

The assassin's bullet became known as 'the shot that was heard around the world'. Identifying Serbia with the actions of the Black Hand and bolstered by an expression of support from Germany, the Austro-Hungarians issued an ultimatum to their neighbour – a reminder of an earlier agreement between them to live with the Austrian annexation of Bosnia. The 'July Ultimatum' required the Serbs to suppress all publications that 'incite hatred and contempt of the Austro-Hungarian monarchy' and remove such materials from schoolbooks and public works. It demanded the removal from public office of all those deemed negative to the Hapsburgs. And it required direct action against the plotters and the acceptance of Austrian involvement in the investigations. On this last point, the Serbs, backed by their Russian allies, balked. War was to follow. The Austrians declared war against the Serbs at 11.00 a.m. on 28 July 1914. Another famous phrase, attributed to the British foreign minister Sir Edward Grey, aptly noted, 'The lamps are going out all over Europe.'

Durch dick und dünn
Durch Not und Tod.

Kriegs-Erinnerungs-Karte

Feldpost.

Lieber Adolf!

2

The two kaisers: *Kriegs-Erinnerungs-Karte*

Durch dick und dünn, Durch not und tod
Through thick and thin, through hardship and death

THE TWO EMPERORS, Wilhelm II of Germany and Franz Josef I of Austria-Hungary, were totemic figures in their respective countries and were pivotal in directing the war in its early stages. This *Kriegs-Erinnerungs-Karte* (War-Memorial-Card) was sent on 9 October 1914 from Alfred Klieber in Leipzig to Adolf Albrecht, a grenadier of the *Ersatz* Battalion, Reserve Grenadier Regiment 100, who was in hospital. Though its personal message of greetings was anodyne, its visual message was plain: that come what may, the two autocratic emperors would tough out the storm that had been created since the assassination of Archduke Franz Ferdinand, heir to the throne of Austria-Hungary, in 1914. With the Austrian declaration of war on Serbia and the mobilisation of Russian support of its ally, the path for the German Empire was clear: it would have to put into action the Schlieffen Plan, which would ensure that a much-dreaded long war on two fronts would be prevented. With the German states effectively sandwiched between the vice-jaws of France and Russia, fighting a war simultaneously against two of the most important military nations in the world was not ideal.

Country of origin:
Germany

Date of printing:
1914

Location: Private
collection

The German Empire was created from a federation of states united by its first chancellor, Otto von Bismarck, in the wake of France's victory in the Franco-Prussian War of 1870–71. Bismarck was aware of the need to isolate France – bent on revenge in the aftermath of the war – from potential allies, thereby garnering power and bolstering its position. His fears over a two-front war meant that the German chancellor's sights were set on enticing the emperors of both Russia and Austria to join Kaiser Wilhelm I in the *Dreikaiserbund* – the Three Emperors' League. But like so many alliances before it, this was to fall apart as the power balance in Europe shifted. With Russia's defeat of the Ottoman Empire in 1878, Bismarck was quick to try to contain the power of his former ally and guarantee the security of the Ottomans; with this came the loss of Russia from the league and the creation of the Dual Alliance in October 1879 that locked together Germany and Austria-Hungary in a relationship that would guarantee military aid in the face of attack by Russia. It also promised 'benevolent neutrality' should 'another European country', namely France, attack either of the nations. Bismarck's diplomatic manoeuvrings would ultimately come to nought, however. With the accession to the German throne of a new kaiser, the brash Wilhelm II, came the rejection of the old statesman, who was forced into retirement in 1890.

The relationship between the two empires of Germany and Austria-Hungary was uneasy, however. Franz Josef I of Austria had lived through sixty-eight years of rule and had seen his country's fortunes wax and wane – falling from a position of leading the German Confederation of States in the 1860s to a point where Austria had to recognise the importance of Hungary in the dual monarchy. Still, the need for protection against Russia was significant, given the powershift in the Balkans following the defeat of the Ottomans in 1879. This led to the creation of Bulgaria and the increasing growth and influence of Serbia, Montenegro and Romania, principalities that would grow into kingdoms in the earliest years of the twentieth century. Jealous of

Kaiser Wilhelm II.

the shifting scenes in the Balkans, from this confused stage Austria-Hungary annexed Bosnia in 1908, adding to the instability – and ultimately leading to war.

Although the alliance between Germany and Austria remained strong, the power base had shifted. The German emperor's desires to contain both France and rival Britain – through the construction of its navy – meant that new understandings were formed between France and Britain in 1904, followed by France, Britain and Russia in 1907 – the Triple Entente.

The assassination of Franz Ferdinand, heir to the Austro-Hungarian imperial throne, in June 1914 put the old emperor in a difficult position. Naturally cautious, he held doubts over the logic of attacking Serbia, when it might mean drawing Russia into the conflict. With this in mind, the Austrians sought German support prior to action. This they received on 5 July 1914; Franz Josef could 'rely on Germany's firm support'. This famous 'blank cheque' ensured the Austrians could go ahead in the knowledge that, in a wider conflict, they would not stand alone.

Bismarck's fear of a war on two fronts had started to materialise, and the kaiser and his chief of the general staff, Helmuth von Moltke, fell back on the plans of Alfred von Schlieffen, formulated in 1905, to contain the two-front nightmare via a direct attack on France. And with the relationship between the two allies severely tested, the two emperors were faced with sticking it out, through thick and thin, hardship and death.

3

The Triple Entente: patriotic badges

THE TRIPLE ENTENTE of 1907 bound together three European nations in a defensive understanding that would guarantee protection in the face of attack, with the focus on the Central Powers of Germany and Austria-Hungary – situated at the heart of Europe – each with its own interests. With the opening and outbreak of war, it is not surprising that cheaply produced patriotic badges were worn by the British public as an expression of patriotism and solidarity of nations in arms. Similar devices would be worn in other European states.

Differing in style from celluloid pin badges to simple enamels, these devices were cheap to produce and purchase. Celluloid 'button' badges had first appeared in the 1890s, produced in America as a way of creating reasonably durable shiny alternatives to the much more expensive process of enamelling. Celluloid – a cheap thermoplastic sheeting – could be stamped out, printed on or simply used to cover printed paper designs that were then bonded into a cheap metal frame with pin. All three examples illustrated – from unknown manufacturers – show the Union Flag at the centre, in partnership with France. Aligned with these is the wronged nation of Belgium, invaded by Germany in August 1914 in prosecution of its Schlieffen Plan, and Russia, an important member of the Triple Entente. For Russia,

Country of origin:
United Kingdom

Date of manufacture:
1914

Location: Private collection

Button badge with flags of the Allies, c. 1914.

both national tricolour and black and yellow Imperial Standard flags are used, signifying the importance of the tsarist autocracy. And with Japan aligned through agreement with the Triple Entente (and its former enemy, Russia), it is not surprising that its flag should appear alongside its allies – in this case, its naval ensign, an off-set rising sun with sixteen rays.

With Germany under Kaiser Wilhelm II threatening British hegemony on the high seas through his desire for a new navy, and the dual monarchy of Austria-Hungary under threat from the emerging and belligerent Balkan states in the late nineteenth and early twentieth centuries, there was growing uncertainty over the security of Europe. The defeat of France in 1871 and the collapse of the Three Emperors' League just seven years later saw the growth of insecurity in central Europe. The Franco-Russian alliance of 1894, signed in secret, guaranteed military support if either country were attacked by nations of the Triple Alliance of Germany, Austria-Hungary and Italy. For France, there was the possibility of restitution of the provinces of Alsace and Lorraine, lost following its disastrous defeat in 1871; for Russia, there was the maintenance of its influence in the Balkans.

For Britain, traditionally isolated and aloof from continental neighbours, the development of the *Entente Cordiale* of 1904 settled many simmering and long-standing resentments over colonial possessions, hangovers from a century or so before. It marked the end of Britain's isolationism and the birth of the nation's involvement in mainland Europe. And with the German kaiser's increased interest in building the *Kaiserliche Marine* to threaten the power of the Royal Navy, there was added security in aligning with another major power: France. Having tidied up colonial issues with France, Britain did the same with Russia, partitioning interests in the Middle East and Central Asia – and particularly Afghanistan and Iran (then Persia) – as part of the Anglo-Russian Convention of 1907. From these steps was born the Triple Entente: all three nations bound together by intent to counterbalance the threat of the central European nations' Triple Alliance.

With this, in 1914 came the response to the enactment of the Schieffen Plan that would see Belgian neutrality and sovereignty ignored and would bring Britain to the war. And if the people at home could not fight, they could at least show support for their brothers in arms through the wearing of simple devices such as these.

4

Austrian *feldkappe*

THE AUSTRIAN *FELDKAPPE* was a distinctive piece of uniform that was to influence military style in the twentieth century. First introduced in 1870, it was the standard headgear of the Austro-Hungarian Army at the opening of the war in 1914. The battered cap illustrated dates from *c.* 1916 and is much simplified from its predecessors. Consisting of a woollen body with a neck apron buttoned at the front that could be let down to provide some protection from the elements, the standard 1908 pattern cap was issued in a bright blue-grey colour known as 'pike grey' (*hechtgrau*) and was linen-lined and equipped with a black leather liner. For enlisted men, the only distinguishing insignia was a large button-like 'rosette' bearing the monogram of the emperor: FJI for Austrian *Heer* and *Landwehr*, and IFJ for Hungarian *Honved*. Like all Austrian uniforms, the cap was stylish yet functional. It was also the substrate for a great variety of cap decorations (*abzeichen*), which were worn to commemorate Christmas in the trenches (*Weihnachten im Feld*) and the operations of individual units.

The Austro-Hungarian Army that wore this cap was pitched into a war that involved not only the assault on Serbia – in an attempt to gain vengeance for the affront on the Hapsburgs in Sarajevo and to silence the Balkan rumblings in its crumbling empire – but also the

Country of origin:
Austria-Hungary

Date of manufacture:
c. 1916

Location:
Museum 1915–18, Kötschach-Mauthen, Austria

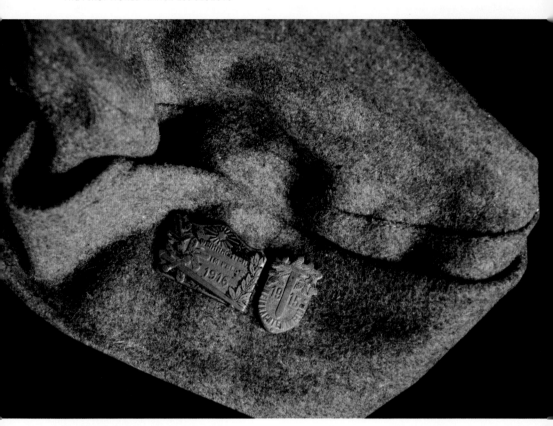

Russians, who placed themselves squarely in the role of defenders of the Slavic nations. The Austrian general staff had drawn up war plans based on two eventualities of war – against Serbia alone or including its much more mighty foe. War Scenario 'R' required a mobilisation that would, in the first instance, pit nine army corps and ten cavalry divisions against the Russians in Galicia, backed up by a further four army corps and a single cavalry division. Facing Serbia and Montenegro would be just three army corps. With general mobilisation on 31 July 1914, some 2.9 million Austro-Hungarian citizens of many ethnicities were drafted into the army – an increase on its peacetime strength of some 450,000 soldiers. This split between the two fronts was to prove disastrous, and by mid-September, the Austro-Hungarian forces had been pushed back disastrously in Galicia, the fortress of Przemysl surrounded. It was only in December, at the Battle of Limanowa–Lapanow, that the

Austrian cap with Christmas *Kappenabzeichen.*

An Austrian soldier wears the *feldkappe* in c. 1915.

Russian advances were halted. In the Balkans, things were no better, with Serb resistance stronger than imagined. By the end of 1914, some 1,268,696 Austro-Hungarian troops had been killed, wounded or taken prisoner. And though fortunes had been revived in the early part of 1915, the declaration of Italy for the Triple Entente – turning its back on its former friends in the Triple Alliance of 1882 – was a severe blow. The Austro-Hungarians now faced a war on three fronts and the prospects of facing the Italians in a defensive campaign across the severely mountainous terrain – while numerous battles were fought on the Isonzo River that drained manpower and resources from both sides.

Our field cap derives from the Austro-Italian Alpine front of 1915–16. It has been simplified; no longer in 'pike grey', it has adopted the 'field grey' colour of its German allies. It has simple buttons and a felt peak. Suited to Alpine wear, it was undoubtedly worn under the severe conditions dictated by Alpine warfare. In itself, the cap tracks the fall of grand ideals in the gritty realism of modern warfare.

5 *Pantalon garance*

BY 1914, THE LEGS of French infantrymen had been clad in bright red trousers for more than eighty years, this conspicuous item of clothing having been introduced in 1829. Originally called *pantalon garance*, this name refers to the fact that the distinctive red colour of the trousers was achieved using a vegetable dye produced from the herbaceous madder plant. Worn with a blue jacket or vest, long dark blue coat (the *capote*) and a red-and-blue *kepi*, the profile of the French soldier represented the national colours of the flag – a factor that was to create some debate and dissent among those modernists who viewed the clearly visible uniforms as a distraction in a modern army. Nevertheless, the French soldier was distinctive, and in common with the military fashions of other nations, his brightly coloured uniform was used throughout the nineteenth century, including at the ill-fated battles of the Franco-Prussian War of 1870–71. By the end of the nineteenth century, however, this style of dress had become a severe drawback as the effective ranges of rifles increased and as smokeless powder increased visibility on the battlefield.

The red trousers illustrated are a pair marked with many acceptance and issue stamps. Mothballed in 1914, this model of trouser had been first issued in 1867 and was characterised by pockets and a short belt at the rear that could be tightened to improve fit. The 1867 model trousers had been modified a few times since then,

Country of origin: France

Date of manufacture: *c.* 1914

Location: Private collection

but not radically; for instance, in 1897, internal pocket openings were removed, and the hem of the trousers was reinforced in order to prevent wear from boots and leather gaiters. The fact that these trousers have survived for 100 years is perhaps a testimony to both the level of manufacturing skill and the garishly bright colour that precluded easy wear in any setting other than a military one.

It was the very brightness of the colour and the depth of the contrast that were to seal the fate of the *pantalon garance*. In the late nineteenth century, the madder-based vegetable dyes were replaced with those created through a chemical process, the cultivation of the plants superseded by a chemical process producing alizarin red, a dye that had been perfected and developed, ironically enough, in Germany. With the madder industry dead and the dangers inherent in retaining a garish uniform apparent, alternatives were sought – but the grey uniform versions suggested in 1902–03 were too close for comfort to those of the Germans. Modernisers had an even greater challenge, as the question of the retention of the red trousers became a debate between the radical left and conservative right in government. As late as 1913, the French minister for war, Eugène Étienne, exclaimed, 'Red trousers are France!' It is not surprising, then, that the French went to war in the opening campaigns of 1914 dressed almost as they would have been in the opening campaigns of their last war against Germany. With France taking massive casualties, it was only in late August that a new uniform shade was produced – light blue or *bleu clair* (soon to be christened 'horizon blue' or *bleu horizon*) – which would become standard. This colour was achieved by pure accident; efforts to produce a homogenous 'tricolour' cloth that would embed the Republican ideals into the uniform cloth – using red, white and blue threads – came unstuck with the recognition of the German origin of the red colour, leaving just blue and white. These, combined, were the origin of the colour that would come to personify the uniform of the French *poilu*: horizon blue.

6

Pickelhaube

IN 1914, ALL ARMIES were equipped with some form of uniform cap or ceremonial helmet, but it is perhaps the German *helm mit spitze*, popularly known as the *pickelhaube*, that is the pre-eminent example of the type: gaudy, impractical and affording little protection from either the elements or from shell fragments and bullets. This headdress was adopted in 1842, reputedly the design of König Friedrich Wilhelm IV of Prussia. Presumably adopted for its martial appearance, the spiked helmet drew on several possible antecedants. With the Prussians adopting the helm, most of the German states followed suit, distinguished by their own distinctive helmet plates (*wappen*). With its long history, the *pickelhaube* was a prominent part of the military imagery of the Prussian state and, with the unification of Germany following the Franco-Prussian War, of Germany itself. The image of the strong German soldier in a spiked helmet was a striking one; with military fashion following the victors, it is possible to identify the emergence of spiked helmets at the expense of French-style *kepis* in the late-nineteenth-century armies of many countries, including Britain and the United States.

Country of origin:
Germany

Date of manufacture:
c. 1915

Location: Private collection

The basic component of the German 1895 pattern *pickelhaube* was a glossy, hardened leather helmet shell,

31

Tommy's Kiddie

PATRIOTIC
1177

G Morine

A crude French postcard aimed at British soldiers; the *helm mit spitze* is used to represent Germany.

the *helmkopf*, which had been pressed into a mould and covered with layers of lacquer to gain a high shine, with leather front peak (*vorderschirm*) and neck guard (*halswache*) sewn on, both finished in brass with a rear spine. The shell was then furnished with bright brass fittings, the spike (*spitze*) complete with ventilation holes (*luftlocher*) and the ornate state *wappen*. Artillerymen wore a ball (*kugel*) representing the cannonball. Both were finished with a mostly ceremonial leather chinstrap and a pair of cockades sporting the national and state colours. To protect it, and reduce its visibility, a cloth cover (*überzug*) was created for field use. All in all, the helmet was expensive to make, complex and used many important war materials. In an army that grew rapidly, its production was unsustainable. *Ersatz* or replacement materials were quickly utilised – steel, or even felt, to create the complex helmet shell.

The example illustrated is Prussian, of a type first issued in June 1915. Gone were the shiny brass fittings, a metal much in demand to serve the munitions industry. In their place were oxidised steel fittings, cheaper to produce and less visible. The helmet spike was also removable. To some, the *pickelhaube* helped define the image of the German soldier as an aggressor, particularly with its prominent spike. On the front line, the *pickelhaube* was the natural target of souvenir hunters, and there are countless photographs of British soldiers 'larking about' in what they termed 'hunnish' headgear. This helmet was one such soldier's haul, brought back to entertain the people at home.

A German soldier, equipped with a *pickelhaube*.

The alien appearance of the *pickelhaube* made it the target of Allied propaganda, and the helmet appeared in images intended to invoke national hatred. The spiked headgear was worn by snarling beasts, inhuman ravishers of women and despoilers of Europe's cultural heritage. Political cartoonists such as Louis Raemaekers had a field day with its ungainly image. It was destined to be replaced in 1916 by the steel helmet (*stahlhelm*), and with it, fatalities from head wounds declined dramatically. With the passing of the *pickelhaube* came the birth of industrialised warfare; there was little room for the ceremonial in the killing fields of Flanders, Artois or the Argonne.

7 Iron Cross

THE IRON CROSS was first founded on 10 March 1813 in Breslau and was awarded to soldiers during the Wars of Liberation against Napoleon. Awarded only for actions in this war, the medal was reauthorised by König Wilhelm I of Prussia on 19 July 1870, during the Franco-Prussian War, and the distinctive medal would make its symbolic reappearance at the very outbreak of the Great War, on the authority of Kaiser Wilhelm II. In all cases, the Iron Cross was an award of the Kingdom of Prussia, but given Prussia's pre-eminent place in the German Empire, formed in 1871, it was awarded across the empire and was widely parodied by the Allies, who claimed that it was 'brought up with the rations'. There was little truth in the allegation.

The Iron Cross was awarded in three classes. Although the medals of each class were identical, the manner in which each was worn differed. Employing a pin or screw posts on the back of the medal, the Iron Cross 1st Class was worn on the left side of the recipient's uniform. The Grand Cross and the Iron Cross 2nd Class were suspended from different ribbons. The Grand Cross was intended for senior generals of the German Army. An even higher decoration, the Star of the Grand Cross of the Iron Cross, was awarded only twice, to Field Marshal Gebhard von Blücher in 1813 and to Field Marshal Paul von Hindenburg in 1918.

Country of origin: Germany

Date of manufacture: 1914–18

Location: Private collection

The Iron Cross 1st Class and the Iron Cross 2nd Class were awarded without regard to rank. One had to already possess the 2nd Class in order to receive the 1st Class (though in some cases both could be awarded simultaneously). The egalitarian nature of this award contrasted with most other German states, where military decorations were awarded based on the rank of the recipient. In the First World War, approximately 4 million Iron Crosses of the lower grade (2nd Class) were issued, as well as around 145,000 of the higher grade (1st Class).

The Iron Cross (2nd Class) illustrated here was kept by its recipient in its original paper of issue. Makers provided the crosses in these small folds of blue paper, protected by a thin piece of tissue; each was packed in boxes typically containing thirty examples at a time. This cross was either never issued or, in common with many others, never worn. In contrast to many other medals, the Iron Cross has a very simple design and is made from relatively cheap and common materials. It was designed by the neoclassical architect Karl Friedrich Schinkel and was based on the Cross of the Teutonic Order, used as their symbol since the thirteenth century. When Schinkel designed it, he consciously avoided using gold and went for silver and iron instead. These materials stood for chivalry, purity and the self-effacement and modesty of the Prussian soldier.

German soldiers receive their Iron Crosses.

The Iron Cross itself was far more than a medal or combat award. It was awarded only in times when the Fatherland was in danger (in 1866, it obviously was not). For the soldiers and Prussian people of the nineteenth century and up until the First World War, it symbolised the cause: the protection of the homeland and the will to shed the last drop of blood for it. To all those who received it, it was coveted, cherished and valued.

8 Propaganda Cross

IN 1914, THE INVADING German Army swept through Belgium and northern France en route to encircle Paris. In 1870, a Prussian army had invaded France and had suffered at the hands of armed irregulars, of *Francs-tireurs*, who had grown out of rifle clubs and were intent on defending their country from the invader. For the Prussians, these irregulars had doubtful military legitimacy and had acted 'illegally' according to standard military practices. For the French, the *Francs-tireurs* had a perfect right to defend their homeland from invasion. It is not surprising, then, that with the enactment of the Schlieffen Plan, the Germans would be sensitive to any civilian involvement in the defence of Belgium and northern France.

As the German armies swept through northern Europe, any suspected acts of 'terrorism' were dealt with severely. Where shots had been heard from buildings – or had been suspected as such – occupants were taken out and summarily executed, their homes burned. In all, it is estimated that 6,000 Belgian civilians were killed and some 25,000 buildings destroyed. In Dinant alone, 674 civilians were shot, and the university city of Louvain (Lueven) was sacked and burned. Elsewhere, in

Country of origin: United Kingdom

Date of manufacture: c. 1914–15

Location: Private collection

northern France, cultural centres were bombarded as the armies wheeled in their arc in an attempt to encircle Paris. At Rheims and Amiens, the great gothic cathedrals were bombarded and badly damaged. In the wake of these actions, the Allied propaganda machine moved into top gear. The crimes perpetrated by the Germans were given a new spin and were presented as inhuman acts of savagery against the innocent. Lurid tales of murder, mutilation and sexual depravity were commonplace, and the invasion of Belgium was transformed into the 'Rape of Belgium'. For the British, the opportunity to castigate the Germans as the 'Hun' ravaging Europe was too much. They turned to the task with gusto: posters, political cartoonists and leader writers all fell on the ever-more extreme 'horrors and atrocities' in an attempt to build up national indignation and bolster recruitment.

One output was the production of cast-iron propaganda 'Iron Crosses'. With both iron and the Iron Cross symbolising purity and chivalry within German culture, it was inevitable that this medal would be selected as a means of ridiculing the enemy. The most common examples, like those illustrated, depict the cross with the words 'For Kultur'. *Kultur* was a concept of German supremacy in the arts and other high ideals of Western civilisation. It was not surprising that the Allied propagandists quickly siezed on this and depicted half-crazed, jack-booted madmen striding across Europe, all 'For Kultur'. Some of the crosses simply state, in heavily ironic overtones, 'For Brave Deeds', while others list the cultural sites damaged by the invasion: Louvain, Rheims, Amiens. Later additions, like the other example pictured here, even reflect on the naval bombardment of the north-eastern coast of England in late 1914. Who produced the crosses is unknown; perhaps Gordon Selfridge, later responsible for reproducing the *Lusitania* medal. Probably sold in order to propagate hatred and sponsor recruitment, these simple devices are material evidence of the anti-German campaign waged by the Allies in the opening months of the war. The selection of the Iron Cross was surely intended to be the greatest insult to the integrity of German deeds.

DON'T IMAGINE YOU ARE NOT WANTED

EVERY MAN between 19 and 38 years of age is WANTED!

Ex-Soldiers up to 45 years of age

MEN CAN ENLIST IN THE NEW ARMY FOR THE DURATION OF THE WAR

"YOUR COUNTRY NEEDS

YOU"

RATE OF PAY: Lowest Scale 7s. per week with Food, Clothing &c., in addition

1. Separation Allowance for Wives and Children of Married Men when separated from their Families (Inclusive of the allotment required from the Soldier's pay of a maximum of 6d. a day in the case of a private)

For a Wife **without** Children	-	- 12s. 6d. per week
For Wife with One Child	-	- 15s. 0d. per week
For Wife with Two Children	-	- 17s. 6d. per week
For Wife with Three Children	-	- 20s. 0d. per week
For Wife with Four Children	-	- 22s. 0d per week

and so on, with an addition of **2s.** for each additional child.

Motherless children 3s. a week each, exclusive of allotment from Soldier's pay

2. Separation Allowance for Dependants of Unmarried Men.

Provided the Soldier does his share, the Government will assist liberally in keeping up, within the limits of Separation Allowance for Families, any regular contribution made before enlistment by unmarried Soldiers or Widowers to other dependants such as mothers, fathers, sisters, etc.

YOUR COUNTRY IS STILL CALLING.
FIGHTING MEN! FALL IN!!

Full Particulars can be obtained at any Recruiting Office or Post Office.

No 0200
DAVID ALLEN & SONS
HARROW

9

Kitchener poster

FOR CENTURIES, BRITAIN had been reliant on volunteers to join its armed services. Unlike many European nations, which had introduced conscription in the nineteenth century, Britain's army was a small one and the nation's commitment to land warfare limited. Since 1881, the British Army had been composed of sixty-one infantry regiments and twenty-nine regular cavalry regiments (supplemented by units of volunteer Yeomanry cavalry), together with major arms such as the artillery and a host of ancillary units destined to keep the army in the field and fighting fit. Each infantry regiment had at least two regular, professional battalions (the norm); a 'special reserve' battalion that was there to receive and train recruits; and at least two part-time 'territorial' battalions, intended for home service but entitled to volunteer for overseas service, too, on what was known as their 'Imperial Service Commitment'.

Country of origin:
United Kingdom

Date of printing:
1914

Location: Private
collection

The regular battalions available at home in 1914 were to form six infantry divisions; each division was to have three infantry brigades, with each brigade in turn composed of four infantry battalions. Brigades rarely had more than one battalion from a given regiment. The typical infantry division of 1914 would also have a significant artillery presence and an attached cavalry squadron, as well as components from all the other arms and services required to keep it operating in the field – a massive undertaking with around 15,000 men in a typical, full-strength British division.

When Field Marshal Earl Kitchener of Khartoum – revered as a national hero for his exploits in Africa – took over as Secretary of State for War in August 1914, he was quick to understand that this war would be costly in manpower. Not confident that the territorial battalions could be sufficiently flexible to allow rapid expansion, Kitchener made a direct appeal to the public, his sights set on expanding the army by 500,000 men. He made separate appeals, in 100,000 tranches, to be numbered successively K1, K2 and so on. The 'First Hundred Thousand', or K1, were recruited within days of the appeal. Kitchener was to issue four further appeals through the late summer and early autumn of 1914, the final 100,000 – K5 – being sanctioned by the government in October of that year. In the days before wireless and mass media, this appeal for manpower was made through newspapers and, most effectively, the use of posters seen in every public space.

Most famous is the image by Alfred Leete of the head and pointing finger of Field Marshal Kitchener, an image that was first published as a cover of the magazine *London Opinion* in September 1914, with the phrase 'Your country needs YOU'. This image was destined to appear on a poster that was to become one of the most famous of all time. The first to bear Leete's image of Kitchener was printed by the Victoria House Printing Co. Ltd, Tudor Street, London. Under the arresting title 'BRITONS', Kitchener's pointing finger and staring eyes were accompanied by the phrase 'WANTS YOU'. 'JOIN YOUR COUNTRY'S ARMY!' and 'GOD SAVE THE KING' were printed below. September 1914 was to see the greatest number of volunteers come forward to join, but for the remainder of the year, a fall-off in recruiting was noticeable. In November 1914, a larger, more elaborate poster bearing Kitchener's image and the original cover image phrase 'Your Country needs YOU' was printed by David Allen and Sons Ltd. Adorned with the national flags, the poster details rates of pay and other information, including the additional words 'YOUR COUNTRY IS STILL CALLING. FIGHTING MEN!

FALL IN!!' Recent research suggests that the design of the poster, incorporating Leete's Kitchener image as its central feature, might have been the work of the famous poster designer John Hassall or, alternatively, one of the in-house designers of Allen's company.

There is no doubt that such posters had a dramatic effect on passersby and on the numbers of men who came forward to 'join the colours'. The poster also had undoubted influence on other nation's designs, such as James Montgomery Flagg's 1917 version featuring a top-hatted 'Uncle Sam' querulously pointing over the slogan 'I WANT YOU FOR THE U.S. ARMY'. (This poster, in its own right, is recognised as a 'national treasure' by the Smithsonian Institution.) Yet, despite this, actual examples of the original Kitchener poster are scarce, and the one illustrated is a rare survivor in a private collection. The chances of individuals being directly addressed by Kitchener's stare and his pointing finger in the early stages of the war are therefore relatively remote. Nevertheless, this image had become firmly engrained in the psyche of the British people.

More common than what has become known as 'the Kitchener poster' are the outpourings of the Parliamentary Recruiting Committee (PRC), which by March 1915 had produced 20 million leaflets and 2 million posters. All posters produced by the PRC were labelled 'Issued by the Parliamentary Recruiting Committee' and were produced in a variety of styles and with a variety of images. None reproduced Leete's original Kitchener image, however, though many alluded to the 'Your Country needs YOU!' message of both the *London Opinion* cover and the Allen-produced poster. A great many attacked the conscience of the average man: 'Are You in This?', 'Daddy, what did you do in the Great War?' or 'Be certain that your so-called reason is not just a selfish excuse'. Despite the tone of these posters, that they were effective is clear, with 1.2 million men joining in the first months of the war. However, the potency of the posters was to decrease as the war dragged on, and the PRC ceased its work on the advent of conscription in 1916, having produced over 6 million posters in its term of office.

10

Liverpool Pals badges

INITIAL RECRUITMENT TO 'Kitchener's Army' was steady if unspectacular – though it was significantly boosted in the aftermath of the British retreat from Mons in August. The men of K1, K2 and so on took their places in the ranks of the existing army system, but very soon energetic and influential individuals were forming whole battalions, men intended to train together and serve together. The concept was born following a request from the City of London to raise a whole battalion of 'stockbrokers' in August 1914. But the proliferation of the concept was in large part due to the action of Lord Derby, the so-called King of Lancashire, who introduced the notion that men of the 'commercial classes' might wish to serve their country in a battalion of their comrades, their 'pals'. The 'Liverpool Pals' was the result. The implication was that middle-class men would not be forced to serve alongside men they would neither know nor understand – men of 'lower social class'. Based on the snobbery of the time, it was a resounding success, though it would lead ultimately to the decimation of local communities. Ultimately, it was these men who would contribute to the much-debated 'lost generation', men of all walks of life who 'answered the call' to be decimated on the Somme in July 1916.

Country of origin:
United Kingdom

Date of manufacture:
1914

Location: Private collection

The first of the 'pals' phenomenon, the Liverpool Pals – or, more properly, the 1st–4th City Battalions of the King's (Liverpool) Regiment – were born of Lord Derby's initiative. In a letter published in the Liverpool press on 27 August 1914, Lord Derby introduced the notion of men serving with their 'pals'. At a public meeting held the next day, Lord Derby was to announce that he would be sending Lord Kitchener a telegram to say that not one, but two, battalions of like-minded men would be offered to the nation. In fact, in just over a week, sufficient men would be found for three battalions, the fourth being added within weeks.

Lord Derby was to take a personal interest in his 'pals', the example of which was emulated up and down the country. At his own expense, he was to commission in silver a badge bearing his 'eagle and child' emblem, which he gave out personally to each original member of the four Liverpool Pals battalions. Edward and Stanley Cole of Bootle, Liverpool, served in Number 4 Company, 19th King's (Liverpool Regiment) – the third of the 'Pals' battalion to be raised. When Edward was presented with his silver badge, he crudely scratched his initials – 'EC' – on the rear and had a pin fitted so that it could be worn with civilian clothing (or perhaps given to his sweetheart). In its place on his cap was the brass version. Both brothers arrived in France on 7 November 1915, in time to take an active part in the Battle of the Somme. Stanley was killed on 30 July 1916 while attacking Guillemont. Some 500 men were killed in this attack – 'Liverpool's blackest day'.

An avalanche of 'City' and 'Pals' battalions were formed from men with similar backgrounds and circumstances, the concept spreading like wildfire throughout the industrial north of England and the Midlands. Becoming a matter of civic pride, each battalion was raised by local dignitaries, who fed, clothed and equipped them until the unit was taken over by the War Office – only then would the costs of raising them be met by the government – to become service battalions (numbered in sequence after the territorials) of the county regiments.

The
Soldier

II

'Les Poilus' postcard

Country of origin:
France

Date of printing:
1914

Location: Private
collection

EACH COUNTRY HAD its image of military perfection
and its name for the military defender of the nation. For
the German soldier (*soldat*), it was the transformation
from simple soldier to trained *Landser* that was revered,
and only those men experienced enough in war could
hope to attain this status amongst their comrades (*kama-raden*). Slang versions used by the soldiers themselves
included the obvious *landratte* (land rat). The reverence
for the soldier in Germany contrasts somewhat with the
approach adopted by the Entente countries, particularly
Britain and France. Here, the popular imagination did
not frame soldiers as upright individuals fully equipped
with rifle and bayonet, and ready to take on the foe;
instead they were portrayed as more individual, perhaps
in keeping with perceived national characteristics.

For the British, the name most commonly applied
was 'Tommy', or 'Tommy Atkins'. This mostly affec-
tionate term appeared originally in the early part of the
nineteenth century, applied as shorthand for the British
soldier in official correspondence, but by the late
nineteenth century, it was widely used in the popular
press, made famous in part by the writings of Rudyard
Kipling. Tommy Atkins appeared in songs, in the press
and on postcards. Although there were some dissent-
ing voices from the ranks, the name stuck. Amongst

The rear of the card, expressing good wishes.

other English-speaking soldiers, 'diggers' was applied to Australians and 'doughboys' applied to Americans. The origins of both of these are obscure. 'Digger' possibly derives from advice given by General Sir Ian Hamilton to the Australian and New Zealand Army Corps (ANZAC) during the Gallipoli landings in 1915 – that they should dig in in order to consolidate their positions – but others argue it relates to nineteenth-century Australian gold mining. 'Doughboy' is even more ambiguous, possibly stemming from the dusty uniforms worn by American soldiers in the mid-nineteenth-century Mexican-American War. In any case, all the terms were applied in an effort to give familiar names to the average soldier.

The object in this case is a photograph – one of many hundreds of thousands (if not millions) that were produced of soldiers during the war. With photography well established, it was commonplace that families visited photographic studios in order to gain a likeness they could pass on to family members. Usually set in formal poses, families stare at the camera or beyond it, careful not to move so that slow shutter speeds could capture their poses without blurring. With the coming of war, photographers were called upon to supply images of soldiers in uniform, an opportunity to record that men or women were 'doing their bit' for their country. Common to all nations, studios did brisk business in supplying these needs, and in the battle zone, enterprising photographers were on hand to capture the likeness of men in uniform, to be sent home with a brief comment: 'I am well, hope you are too.' The sadness is that in many cases the soldiers depicted were killed before they could return to pick up their orders.

The photograph shows three men of the French 31st Infantry Regiment at a camp in 1914. Relaxed in pose, the men are equipped with *pantalon garance*, red-topped kepis and dark blue *capote* (the typical greatcoat of the French soldier, buttoned back to allow for marching), together with the standard black leather pattern 1888 equipment and Lebel rifles. The photograph gives few clues about the men's names or, ultimately, their fates. The term *poilu* (meaning 'hairy' or 'shaggy') was used widely for the French soldier, both amongst the French and occasionally by his British and, later, American allies. The three men in the photograph are typical, if perhaps more groomed than would be seen commonly in the trenches, with flamboyant moustaches and goatee beards. With France mostly an agricultural country, the adoption of the name *poilu* might have resonated with the wider agrarian population of the country. Yet the name is supposed to have originated in a story by Honoré de Balzac, *Le Médecin de Campagne* (1834), in which a group of French soldiers are required for a deed demanding particular courage. Only forty soldiers in one regiment are deemed to be *assez poilu* ('hairy enough'). *Poilu* was also commonly familiarised as *piou-piou*.

Piou-Piou
The British Tommy Atkins to the French

YOUR trousies is a funny red,
Your tunic is a funny blue,
Your cap sets curious on your 'ead–
And yet, by Gawd, your 'eart sits true, Piou-piou!

Second Lieutenant Joseph Lee,
KRRC Ballads of Battle, 1919

12

Russian *furazhka*

THE ARMIES OF 1914 were distinguished from one another in form of dress, equipment and munitions. Typical of all Allied nations was the use of some form of soft cap, the style of which was influenced by national characteristics. These caps contrasted heavily with the imperial German spiked helmet, the *helm mit spitze* or *pickelhaube*, which provided little in the way of protection and was parodied mercilessly in propaganda to send up the 'German hordes'. In 1914, Belgian and French infantrymen wore similarly archaic headgear: the Belgian shako, complete with pompom, that, in design terms, harked back at least a century, and the French kepi, practical in design yet dramatic in colour, with red top and dark blue band, first introduced in 1884. The British and Russians, in contrast, wore simple khaki-coloured peaked caps that had been born out of their experiences in the earliest wars of the twentieth century, in South Africa and the Russo-Japanese War.

The defeats suffered in the Russo-Japanese War of 1904–05 took a heavy toll on the Russians; no longer could they afford to go to war with outdated equipment and tactics. The Russian uniform was distinctive: a long pullover tunic shirt with stand-up collar known as the гимнастёрка (*gymnasterka*). Without direct equivalents (other than the tunic worn by the British Indian

Country of origin: Russia

Date of manufacture: c. 1914–17

Location: In Flanders Fields Museum, Ieper, Belgium

Russian *frontovik* prisoners of war in Germany, wearing the *furazhka*.

Army), this item, first introduced in 1870, drew on peasant traditions to become one of the most distinctive items of the Russian Army. But in its original form – as a distinctly white uniform – it was vulnerable, and it was replaced by a khaki version in the prelude to war. Accompanying this was a peaked cap known as the *Фуражка* (*furazhka*), which was introduced in 1907. Both items were theoretically issued in cotton for the hot continental summers and wool for winter –

though this would be replaced in the depths of winter by a fleece known as *nanáxa* (*papakha*). Our example is a rare survivor of the *furazhka*.

It is simple in design, similar in many ways to the British Service dress cap – introduced in 1905 – though it was less formal and was easily moulded to fit the wearer's head comfortably. The British cap was stiff, and it was only the rigours of the front-line trenches that transformed it into something more malleable that could be modified and shaped. Our cap retains something of its original shape and probably did not see much service in the front line, worn by a veteran soldier (*frontovik*). Lacking a chinstrap, and with a distinctive short leather peak, the cap was there to demand uniformity of dress and to act as a platform for the distinctive regimental insignia – the imperial cockade. For ordinary soldiers, the cockade was nothing more than a simple pressed-metal disc that was painted in the Russian imperial colours of orange and black; for officers, it was more ornate, better made and distinctly raised in style. Our cap is an ordinary infantryman's.

The transformation from cap to steel helmet in most armies in 1915–16 marks the transition from open warfare to the entrenched positions that were ultimately to blight the landscape of Europe and, in the west at least, turned the war into the longest extended siege in history. In Greater Russia, trench warfare was less sustainable, and troops moving in open fields were still a distinctive feature of the war there. Without long trench lines, positions were more easily outflanked, but the attackers were more often than not dangerously exposed, with limited opportunity to supply and reinforce. With trenches so prevalent in the west and with head wounds consequently so common – as soldiers were tempted to put their heads above the parapet or tall soldiers forgot to duck – steel helmets had become the norm by the close of 1915. In the east, the helmet took longer to appear, the cap lingering on as supply issues began to bite, an echo of the open warfare that persisted in the wide, rolling landscapes of the Eastern Front.

13

Canadian insignia

REGIMENTAL DEVICES ARE of the greatest importance in warfare. In a military sense, distinguishing friend from foe on the battlefield has long been an important expedient, and the use of some identifying device in the years before uniforms was essential. Though temporary 'field signs' (i.e. branches, foliage, paper scraps) had been used since at least the Middle Ages, perhaps the earliest metal military uniform badges were one-sided silver badges sewn directly to the clothing by Royalist soldiers during the English Civil War – but it would be some time before real 'cap badges' would be worn. In the British Army, the wearing of metal headdress badges followed the introduction, in 1800, of the shako – an unwieldy piece of headgear that was finally abolished in 1878.

In the British and Imperial Armies, with the arrival of khaki service dress in the early twentieth century came the adoption of a cap. New badges were called for, and from 1898, new designs were in place that would come to personify the regiment, widely used and reproduced in a number of settings, both domestic and military. This practice differs from most other nations at the time. For France, Italy, Belgium or Germany, for example, infantry battalions were simply identified through the use of numerals most often displayed on shoulder

Country of origin:
Canada

Date of manufacture:
1914–18

Location: Private collection

straps or collars – though branches of service, such as the artillery, were commonly identified by the tools of their trade (i.e. crossed cannons).

Pragmatically, the use of regimental insignia on caps and other headdress was intended to identify the unit to the casual observer, but there is more to it than that. Propagation of the 'love of one's regiment' was a very real principle in cementing the solid relationship between a soldier and his unit. Recruits to a regiment were (and are to this day) taught to respect its traditions and honours, and cap badges represent in miniature a compressed time capsule of the achievements of the regiment. But in truth, they mean much more: *esprit de corps*, difficult to measure but deemed essential in a well-trained force. Of all the cap badges associated with the armies of the British Empire, perhaps the most identifiable are those that bear the maple leaf.

The maple leaf has been associated with Canada since the early part of the nineteenth century, when it was adopted by French Canadians, typifying the dominance of the maple tree in the forests of this new nation. By the latter part of the century, it had been adopted as a symbol of the most populous and adjoining regions of Ontario (in gold) and Québec (in green). The distinctive leaf became the subject of patriotic songs and first appeared on Canadian coinage in 1876. In military usage, the maple leaf was deployed with soldiers forming the Canadian contribution to the Boer War of 1899–1902. It is hardly surprising, then, that the maple leaf became the dominant symbol of Canada's contribution to the Great War, with the overwhelming majority of the young country's forces wearing the device to distinguish them from other soldiers. The badges illustrated are typical. The maple leaf is prominently displayed in what was the standard 'general service' badge; most of the 260 or so infantry battalions that served in the Canadian Expeditionary Force had a distinctive badge – more often than not bearing the maple leaf. And if this did not sufficiently distinguish the soldier as a Canadian, then the simple titles bearing the name 'Canada' worn on the shoulder

Canadian
shoulder title.

straps would confirm this. With the standard uniform of the average 'Canuck' looking very much like that of the British soldier, wearing distinguishing badges like these was important.

The Canadian contribution to the Great War was huge. By the end of the war, there were some 665,000 Canadians in uniform. More than 470,000 Canadians served overseas, with 60,000 dead and a further 172,000 wounded. Though the majority of Canadian soldiers who served overseas were British born, they were mostly fiercely loyal to their adopted land. Canada joined the war on 5 August 1914, and the Canadian Expeditionary Force that crossed the Atlantic was soon to figure in many of the most significant battles on the Western Front. Canadians held the line in the first gas attack, in the Ypres Salient in May 1915; they would serve on the Somme in 1916 and would take the village of Passchendaele in November 1917. In 1918, they would be in the vanguard of the armies that drove the Germans back to their Armistice Line. And at Vimy Ridge in April 1917, the four divisions of the Canadian Corps acted under Canadian generalship for the first time, and the seeds of the independent nation were born. In all cases, the maple leaf was worn proudly into battle and would figure heavily on the white headstones of the cemeteries still that plot their progress.

14 Khaki uniform

THE SYMBOLISM OF the movement from red coat to khaki jacket in the British Army serves as a metaphor for the transition from the choreographed warfare of the Napoleonic times to the wholesale butchery of modern warfare. The change from a conspicuous uniform to one that blended with the battlefield was one that was widely considered in all the dominant armies of Europe at the turn of the nineteenth century. The 'field grey' (*feldgrau*) of Germany, 'pike grey' (*hechtgrau*) of Austria and 'khaki' of Britain were all responses to the need for anonymity on the battlefield.

Prior to the Anglo-Boer War of 1899–1901, the British soldier had worn the red coat, which, coupled with the white, pipe-clayed, leather equipment of the time, made Tommy somewhat conspicuous. The need to blend into the veldt was recognised early on in South Africa, where the dun-coloured cotton khaki drill had been issued; this was seen to be inadequate, as it was not hard-wearing and was not warm enough in the cooler periods. As such, a wool serge version was produced that was to be embodied in Army Orders in 1902 as service dress. Service dress went through several modifications in the 'Lists of Changes' issued periodically by the War Office, but by 1914 it had settled down to a pattern that was used more or less throughout the war, issued from 1907 onwards.

Country of origin: United Kingdom

Date of manufacture: *c.* 1917–18

Location: Private collection

The British 1902 service dress jacket illustrated here was worn by a lance corporal in the Honourable Artillery Company in 1917–18. Its design and development were the products of a basic military requirement to have a comfortable and serviceable uniform that would be suited for field conditions in all weathers. The jacket was meant to be loose-fitting (if it fitted at all – a fact not lost on contemporary cartoonists), with a turned-down collar, patches at the shoulder to bear the extra wear from the position of the rifle butt in action and pleats to improve fit to the rear of the jacket. It had a pair of box-pleated patch pockets with button-down flaps at the upper chest and a pair of deep pockets let into the tunic skirt, again with button-down flaps. A simple pocket was also sewn into the inside right skirt of the tunic to take the soldier's first field dressing. Two brass hooks, often removed or lost through use, were intended to support the belt in its correct position between the sixth and seventh tunic button. Shoulder straps bore regimental insignia in the form of brass or, later, as brass shortages were felt, cloth shoulder titles. Throughout the war, insignia were added to the sleeves, including rank badges, specialist proficiency badges and so-called battle patches and divisional insignia.

British soldier in Service Dress, c. 1915.

The khaki uniform was worn in the trenches, on parade and while home on leave. Worn and dirtied, typically it would become infested with lice while in the trenches – an inevitable consequence of the close quartering of men in squalid conditions. Brushed down and repaired, this jacket would be worn with pride – and would be instantly recognisable, emblematic of the 'man from the trenches'.

15
Puttees

PUTTEES ARE A peculiarity of the Great War, a military fashion adopted by many countries that helps define the profile of the typical soldier. The *Encyclopaedia Britannica* for 1911 offers a definition:

> PUTTEE adapted from the Hindi patti, bandage (from *patta*, strip of cloth), for a covering for the lower part of the leg from the ankle to the knee, consisting of a long narrow piece of cloth wound tightly and spirally round the leg, and serving both as a support and protection. It has been adopted as part of the uniform of the mounted soldier in the British army.

Country of origin: France

Date of manufacture: 1915–18

Location: Private collection

For the British, puttees were derived, like the khaki service dress, from the British experience in India, and were introduced in 1897. These 9ft-long strips of cloth, tied with long tapes, replaced the black leather leggings or gaiters that had distinguished the soldier of the Anglo-Zulu War. Worn with the first British khaki uniform to be introduced, they saw service on the North-West Frontier and in the Second Boer War, and would be adopted for service with the khaki serge uniform introduced at the end of that war, in 1902.

But the puttees illustrated are a pair that are peculiarly French. Manufactured in *bleu horizon* (horizon blue),

61

the French versions were more prosaically named, simply explaining their use: *bande molletière* (calf bandages). Like the British puttees, the French *bande molletière* were introduced as part of a shake-up in French uniforms, the replacement of the almost sacred red trousers and dark blue jacket that was finally deemed obsolete at the end of 1914. This pair have seen service, and are frayed and dog-eared. Images of French soldiers for the most part show soldiers with untidy *bandes*, despite the reinforcing that was typical of the French version of this military fashion. In fact, most combatants wore puttees as part of their front-line service uniform:

Puttees were a fascination to the British public.

British Empire troops; French and Colonial French; Italians; Austro-Hungarians; the Americans, after jettisoning their canvas gaiters as unsuitable to trench warfare in 1917; and the Germans as the supply of leather became difficult. With only the Belgians – and specialist troops such as artillerymen – relying on leather gaiters, the leg clad in wound puttees became an icon. In Britain, china models of puttee-clad legs were sold in souvenir shops and displayed on mantelpieces. In Newfoundland, the issue of dark blue puttees worn with otherwise khaki uniform has come to symbolise the efforts of this proud Crown colony, that as yet was not a formal part of Canada. Newfoundlanders would not surprisingly be called 'blue puttees'. This military fashion staggered on in one or two armies in a second world conflict.

Consisting of long wool cloth strips provided with cotton tapes, puttees were wound tightly around the leg, generally tied just below the knee by tapes. There was an art to tying them, and some soldiers were none too adept at doing so. Contemporary images show the smartest soldiers with the smoothest-looking calfs, while other images show the long bandage-like strips tied any which way. The best fitting were shaped to allow for the bulge of the calf muscles, and were graduated along their length; these French examples do just that. They are also reinforced to allow for wear and tear, and to prevent fraying. An English company, Fox, produced puttees commercially that not only took in these features, but also provided leg-specific left and right versions, carefully marked with 'L' and 'R'. Officers wore these in the trenches.

In British service, puttees were tied from the ankle to the knee for the infantryman, while mounted soldiers were distinguished by their practice of winding the puttee from the knee to the ankle, the tapes wound close to the ankle. This became a mark of distinction between the services. To find ways of exerting their own personality, soldiers would also create – using judiciously applied folds – fancy patterns with their puttees. But the simple purpose of puttees was to deal with an issue that had plagued infantrymen for centuries: to ensure that the junction between the trousers and the boot is not exposed to the elements, thereby allowing water, mud, dust and any number of objects to enter the boot and cause the soldier discomfort on the march. Though doing a valuable job in keeping out at least the worst of the elements, tying the puttee too tight was found to exacerbate the problem of 'trench foot', a condition akin to frostbite, resulting from restricted blood circulation and prolonged water immersion.

The stiff leather gaiters used by many nations in the run-up to the war served a similar purpose, but leather tends to hold water, become weighty and stretch, thereby increasing the burden on the soldier. Puttees have a natural advantage; they are light, easy to roll up and capable of being washed. More puttees provided the desired effect of a covering for the lower leg that would give greater support and protection. They would, of course, become sodden and muddy very quickly indeed.

16 Lebel rifle

ALL THE PRINCIPAL combatants went to war with a bolt-action rifle. For the British, it was the .303 calibre Short Magazine Lee–Enfield. For the Germans it was the *Gewehr 98 Mauser*. Both systems had the capability of loading rounds from clips (or chargers, in British usage): ten for the British, held in a detachable magazine, and five for the German. The French rifle operated a different system: each 8mm cartridge was loaded individually, eight cartridges stored in a tube within the forestock of the rifle.

On its introduction in 1887, the *Fusil Modèle* 1886, or simply the *Fusil Lebel* rifle, was revolutionary. Named after the colonel director of the *École normale de Tir*, who was chairman of the 1886 commission that selected the rifle, its cartridges used smokeless powder, and its overall design was robust and capable of some tough handling. The Lebel was more superior in handling and rate of fire than the *Mauser M-71/84* then in service. The introduction of this rifle sparked an arms race; the Germans were quick to replace their outdated weapon with a rifle that would eventually evolve into the standard infantry arm of the Great War, the *Gewehr 98*, which fired a 7.92 x 57mm rimless Mauser cartridge and was equipped with a spring-loaded box magazine. This gave the Germans an advantage over the Lebel, which was slow to reload. It was also only accurate to 400m and suffered by having poor sights. Nevertheless, the fact

Country of origin: France

Date of manufacture: 1890

Location: Private collection

that the French weapon had a greater capacity – with eight rounds compared to five, was a distinct advantage – and the rifle was robust and well made.

Weighing 4.18kg, and with a length of 1.3m, the wartime Lebel was designated the *Fusil Modèle* 1886–93 following a modification of the receiver in 1893. The rifle illustrated is typical of that carried by the *poilu* during the war. It was made at the Châtellerault St Étienne arsenal, and is marked as such, made in 1890 with the designation '*Manufacture d'Armes*' above the arsenal symbol, and the designation '*Mle 1886 M93*'. It is one of very many rifles that formed part of the French infantryman's standard equipment.

In fact, the Lebel was made in large numbers – some 2.8 million – and, on mobilisation, it was issued to the regular *Infanterie Métropolitain* and to the reserves; from the opening Battle of the Frontiers in 1914 to the Battle of Verdun in 1916, the rifle remained the only type used by the French *poilu*. Eventually, though, the strains of the Lebel would be replaced – at least in some arms – by a charger-loading rifle, the Berthier, or *Fusil 07/15*, which was developed from a cavalry carbine and equipped with a three-round magazine. This weapon had originally been designed as a direct response to German designs in the latter part of the nineteenth century, but was slow to be adopted; the French were planning to develop a semi-automatic rifle that would have been revolutionary. These plans were interrupted by war, and the sturdy Lebel remained in the hands of the French infantryman until its end. Equipped with the épée bayonet 'Rosalie', the Lebel helped define the image of the *poilu* in popular culture.

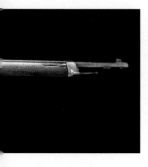
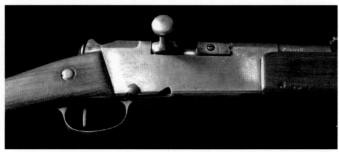

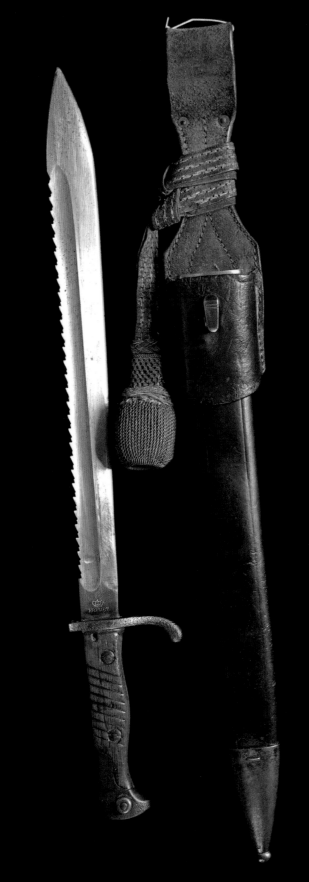

17

'Butcher' bayonet

BAYONETS ARE A throwback to medieval warfare. Fixing the naked blade to the front of the rifle transforms it from a firearm to a pike; instruction in the use of the bayonet was instruction in fighting a determined enemy in a personal battle. The British Army instruction manual *Bayonet Training* (1918) was clear: 'Hand-to-hand fighting with the bayonet is individual [...] killing is at close quarters, at a range of 2 feet or less, when troops are struggling corps á corps in trenches or darkness.' When the European nations went to war, they did so equipping their soldiers with a bayonet. As the British instruction manual *Bayonet Fighting* (1915) put it: 'The bayonet plays a most important part in modern warfare, and it is believed that it will only by a series of bayonet assaults carried out by men skilled in the use of the weapon [...] that positions held by a brave and determined enemy can be captured.' This doctrine was common to both sides of no-man's-land.

The British soldier was equipped with the fearsome 17in sword bayonet, the 1907 pattern. This was intended to maximise the reach of the soldier, particularly as he was issued with a rifle – the Short Magazine Lee–Enfield – that was shorter than most other protagonists. The bayonet of the average French infantryman was somewhat different; instead of a sword, he was

Country of origin: Germany

Date of manufacture: 1914–18

Location: Private collection

67

equipped with a 520mm cruciform-sectioned, rapier-like épée bayonet (the Mle. 1866) that was christened 'Rosalie', and which figured in folklore and poems:

> Farewell, my wife, farewell, Marie,
> I am going with Rosalie
> On the long march you will cling to me
> And I shall love you Rosalie.

Grace Fallow Norton, 'Roads', 1916

For the Germans, the most common bayonet was the S98/05, introduced in 1905. Like its rivals, it was distinctive. Replacing the longer S98 sword bayonet introduced with the *Gewehr 98* rifle, the S98/05 had a distinctly bulbous profile to the blade that gave it a noticeable 'butcher knife' look. It was designed to do exactly what the other nation's blades were intended to do: kill the enemy at close quarters. But the S98/05 had another version. A proportion were equipped with a 'sawback', a move that took the bayonet from killing blade to multi-tool. Running along the back of the bayonet was a fearsome set of teeth that allowed it to be used as a wood-cutting tool, creating a compromise between killing weapon and pioneer tool. Issued to pioneer battalions and non-commissioned officers (NCOs), this blade was given to only a small proportion of German troops. The example illustrated is typical of the type. Most were in the traditional sword-manufacturing town of Solingen – 'the City of Blades', situated in Nord Rhine-Westphalia – but this is from the *Königliche Gewehrfabrik* in the Thuringian city of Erfurt. The weapon is equipped with an original troddel or 'sword knot', an item that was originally functional but had now become a component part of the identification system for a unit. No doubt it was the trusted tool of a pioneer, or an item of status for an NCO. But as it was equipped with the same means of attaching it to the rifle as the normal version, the sawback S98/05, still functioning as a weapon, was held up as evidence of the 'dastardly Hun' intent on wreaking havoc across Europe.

British soldier equipped with SMLE rifle and 1907 pattern bayonet.

Undoubtedly such weapons/tools could inflict terrible wounds if used in an assault. Yet multifunction bayonets were not new; the British themselves had, on the same multifunctional principles, issued a sawback sword bayonet for their artillerymen, who were equipped with short carbines, in 1879. This was conveniently forgotten in the propaganda battleground. That this propaganda had an effect is evident from Erich Maria Remarque's classic 1929 novel of the German experience of the war, *Im Western nichts Neue*, translated as *All Quiet on the Western Front*. Here, the hero, Paul Baumer, describes the act of removing the sawback in the face of the fear of retaliation:

> During the day [...] we overhaul the bayonets – that is to say, the ones that have a saw on the blunt edge. If the fellows over there catch a man with one of those he's killed at sight. In the next sector some of our men were found whose noses were cut off and their eyes poked out with their own saw-bayonets.

The utility of the sawback blade was soon forgotten, as pressure mounted. From 1917, the saw itself was ground from the blunt edge of the bayonet, and the blade returned to its sole purpose, a purpose in keeping with all similar weapons used in the war – the closing and taking of enemy positions by force.

Fritz Braune
Neudorf Kr. Twiste
2. 7. 98
Fritz Braune
Neudorf Kr. Twiste
2. 7. 98

18

German identity disc

IDENTITY DISCS HAVE not always been part of the soldier's traditional accoutrements. In the American Civil War, combatants carried small pieces of paper with their names on them in order that they should receive a named grave if killed, and later bought engraved badges that could be attached to their uniforms. Yet few nations thought clearly about the importance of being able to identify their dead, if only as part of an accounting procedure, until the latter part of the nineteenth century. The first to do so were the Prussians, who in 1870 issued a simple rectangular tag suspended by a cord that was marked with the regimental details and regimental numbers. This tag was specified in the Prussian regulations of the Army Medical Corps, with the simple aim of identifying the dead or wounded. Other nations followed suit, slowly: France in 1881; Austria and Russia in 1902; Britain in 1907.

The choices available to these nations were many. Most went for a tag or disc that was suspended from the neck on a cord. These options were understandable; the grim reality of war was that with so many awful artillery wounds, limbs would be wrenched from bodies, negating the use of wrist bracelets. During war conditions, the fear that a soldier's body could be left unidentified on the field of battle meant that men more often than not

Country of origin: Germany

Date of manufacture: c. 1916

Location: Private collection

71

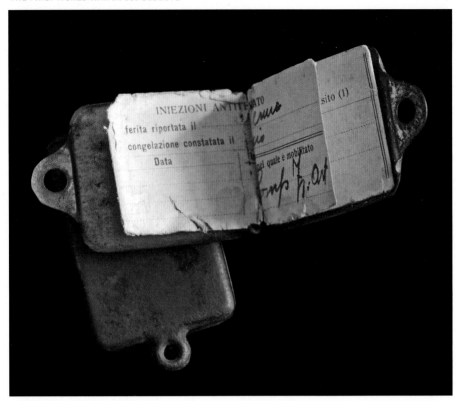

INIEZIONI ANTITE...ATO
ferita riportata il
congelazione constatata il
Data

...sito (I)

...el quale è mobilitato

Italian (top) and Austro-Hungarian (bottom) identity capsules.

made their own wrist bracelets, or commissioned them from jewellers; and in 1918 the French finally adopted an official pattern that was intended to be worn around the wrist. The Austrians had a complex metal capsule – the *Legitimationkapsel* – which contained a paper insert with the soldier's details, but which was intended to be clipped to the inside of the trouser pocket. This was copied by their direct enemies, Italy, when they joined the Allies in 1915.

In this way, patterns varied considerably from nation to nation. The British used three different types: a single stamped aluminium disc, which carried the name, rank, serial number, unit details and religion issued on mobilisation in 1914, before being replaced by a single red fibre disc. Once this single disc was removed from the body, as stipulated in the 1914 *Field Service Regulations*, the chances of identification were much reduced. As such, in August 1916, a two-disc system was evolved, the discs themselves carrying the same information as before, in duplicate, but this time stamped on compressed fibreboard discs: a green octagonal one which, it was intended, would stay with the body, and a red disc which would be taken as part of the accounting procedure. Both were to be worn on a string around the neck – but as this often became dirty and clammy, some soldiers carried the discs separately in their haversack or pack. All were to be given the brutally frank name 'cold meat tickets' (resembling as they did the tags used in butchers' shops); post-war, the term 'dog tag', from American usage, became commonplace.

But our example is German, of a pattern that was issued in 1916 to all soldiers. Stamped in simple zinc alloy, this disc was worn around the neck on a cord that was sometimes in the colours of the state; typical was the white and black of Prussia. The details of its owner are stamped twice, one above the other. There is a simple reason for this: the disc could be broken along its centre line, leaving one half with the body, the other removed for 'accounting' purposes. Fritz Braune came from Neudorf in Hesse and was born on 2 July 1898. He was just 18 years old when he joined his regiment, the *Grenadier-Regiment König Frederich 1 (4. Ostpreußisches)* nr. 5. All these details are stamped on the tag, or *Erkennungsmarke*, that was carried by Grenadier Braune throughout his service in the field. And it saw some action: attached to the 36th Infanterie-Division, his regiment was pitched into the Somme battle front on 24 July 1916, and would see action in all the major battles in 1917 before moving south to the Marne. Fritz survived; his disc remained intact. So many others are buried with their owners, periodically surfacing as the ploughs break the surface for cultivation; sad reminders of young lives lost.

19

Ottoman belt buckle

WHEN WAR WITH Germany was declared on 4 August 1914, the Ottoman Empire ostensibly remained neutral; yet already this ancient state had signed a treaty with Germany that would bind it to the Central Powers. For the kaiser, the greatest possibility of a Greater Germany, and an influence that would spread through the Balkans and into the Middle East, was an unbridled dream that would manifest itself in the construction of an unbroken railway link from Berlin to Baghdad, passing through Thracian Turkey and into Anatolia, passing over the Bosphorous at Constantinople. This would travel through aligned nations, with Bulgaria and the Ottoman Empire pivotal in this; it was inconvenient, though, that belligerent Serbia sat squarely in the way.

German influence in European Turkey was strong, with military missions to the Ottomans from the late nineteenth century; its influence was to grow when, on 3 August 1914, the British clumsily requisitioned two warships being built in British shipyards, at great cost to the populace. Tensions came to a head when on 10 August the German warships *Goeben* and *Breslau* were granted passage through the technically neutral Dardanelles straits to Constantinople, to become symbolic substitutes for the ships 'stolen' by the British. A final blow to British influence was the appointment

Country of origin: Ottoman Turkey

Date of manufacture: 1914–18

Location: Private collection

of the German Admiral Souchon to the command of the Ottoman Navy – the *Goeben* and *Breslau* were now technically Ottoman ships, the *Yavus Sultan Salim* and the *Midilli*.

Committed to the Central Powers, the Ottomans' position was originally defensive, holding the Russians in the Caucasus and ensuring that the Dardanelles defences were intact and supported by the laying of minefields. The Ottoman forces mobilised in August 1914 initially with three armies, growing to five in 1915. In 1914, the 1st and 2nd Armies were serving in Thrace to the west of Constantinople, facing their old enemies of the Balkan Wars and, in 1915, defending both shores of the Dardanelles and Bosphorus (the 2nd Army later serving in the Caucasus); the 3rd Army served in north-east Anatolia throughout its existence; the 4th Army, formed in September 1914, was sent to Syria, taking part in the expedition against the British in the Suez Canal Zone in late 1914; and, finally, the 5th Army, raised on 25 March 1915, was to form the main defence of the Dardanelles against the Allied attacks. Three other armies, the 6th, 7th (both formed in 1915) and 8th (formed in 1917), would see service in Mesopotamia (Iraq), Palestine and Syria.

The profile of the Ottoman soldier had changed through the experience of the Balkan Wars and had experienced a shift in influence away from the French to the Germans, a by-product of the crushing defeat of the Franco-Prussian War of 1870–71. The belt buckle illustrated belies its German influence. Prior to the Young Turk revolution, the *Mehmetçik* (the Ottoman nickname for the private soldier; he would be 'Johnny Turk' or simply 'Abdul' to the British and Anzacs) wore a blue uniform with red *tarbush* ('fez'). With the reforms of the army, and in line with most other military forces, the standard uniform, introduced in 1909, was drab in colour ('khaki', but varying considerably in shade, from beige to brown, and in quality, particularly as the war progressed), its tunic resembling that of the German Army. The *tarbush* was replaced with a unique piece of headgear, the *kabalak*, sometimes called the *Enveriye* after Enver Pasha, who introduced it. The *kabalak* consisted of

Ottoman troops present arms.

a long cloth that was wound around a wicker base, forming a kind of solar topee. The soldier was armed with a Mauser pattern rifle, known as the Turkish Mauser, with an appropriate bayonet, both made in Germany.

The soldiers' personal equipment, also supplied by their allies, was based on the standard German pattern of leather belt and ammunition pouches, entrenching tool, water bottle and bread bag. Characteristic of this set was the use of a distinctive brass belt buckle with white metal centre. The belt buckle illustrated is a handsome adornment to the Ottoman soldier, its star and crescent – the *Ay-yildiz* – its central device. In this, the buckle differs from its German version, which bears the Christian statement *Gott mit Uns* (God with Us). Irreverent British soldiers would poke mild fun at this with signs stating 'We've got mittens too'. This equipment set represents the ideal; in reality, the Ottoman soldier would have to suffer extreme shortages and would present a rag-tag image to the usually well-equipped Allies.

20
US field equipment

THE PROVISION OF appropriate load-bearing equipment for the soldier has been a question that has taxed the military mind ever since the infantryman was first conceived. For centuries, the design of equipment – to include ammunition carriers, haversacks for accoutrements, ration carriers, and so on – has centred on the belt, with shoulder straps and braces designed to spread the weight. Both German and French equipment were founded in an archaic design, with the belt supporting much of the weight of the ammunition. And both used leather as a primary material. Though leather is relatively tough and easy to source, it is liable to stretch when wet, and this was a problem in the mid-nineteenth century when equipment relied upon belts with loops to contain cartridges. All too often, these cartridges would be lost in the field as the loops deformed. Something better suited to field use was required.

One of the greatest innovations in soldiers' load-bearing equipment was the discovery and use of thick woven cotton strapping, known as webbing, which was invented by the Mills Equipment Company in the United States in the late nineteenth century. In 1880 the US Army became the first to adopt webbing as an item of universal issue, with a webbing cartridge belt designed to hold the .45–70 cartridges for the Springfield rifle

Country of origin: USA

Date of manufacture: c. 1910–18

Location: Private collection

then in use. Webbing belts formed part of the American soldiers equipage in the Spanish-American War (1898–1902); duly waterproofed they served well in the tropical climates of Cuba and the Philippines. With this success, the use of webbing expanded, and by the early twentieth century the open webbing belts had developed into pocketed belts to hold chargers or clips of ammunition for the 1903 Springfield rifle. Supplied with 'suspenders' – shoulder-strap braces – the 1903 pocketed belt was the basis for the American equipment set that would serve through two world wars.

Private Johnson was a member of the HQ Company of the US 89th Division – 'the Rolling W' – which was first raised in August 1917 to serve in Europe in the First World War. Arriving in June 1918, the division was placed in the line in the St Mihiel Salient, a bulge in the line to the south of Verdun. The salient was taken in September 1918; the 89th, a component part of the US IV Corps, formed the mid-part line in the southern limb of the salient. Private Johnson was equipped as any 'doughboy' (a term of obscure origins, but possibly deriving from the Spanish-American War), with uniform, gas mask and steel helmet – as well as a full set of infantry equipment. Like so many other US soldiers returning from the war, Johnson's effects were simply stored in a trunk on his return from Europe, forgotten for some eighty years. Packed away were parts of his webbing and canvas equipment set, designated the M1910 Equipment – which had served well this member of the American Expeditionary Force (AEF).

Surviving are Pte Johnson's cartridge belt, canteen (water bottle), haversack with slung pouch for his 'meat can' (mess tin), his gas mask (called the 'American Corrected English Box Respirator') and steel helmet. This equipment was carefully packed with his full uniform – as if kept in readiness for future conflict.

As originally planned, the equipment was required to carry around 50lb of equipment and clothing, comparable with most other infantrymen of the day, though at the lower end of the normal 50–60lb of equipment. In fact, in field use more would be needed – especially as in the

US soldiers in the
Rhineland, 1919,
part of the Allied
occupation force.

trenches the soldier had to be self-sufficient. In fact, the
amount and manner of carriage of equipment is controversial, and has been the subject of much debate: just how
much was the average soldier hindered in moving forward over the freshly shell-blasted battlefield? And how
much did the equipment weigh him down? With Private
Johnson serving in the HQ, he may never have had to test
this out in action, but very many of his comrades did.

The arrival of the Americans in France in 1918
announced to the Central Powers that their time was
about to expire. The vast resources of the United States
would surely bolster the Allies and ensure the defeat of
the Central Powers. The Battle of St Mihiel (1918) saw
the Americans 'blooded' with some 7,000 total battle
casualties; ultimately they would lose 50,280 men killed
in battle – and 57,460 who succumbed to the influenza
pandemic of 1918.

21 Austrian water bottle

FINDING AND SUPPLYING adequate sources of water in wartime was a major preoccupation for the military engineers of all nations. On the Western Front, water was plentiful, but it was often the case that surface water supplies were contaminated and tainted by everything from gas shells to dead bodies, and maintaining a plentiful supply to thirsty troops meant drilling for water at depth, tapping into uncontaminated supplies of fresh ground water. Much of the efforts of military engineers of all the armies were expended on searching for supplies, the effects of which were magnified in the arid desert environment of Palestine,

Gallipoli and Mesopotamia (Iraq). As the British *Field Service Regulations* (1914) put it: 'As the health of a force depends largely on the purity of the water provided, everything must be done to ensure an ample supply of pure drinking water.' In Gallipoli, water had to be supplied to the British and ANZAC troops from Alexandria in Egypt, as opportunities to obtain plentiful supplies were limited – though not for the Ottomans. And water was not only required for men; with the armies of the Great War so dependent upon horses, ensuring that they were well supplied and watered was an equally challenging task.

Part of the field equipment of all combatants was a water bottle. The bottle itself had to be hardy, capable of

Country of origin: Austria-Hungary

Date of manufacture: 1916

Location: Private collection

taking some punishment while supplying the needs of the average soldier. For the most part, soldiers were discouraged from drinking while on the march, with the prevailing doctrine being that regular intakes of water led to a propagation of thirst: instead, soldiers were encouraged to suck on stones in an attempt to promote salivation. The British *Manual of Elementary Military Hygiene* (1912) stipulated that to make up loss of fluids from the body, in temperate climates a man would need to drink 3.55 to 5 pints daily (approximately 1.75–2.5 litres), and considerably more in hot climates. For this reason alone, most water bottles carried by combatants were capable of taking at least 2 pints (1 litre) of fluids.

This makes the standard Austro-Hungarian issue water bottle all the more surprising. Attractively produced, neat and self-contained, the enamel *feldflasche* illustrated is typical of its type. Battered – with some loss of enamel, missing its cork and matching cup – the flask was made by the Austrian company BGB Brunn in 1916. The water bottle itself was normally carried in the 'bread bag', and was carried without much of a cover – though soldiers often improvised them from wool, canvas and so on. For Alpine troops, the bottle was carried in a skeleton strap made of leather – though in many cases the strap was simply replaced by cord. What is most surprising, however, is how little water could be carried by the Austrians in one of these objects, just 0.5 litres: they must always have been on the lookout for a water source. This would be fine in static warfare on the Alpine front; fighting against the Russians in the summer sun of Galicia would be another matter all together. It is hardly surprising, then, that Austro-Hungarian soldiers often carried more than one water bottle. Of the Allies, the best equipped in terms of quantity were the French, with their distinctive *bidon modèle 1877*. Featuring two spouts – a large cork-stoppered one and a smaller wooden-plugged one – the bidon issued to most troops had a capacity of 2 litres, though the rumours were that this was more often than not filled with something a little more strong than simply water.

22 French field kit

THE ABILITY TO store, eat and supply food is of paramount importance to the average soldier. Food was a particularly important issue in maintaining morale while men were in the trenches – and the supply of hot food was recognised as one of the major aspects supporting the morale of the average soldier. Getting hot food to the trenches was challenging for all sides; ration parties would bring up rations at night, usually men 'out at rest' detailed for work up the line at night. With increasing sophistication of the military machine, hot rations in specially designed ration carriers were brought up the line; an arduous duty, but one much appreciated by the front-line troops all the same. Other rations would be commonly brought up in sand bags, often in a hopeless jumble.

For most nations, the supply of field kit to cook such rations – and carried by the average soldiers – comprised a mess tin with lid and handle, equally capable of being held up to receive rations as it was to cook them

Country of origin: France

Date of manufacture: 1914–18

Location: Private collection

on rudimentary fires. In British use, the lighting of fires was officially frowned upon, but was commonly done in any case, particularly in the trenches, where getting hold of hot food was challenging. Cooking could be done on braziers or small fires in the mess kit provided, placed directly upon the heat source. Its bowl and lid acted as both dish and cooker. But all too often the smoke would bring the attention of mortars and other trench artillery, and was a dangerous business.

Of all the nations committed to the front, it was the French who carried the most in the way of eating and drinking receptacles. In addition to the 2-litre (or 1-litre in some circumstances) *bidon*, or water bottle, there was an enamel cup, a bowl (the *gamelle*) with lid and an integral plate (that served as a frying pan). To this already considerable weight was added a canvas bucket for fetching water, and a large cooking pot, or *marmite* – intended mostly for the campsite, but just as easily finding its way to the front line. These items of a soldier's equipment were so necessary – and so common – that they regularly turn up at flea markets. The items displayed, all relics of the *poilu*'s life in the trenches, were bought at a flea market in the South of France, and all derive from the cooking kit of one man of the Great War.

There were many others: the necessary coffee mill, or the larger cooking pots such as the *bouthéon*, or the *grand gamelle*. These utensils were to be used at company level, with soldiers assigned to cooking detail on a rotational basis: a soldier carrying them up to the front line would be doing so for the use of all his comrades, not just for himself, as happened so often in other armies. Without fresh supplies the utensils would just represent an encumbrance. Though the French were equipped with more cooking utensils than the soldiers of most other nations, in common with the front-line troops on both sides of no-man's-land in the trenches they more often than not subsisted on a monotonous diet of foods that could easily be carried: bread, dubious tinned meat (christened *singe*, or 'monkey', by the *poilu*), wine and sausage, all shared in the spartan and squalid conditions of the trenches.

23 Field dressing

SOLDIERS COMMITTED TO battle placed their trust in their leaders – their NCOs and officers – as well as in blind faith to get them through safely. But with the incidence of random wounding at the front, some 30 per cent of soldiers would be hurt during their service. It is not surprising that soldiers talked of wounds that would get them home to their loved ones, wounds that would not be so life-threatening to be dangerous yet not too trivial to be treated in the field, thereby returning the soldier to action.

The aftermath of an attack would be the suffering of men, many of whom would be stranded in no-man's-land, sheltering in shell holes, waiting and hoping for the arrival of stretcher-bearers. In battle, it was mostly expressly forbidden for soldiers to stop and give aid to their fallen comrades. This would impede the attack. Instead, stretcher-bearers were battalion men who gave up their arms to carry their stretcher, the bearing of arms by medics being expressly forbidden in war. Ideally, at least six men would be needed per stretcher; this was not always achievable, and prisoners were often drafted in to carry wounded soldiers back, as it was an offence for otherwise able-bodied

Country of origin: United Kingdom

Date of manufacture: *c.* 1918

Location: Private collection

men to escort wounded soldiers back without the express permission of an officer. Many were bandsmen, others were infantrymen detailed for the job – a dangerous task, requiring service under fire, usually in no-man's-land.

Field dressings were issued to all soldiers. The British example illustrated, manufactured in 1918, was designed to be kept in a pocket under the front flap of the service dress tunic, specified in the *Field Service Regulations*. The same principle was applied in the German Army. Early on, these pouches also contained safety pins and ampoules of iodine as a form of disinfectant to treat wounds; later in the war, the value of the chemical having been questioned, it was left out of the set. In all cases, the idea was that a wounded man would have his own dressings used upon him; with so many wounds being caused by shell fire, larger dressings were needed than could be carried by an individual, and these special 'shell dressings' were carried by regimental stretcher-bearers in action.

The first field dressing was intended for rudimentary first aid, and consisted of a packet containing two dressings – one for the entry wound, one for the exit (in the case of gunshot wounds). For the British, the regulations were clear:

> The first field dressing applied as a protection against dirt and to stop haemorrhage, with the addition of some support to a broken limb, before removal of the patient, is all that is needed on the field itself. After this first aid, a wounded man should be left where he lies, under as good cover as possible, unless the nature of the ground, a pause in the fighting, or the approach of darkness allows systematic collection and removal.
>
> *Field Service Regulations*, Part II Organisation and Administration 1909 (Reprinted with Amendments, 1914)

With linen and lint becoming a scarce commodity in Germany – with the British blockade in full force – the kaiser's front-line troops were issued with '*ersatz*' paper dressings. With so many men wounded in the war, it is telling that even in their hour of need, German soldiers were asked to give more.

24

Adrian helmet

STEEL HELMETS WERE an innovation that was born out of the necessity of modern war. In 1914, all armies were equipped with some form of uniform cap or ceremonial helmet – the German *pickelhaube* being an example of this type – gaudy, impractical and affording little protection from the elements or from their enemies. In action, this meant that head wounds were common, especially when the attention of snipers was concentrated on the movement of soldiers past loopholes and dips in the trench sides. Men were vulnerable to snipers, but they were also subject to the random tragedies of spent bullets, air-burst shrapnel and shell fragments. Clearly there was a need for increased head protection, and this was to be introduced in late 1915, with innovation by the French, Germans and British producing markedly different steel helmets.

Adrian helmet to the *Chasseurs à Pied*.

Country of origin: France

Date of manufacture: c. 1915–18

Location: Private collection

The first real approaches to developing a steel helmet in France saw the creation of steel skullcaps that could be worn beneath the kepi. This, it was hoped, would reduce the impact of air-burst shrapnel, or deflect nearly spent bullets, which so often led to casualties on the Western Front. The resulting *cerveliere* was ordered in February 1915, with 700,000 ordered and by 27 March some 207,000 had been delivered. It was awkward, ungainly and heavy to wear under the standard kepi.

It was destined to be replaced by one of the most influ-ential designs of the Great War, the so-called Adrian helmet. The helmet takes its name from the man who introduced it, *L'Intendant* General A. Adrian, but its design borrowed much from that worn by the French fire service. With its pleasing, almost streamlined shape, the Adrian helmet soon came to encompass the image and ideals of the French soldier.

German soldiers guard French POWs, most wearing Adrian helmets.

Like the German *stahlhelm* or the British 'Brodie', its image was used in the press, in propaganda and, after the war, in defining veteran's organisations. The Adrian marks the kilometre stones of the *Voie Sacrée*, the 'sacred way' that served as the supply lines for Verdun. Unlike the helmets issued to the British and Germans later in 1915, the French Adrian also provided a means of identifying the branch of service of the French troops that wore them. Seven badges were designed that would identify the infantry, with their flaming grenade; the *Chasseurs à Pied*, or light infantry, distinguished by a hunting horn; the artillery, denoted by crossed cannons; the *Génie*, or engineers, depicted by helmet and breast-plate; a crescent for African *Zouaves* and *Tirailleurs*; the medical service by the traditional Caduceus symbol of serpent and staff; and finally the grenade and anchor for colonial marines.

Our helmet was proudly worn by a member of the *Chasseurs à Pied* in war and peace, identified by its distinctive horn. With the importance of the helmet to the soldier, each one who had served was awarded an Adrian as a souvenir of service by the French government in December 1918. It was intended that this souvenir be individually engraved; an impractical, ornate brass plaque was attached to the visor by veterans, which was worn increasingly at remembrance parades. Marked as a '*Soldat de la Grande Guerre*', all too often, as in this case, no further identification of the individual was given. We are left to muse on the actions of this brave soldat in war.

The Adrian was surprisingly successful. Surprisingly, because it was made from mild steel, and had four main sections in addition to the liner. The steel was just 0.7mm thick, meaning that the helmet weighed just 0.765kg – much lighter than the *cerveliere* it was designed to replace. The first orders were placed in the spring of 1915 and were issued in July 1915; by September, all troops intended for Joffre's great Champagne offensive were equipped with the helmet, and by the end of the war some 20 million helmets were produced by eight main manufacturers across France.

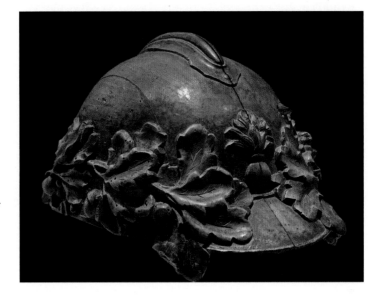

Wooden former for the bronze Adrian helmets that cap the kilometre stones of the *Voie Sacrée*.

25 Colt 1911

THE COLT M1911 pistol – officially the Automatic Pistol, Calibre .45, M1911 – is one of the most famous weapons ever produced, a design classic that has been copied by many manufacturers the world over. Some 2.7 million individual weapons have been produced since it was first designed by John Browning. Weighing some 2.44lb and measuring just 8.25in long, the M1911 is both neat and robust. Semi-automatic, the pistol is loaded from a seven-round box magazine, which supplied the man-stopping .45 calibre bullets.

The M1911 pistol is surprisingly modern in design and look, and was favoured by many for its size and reliability at a time when service revolvers such as those in British service – the .455 Webley Mark VI for example – were extremely cumbersome, weighing in at 2.4lb and with a length of 11.25in. Compared with the Webley, the M1911 was compact, while still delivering firepower equivalent to the large British service revolver.

Country of origin: USA

Date of manufacture: c. 1911–18

Location: Private collection

The example illustrated is typical of the weapon; not marked for US service, it was one of many that were produced for use in those armies whose officers were given a free hand to purchase their personal side arms. This one was the property of a French officer; it could just have easily have been purchased by an Italian, British or Belgian. While many officers might have followed the norm in adopting the standard revolvers of the day, others used a range of automatic or semi-automatic pistols. This was true of several nations, Germany amongst them, with the Luger and Mauser being representative of the type. With much smaller calibre ammunition, though, neither had the stopping power of the Colt.

The M1911 grew out of a need for a weapon capable of delivering this stopping power for the US Army, which was engaged in battles against guerrillas in the Philippines during the latter part of the nineteenth century. The US government initiated weapons trials in 1906 with the specification that the pistol should be 'no less than .45 calibre', and that, ideally, it should be semi-automatic. The Colt bested five other pistols in the trials; and while 6,000 rounds were fired from a single weapon over the two-day trials, it did not misfire or jam. This level of robustness would serve it well in the world conflict, and it entered US service in 1911.

The pistol is also perhaps representative of the weapons the United States brought to the war theatre in 1917. Robust, reliable and no-nonsense, in the right hands the Colt was capable of hard work. In the hands of Sergeant Alvin York – the celebrated son of Tennessee and winner of the Congressional Medal of Honor – while attacking a German machine gun position, it was deadly. Innovative in design, it was joined by the M1895 Winchester 'trench' shotgun, an efficient weapon in the confines of a trench or dugout but one that garnered complaint from the Germans, aimed at the United States through diplomatic channels, as being 'inhumane' – in a war that produced chemical weaponry. Our Colt is representative of the ever more efficient manner in which soldiers were killed in this most industrialised of all conflicts.

26
Trench coat

ONE OF THE most enduring objects associated with the Great War – and one that continues to have an impact on modern life through an incongruous link between the war and fashion – is the 'trench coat'. Though the coat itself may well have had nineteenth-century antecedents, the widespread use and adoption of the coat dates to the First World War.

As we know it today, the trench coat is very much a 'fashion statement'. Stylish, the coat can be worn to good effect by both men and women, and has been seen in all cuts and colours. Not surprisingly, its military antecedents were more commonly light khaki in shade – attempting to blend into the background of the battlefield. The coat has passed into popular imagery as the garment of choice for private detectives, gangsters and spies – as well as *femme fatales*. Yet the trench coat was born out of much more serious purpose – the practical necessity of providing protection to its wearer who, more often than not, would be occupying a hole in the ground open to the elements.

The standard cold-weather protection issued to the average soldier was the greatcoat, or *capote* in France. Both British and French versions were constructed from wool serge, and were a considerable weight, even when dry. Difficult to wear with equipment, and

Country of origin: United Kingdom

Date of manufacture: *c.* 1917

Location: Private collection

prone to fouling with mud and water – creating an even weightier piece of clothing – greatcoats were bulky and long. It is not surprising that the average soldier in the winter trenches was tempted to cut down his coat accordingly, to prevent its skirts trailing in the mud – though the French *capote* had the facility for its skirts to be buttoned back. With ordinary soldiers, though, more often than not they had little choice but to abandon the greatcoat in favour of the groundsheet, or leather jerkin. Allied officers, providing their own uniform, had greater freedom, and adopted the lightweight 'trench coat' as an alternative, thus creating demand – as reported in the *New York Times* in August 1917:

> Trench coats in demand. Military supply dealers here report a growing demand for the British trench coat on the part of the recently-commissioned army officers from Pittsburg. The coat in question has been designed specially for use in trench warfare. It has a high collar with a wide turn-over, and is close-fitting to the waist. Below the waist it flares out [...] as for length, it comes down about to the soldier's ankles. The wide skirt effect gives plenty of leg room for running or climbing in and out of trenches.

> *New York Times*, 29 August 1917

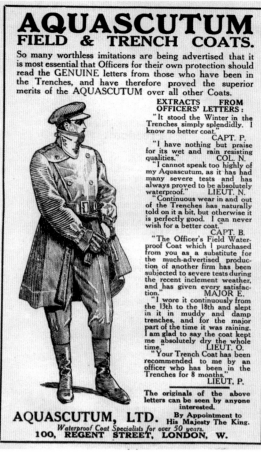

Aquascutum advertises its trench coats.

The garment illustrated is typical. Made by London outfitters Thresher & Glennie, it was the property of a lieutenant in the King's Own Yorkshire Light Infantry, who bought the garment in 1917 and adorned it with rank badges and formation signs. It is in surprisingly good condition – surprising as the coat was deliberately made to withstand the rigours of field and trench life, and to ward off cold and wet. Perhaps the coat was never worn in the field and was packed away after the war, a forgotten relic of the conflict. We might never know. What is clear is that its principal features align with the best of its type, all focused on 'trench use': that it should be made of heavy-duty waterproofed gabardine material (and should be capable of hosting a warmer button-in liner), and that it should not be too long so as to be obstructive. We know from contemporary adverts that the coat cost £4 14s 6d; they trumpeted: 'The Thresher trench coat deserves serious attention [...] two-and-a-half years of war service have stamped it as one of the War's greatest discoveries.'

It is double-breasted, too, with a storm-flap whose purpose was to keep out the cold and wet of the trenches (but in its descendants is now little more than a vestige). Belts at the waist and wrists provide means of closing off the coat from the elements, while at the throat an additional buttoned throat strap gives the chance to cinch the collars together – thereby resisting both the elements and the unwanted attentions of a gas attack, with gas hoods being tucked into outer garments to provide a more effective seal. All in all, the trench coat belies its original martial purpose, even in fashion; brass D rings on the cloth belt meant that this waist belt resembles another piece of officer equipment: the Sam Browne belt. For this is an officer's coat, first and foremost.

Trench coats have a history that spread back before the war, and the premier suppliers of officer's kit all claim to have produced a version, and some claim laurels for invention, including Burberry and Aquascutum. Aquascutum claim the invention for themselves, with its website proclaiming that the company 'played an intrinsic role in the history of the trench coat', its founder working 'in collaboration with the British military to turn his patented waterproof fabric into a garment that offered functionality and protection for the soldiers of the First World War'. Either way, very many outfitters offered their own versions, and tempted young officers with the chance of owning a piece of kit that was marked out as being *de rigueur* for 'the trenches'. Nevertheless, the trench coat was an instant success and was used by officers throughout the war. It is a real example of a military necessity that had direct read-across into modern life. Whether today's purchasers make any direct connection with the lives of the soldiers who originally fought in the garment is a moot point.

First Moves, 1914

27

Moisin-Nagant rifle, Tannenberg

THE MOISIN-NAGANT rifle has become a significant component of the iconography of the Great War.
Images of the massed ranks of the tsar's armies stood
bolt upright with the rifle upon their shoulders are
common, representative of the great mass of men mobilised to form the 'Russian steamroller' so feared by the
Germans and admired by the Allies.

At the outbreak of the war, Tsar Nicholas II appointed
his cousin, Grand Duke Nicholas, as commander-in-
chief. On mobilisation, the Russian Army could boast
some 15.8 million men in uniform – two-fifths of the
male population of service age – and supported some
115 infantry and 38 cavalry divisions. A combined total
of some 78 infantry and 29 cavalry divisions faced the
Central Powers of Germany and Austria-Hungary.

No other nation would mobilise as many men in prosecution of the war. But all was not well. Ensuring that
this impressive number of men each had a rifle and bayonet was a significant challenge to the Russians, whose
economy was not capable of gearing up to maximum
war effort. While Russia headed the tables in the supply
of men, it was very much at the bottom when it came to
military expenditure. While Russia expended some US
$1.8 billion per year on the supply of its military during
the Great War, Germany, Britain and even the United

Country of origin:
Russia

Date of manufacture:
1914–17

Location: Private collection

101

States were to spend at least twice as much on their military consumables during the war. This deficit would have a net effect on the soldiers at the front – many of whom would have to do without a rifle of their own.

The tsar's men: Russian soldiers armed with Moisin-Nagants.

The *Винтовка Мосина*, or Mosin-Nagant, (officially the 3-line rifle, Model 1891) was adopted in 1891 as the standard weapon of the Russian infantryman. The example illustrated is typical. Designed by Captain Sergei Ivanovich Moisin, it employed a bolt action based on the Mauser system and, like the German Mauser, had a fixed magazine capable of holding five rounds of .30in calibre (or three 'lines'), which was loaded using a charger or clip. Initially made under contract in France, Russia was soon producing the M1891 at the Tula and Ishvesk arsenals, though it soon became necessary to place orders with munitions factories in the United States. The Moisin-Nagant rifle was to be used with its bayonet fully attached – Russian soldiers were not issued with a scabbard. The bayonet was a simple cruciform épée that fitted over the barrel with a socket and locking ring that was tightened by means of a screw to securely attach the weapon to the rifle.

Our example is a well-preserved one, which is something of a surprise given the fact that it was most probably captured by the Germans in the aftermath of the Battle of Tannenberg, fought between 26 and 30 August 1914. The battle was intended to cut off the German 8th Army south-west of Königsburg in East Prussia, but it soon developed into a major defeat, with the loss of 92,000 Russians captured and 78,000 killed. Just 10,000 escaped – the Russian 2nd Army was decimated. With such a major defeat, the Russians were in disarray and the Entente powers seriously threatened. While the Russian commander Major-General Samonov committed suicide, the German leaders, in the shape of Generals Hindenburg and Ludendorff, were celebrated. Vast amounts of booty were returned to Germany, reputedly in sixty trains. Amongst them must have been this rifle, manufactured in 1906 at the Tula arsenal. It would be remarked and refitted for German service.

The failure of the Imperial Russian Army at Tannenberg was set to be a metaphor for the battles of the Eastern Front. Driven into the ground, bayonet-first, an upright Moisin-Nagant was taken as a symbol of surrender, each one on the battlefield representing a captured soldier. Perhaps this captured rifle was left just-so, taken from the field by salvage parties. It would be sorely missed by the Russians in the battles that followed.

After the battle – Moisin-Nagants driven into the ground.

28 Short Magazine Lee–Enfield

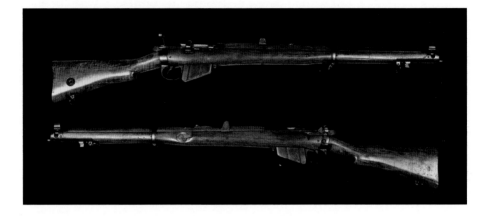

THE PRINCIPAL WEAPON of the British soldier in the Great War was the Short Magazine Lee–Enfield rifle, SMLE to most soldiers. The SMLE was based on its predecessor, the Magazine Lee–Enfield (MLE) first introduced in 1895. The MLE was the first British service rifle equipped with a ten-round magazine, and was famed for its mechanism which cocked the striker when the bolt was closed – a swift action, important in battle, meaning that the weapon could be cocked and fired rapidly. Illustrated is a museum specimen, the SMLE Mark III, preserved in the Swedish *Armémuseum* and looking as it would have done on issue. Most others that served in the war would be considerably more battered and worn.

The design intention was to build on the reliability of the earlier MLE, but to shorten it, lighten it and provide the means of its loading through a charger-fed magazine system – thereby capitalising on its superior bolt action. The resulting rifle, the SMLE Mark 1, was to appear on 23 December 1902. It was 5in shorter than its forerunner (though with three butt sizes fitted to soldiers of differing stature), and was both easier to handle and capable of being used as an infantry rifle and a cavalry carbine.

Country of origin:
United Kingdom

Date of manufacture:
1914–18

Location:
Armémuseum,
Stockholm,
Sweden

The charger system used by the SMLE allowed for five rounds to be loaded at a time, the magazine holding ten altogether. In British service, the 'charger' was a clip that held five rounds of the standard Mark VII cartridges – known as 'ball cartridge'. The charger was discarded when the cartridges were pressed home, forced downwards into the spring-loaded magazine that was capable of holding ten rounds in total. The high-capacity magazine and efficient bolt action meant that in the right hands the rifle had an impressive rate of fire. Well-trained soldiers could fire around fifteen aimed bullets per minute with the SMLE – while the record, set in 1914, was thirty-eight bullets fired in a minute, a prodigious rate of fire.

The SMLE was to undergo several modifications through to its last model, the Mark Vi, in 1926. It would be one of the most admired bolt-action rifles in history. The early Mark 1 rifles have the provision for a long-range volley sight – inaccurate, but capable in the right hands of putting down a volley with an effective range of 1,500–2,000 yards. The SMLE Mark III, introduced in January 1907 with changes to its sights and charger loading system, was the main rifle to be used during the war; from January 1916, simplifications to this rifle were made in order to speed up production for the New Army.

The British soldier who went to war in August 1914 was one of the best trained in the world. A professional soldier, he was well trained in the musketry drill that was set out in the official manual *Musketry Regulations, Part I* 1909, which was reprinted in August 1914 in readiness for war. The SMLE was reputed to have one of the fastest bolt actions; it certainly had a larger magazine than the rifles possessed by the Germans, or by their French allies. With this level of training and equipment, the British regular soldier of 1914 could loose off fifteen aimed rounds per minute, and sometimes considerably more. In the summer of 1914, with the British Expeditionary Force committed to the field at Mons on 23 August 1914 and engaging in the retreat to the Aisne, the Germans experienced firepower they had not expected. Were they met by machine guns? The simple answer was no.

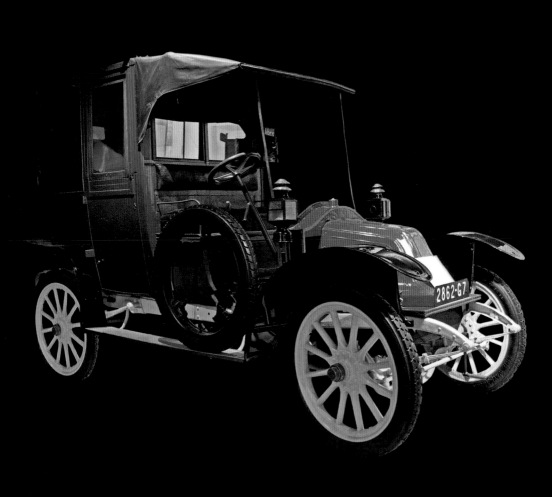

29

Taxi cab of the Marne

THE SCHLIEFFEN PLAN had been developed by Count Alfred Von Schlieffen as early as 1910 in planning for a future conflict with France. Since the crushing defeat of France in the Franco-Prussian War of 1870–71, and the loss of the provinces of Alsace and Lorraine to the new German Empire under Otto von Bismarck, tensions between the two continental powers had been running high. In France, for instance, schoolchildren were taught to regard Germany as their enemy, and propaganda, games and patriotic songs all proclaimed the potency of the French ambition to reunite the lost provinces with mother France.

The diplomatic games played out in Europe had also led to the distancing of Germany from potential allies such as Britain and even Russia. This created power blocks in the early twentieth century that would ultimately lead to the development of the German plan that ensured France would be attacked first in any continental conflict. The alignment of France and Russia in 1892 – and the *Entente Cordiale* of 1904 that settled differences between Britain and its continental rivals – led to the German Schlieffen Plan, the ultimate aim of which was to knock France out of the war before, it was hoped, the considerable armies of Russia could be mobilised and brought to bear on the conflict.

Country of origin:
France

Date of construction:
1905

Location: *Musée de l'Armée*, Paris, France

With the events that unfolded in the aftermath of the shooting at Sarajevo in June 1914, the Schlieffen Plan came into action. Like a swinging door, seven German armies were to pivot in a movement intended to encircle Paris and extinguish the heart of the French nation. The German right wing – comprising the 1st, 2nd and 3rd armies – had to travel the longest distance in an arc that cut a swathe through northern Europe – and that, it was hoped, would quickly trample over the Belgians that stood in their way. The longest distance of all was to have been travelled by General Alexander von Kluck's 1st Army, which was to encircle Paris and its defenders. In reality, with momentum ebbing away, and meeting resistance from the Allied armies, von Kluck made the fateful decision to bring his army around in front of Paris, thereby abandoning the main premise of the pre-war plan. Instead of encircling the French capital, Kluck's 1st Army moved southwards to the east of Paris in support of Bulow's 2nd Army. Here, both German armies were stalled by the French and their allies on the River Marne. On this line the French 6th Army – supported by the British Expeditionary Force on its right flank – faced von Kluck's 1st Army on the outskirts of the city. It was events on the Marne that would turn the whole course of the war.

Our object is a simple Renault G7 taxi cab of the type used in Paris from 1905. One of at least 10,000, this example is preserved in the *Musée de l'Armée* in Paris, donated by an American veteran's association in 1922. It is a rare survivor. In September 1914, with the German 1st Army almost knocking on the gates of the city, the French military governor, General Gallieni, requisitioned the city's fleet of Renault taxis as an auxiliary means of transporting troops to the front. With the French 6th Army in need of reinforcement. Gallieni planned to supply men called from the reserves – and to supply them directly to the front, five at a time, crowded with their equipment into Renaults, as in our example. Some 1,200 taxis were requisitioned by the military governor, with the aim of supplying 6,000 troops to reinforce the beleaguered

French wounded returning from the Marne, September 1914.

armies on the Marne. On 6 September, 600 taxis left the *Invalides* in the centre of Paris for the Marne battlefront some 150km away: on 7 September a further 700 were sent on their way. Taxi meters running, the operation cost the public purse some 70,000 francs.

The Allied line held, the Battle of the Frontiers effectively over. Both sides started their 'Race to the Sea', seeking the possibility to turn each other's flanks in a decisive battle. Though providing a small component of the total number of French troops committed to the Marne – the vast majority being transported by train – *Les Taxis de la Marne* attained mythical status, and were held as an example of French fortitude and ingenuity in time of military crisis.

3O

Cloth Hall, Ypres

The Cloth Hall in
c. 1917, and today.

Country of origin:
Belgium

**Date of
construction:**
1304 (rebuilt
1933–67)

Location: Public
building, Ieper,
Belgium

THE CLOTH HALL (*Lakenhalle*) in Ypres is one of the most iconic buildings to be involved in – and rise out of – the destruction of the Great War. Built in the Middle Ages to house the main trading base of the significant Flemish cloth industry, its destruction and focus for shelling from the German lines crowding the low ridges to the east is representative of the symbolic and strategic importance of the city. The resurrection of the Cloth Hall in the post-war period, rebuilt as a replica upon the residue of foundations, is also symbolic of the rebirth of the city, and the rejuvenation of the shell-blasted landscape of Flanders.

Ypres and its Cloth Hall first experienced war in 1914, when a detachment of German Lancers – Uhlans – passed through the city walls to inspect the city. The Germans being driven off during these days of fluid warfare, the city was soon to become the home of the British Expeditionary Force, or BEF, which deployed here during the Allied victory on the Marne, and the subsequent 'Race to the Sea', during which German and Allied troops struggled to turn each other's flanks. With the entrenchments that appeared along the line stopping progress, there was an urgent need for the German Army to push forwards. The ground from Ypres to the sea was strategically significant, important for centuries as a flat ground that would allow the movement of armies. It was here that the German 1st Army pushed forwards in August as part of the Schlieffen Plan. Thanks to the quick-witted reaction of the Belgian lock keeper Henri Geeraerts at Nieuport, the land close to the Belgian coast and next to the the low-lying Polder plain had been flooded to impede the German progress. From Nieuport to Dixmude, the land was flooded, ensuring that the slightly higher ground to the south, connecting with the city of Ypres, would be a focal point of German intentions. Capture of the city would mean that the channel ports – and the safety of the British Expeditionary Force – would be threatened. It had to be defended at all costs.

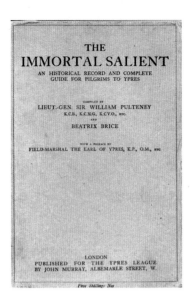

The *Immortal Salient*: a 1925 guidebook for pilgrims to the battlefields.

The Cloth Hall is massive in structure, built from dense hard crystalline sandstones that were capable of withstanding a significant amount of pounding. At street level, even today the Cloth Hall displays its scars, earned some hundred years before; today busy shoppers and eager tourists hurry past the ancient building, without a glimpse, to visit the city's cafes or museums. The British occupation ensured that the Cloth Hall's *belfort* (bell tower) would be the focal point for German artillery. With the Germans occupying the low ridge system, which surrounded the city in a lazy arc on three sides, the tower was targeted day and night. With scaffolding erected, the people still in residence in Ypres hoped to protect their ancient relic, but to no avail.

For their part, the Germans threatened the capture of the city – and the route to the channel ports – on at least three occasions. The First Battle of Ypres, in October 1914, was the first German attempt to take the city and to defeat the Allies decisively. The Second Battle of Ypres, in May 1915, would see the Germans try again – this time with the first-ever mass use of chemical weapons in warfare, with the release of poison gas. Other battles followed, on a smaller scale, until the British attempted an attack on the German lines in 1917. The Germans would try again in 1918 – piercing the British front line before running out of steam before the city.

The Cloth Hall was at the centre of what was known as the Ypres Salient. A salient is a bulge in the front line, and in this case the bulge extended eastwards to mirror the arc of low hills around the city. From the Cloth Hall, and running eastwards through the city walls, was the Menin Road, a straight-as-a-die route that bisected the salient and rose gradually up the slopes of the Passchendaele Ridge. Up this road went armies of men to the front line, passing through the Vauban-designed ramparts at the Menin Gate. From Hellfire Corner to the front line, the road was under continuous observation; transports never paused in their work, a continuous stream of men and materiel moving eastwards.

Salients like this allow the attackers to receive fire poured in from at least three sides, its occupants on the receiving end of directed and continuous artillery fire. It was this artillery fire that reduced the city to a pile of rubble. The destruction of Ypres became an image of the martyrdom of Belgium. The last sizeable city in Belgium still in Allied hands, it was to be defended at all costs. The Cloth Hall and the adjacent cathedral became a focal point of attention for photographers, such as Anthony of Ypres, who painstakingly documented its destruction. It was also a point of great interest to the many soldiers who passed through the city, and who would periodically stop to collect stones, broken religious relics and glass from the wrecked buildings.

Ypres and its 'immortal salient' also became a focal point for pilgrims in the post-war world. With the birth of mass tourism, linked with the rise in post-war pilgrimages to visit the sites of battle and loss, Ypres and its Cloth Hall – still in ruins – was revered. Thousands of visitors came to the site to see its ruined stone walls and to reflect on the 'lost generation' of soldiers who had passed by them. For this reason, Winston Churchill had called for the city to be retained in ruins as a monument to British endeavour. But as the war ended, the people returned to the city and the magnificent gothic structure rose once more from the ruins.

THE COMING OF THE INDIAN TROOPS.

TUMULTUOUS WELCOME.

PICTURESQUE SCENES IN THE STREETS.

By MALCOLM MACASKILL.

MARSEILLES.

15th LANCERS, LAHORE DIVISION.

OUR ANCIENT CITY.

THE NEW SPIRIT.

By A LONDONER.

CHARGE OF BENGAL LANCERS.

SPECIAL SKETCHES FROM LIFE.

GOOD OUT OF EVIL.

3I

'Our Indian Troops'
Scrapbook

THE ARRIVAL IN France of the Army of India – as the British Indian Army was officially called – in September 1914 was viewed with obvious pride. This scrapbook, comprising carefully cut and equally carefully pasted columns from 1914 editions of the *Daily Telegraph* newspaper, records with enthusiasm the arrival of the Indian troops at Marseille in September 1914:

> Rich as the history of our Empire is in scenes that dazzle the mind's eye with their historic colour and significance, can we say that anything in its past quite equals the Spectacle of the coming of the Indian troops to France there to fight with valour and devotion.

Country of origin: United Kingdom

Date of production: 1914

Location: Private collection

The Army of India had been reformed in 1902 through the actions of Kitchener, who created a modern, well-trained force from a range of disparate armies within the subcontinent. The reformed army had a total strength of some 240,000 men in 1914, with nine divisions, each one of 13,000 men with one cavalry and three infantry brigades. This would double during the war. In line with the other British Empire dominions, India quickly came to the aid of Britain in 1914, and brought with it access to the magnificent resource of its army.

The scrapbook cover, harking back to a previous war, in South Africa.

Though the scrapbook records the arrival of the Indians in France on 30 September 1914, this was just one of seven expeditionary forces that the Army of India sent overseas. While Expeditionary Force A was to serve in France, the others would serve in East Africa, Mesopotamia, Sinai, Palestine, Egypt and Gallipoli. In Mesopotamia, Expeditionary Force D made up the majority of General Townsend's forces and was to suffer terribly in 1916. Overextended, Townsend's campaign to invade the Ottoman territory stalled at Kut-el-Amara. Here, in 1916, the British and Indian troops were besieged, finally surrendering to the Ottomans in April. Some 11,012 Indians were killed in the campaign, with an additional 3,985 dying of wounds and a staggering 12,678 dying of disease, many of them through the neglect of their Ottoman captors.

Under the headline 'The Coming of The Indian Troops. Tumultuous Welcome. Picturesque Scenes in the Streets', one cutting records their arrival in France with enthusiasm and makes much of the mingling of the Indians with the range of colonial troops from the corners of the French overseas possessions:

> The good people of Marseilles waited looking more eagerly everyday to see 'Les Hindous' begin to pass. We saw everything else – Tommies and Turcos fraternising [...] Senegalese marching through the streets by the hundreds and thousands [...] But at last one morning the Indians really did come [...] there were cries of Vivent les Hindous!

Transferred from Marseille in October, Indian troops were soon in the thick of the fighting, and took up their position in the developing British line within France and Flanders. 'If anyone had any fears as to how the Indian troops would behave against disciplined Europeans [...] their doubts should now be dispelled, for the turbaned warriors displayed a bravery and dash equal to anything done in war,' commented the newspaper scraps. In March 1915, the Army of India was committed to the Battle of Neuve Chappelle, where it formed around half of the attacking force that was intended to break the line and rush the high ground at Aubers Ridge, in French Flanders. Ultimately, the Indians were to attack without the aid of artillery bombardment (and, in any case, the battle was marred by a shell crisis that would ultimately unseat the government). Almost 1,000 were killed in the battle.

The Indians were ill-prepared for the climate, however, and they were withdrawn from France and Flanders for the warmer climes of Egypt in October of that year. They had served well, and would serve with even greater distinction in Africa.

32

Christmas gift

FOR THE MEN in the trenches, the winter of 1914–15 was trying. In Flanders, with its low-lying damp ground, water was never too far away. As Dr Hugh Mill of the British Rainfall Organisation would remark in a paper to the society in May 1915: 'the abnormal rainfall of the four months November and December 1914 and January and February 1915, gave to the winter just past a character of unusual wetness.' The experts were surely in a position to notice – as were the rain-soaked, freezing men in nearby Flanders. For the British and French soldiers, keeping dry and warm in the trenches was largely impossible; the High Command, not prepared to give ground, gave little attention to improving them, and men lived in squalor. There was ever expectation that Christmas in the trenches (*Weihnachten im Feld*) would be dismal.

For all the soldiers, on both sides, spending Christmas in the trenches had an extra poignancy: separated from their loved ones, soldiers felt a greater sense of longing for home. With the Christmas tradition strong in German culture, Christmas trees (imported to Britain with Prince Albert of Saxe-Coburg and Gotha) would be sought and carefully carried to the front line. Christmas without trees, and without the traditional songs *Stille Nacht* and *Der Tannenbaum*, would have

Country of origin: United Kingdom

Date of production: 1914

Location: Private collection

been unthinkable. Despite the poverty of the conditions, on both sides of no-man's-land cards sent home from the trenches were still able to express the traditional wishes of hope for peace on Earth. Christmas gifts were sent to the trenches from a variety of sources at home, with chocolate, cigarettes and even Christmas puddings being sent from the proceeds of subscription funds. The most famous was that issued by Princess Mary's fund in the first Christmas of the war in 1914. This generosity would never again be repeated.

One of the most commonly encountered items relating to the First World War is the brass Princess Mary's gift box. This brass box, well constructed and with designs inspired by the Art Nouveau movement, was treasured by all who received it at Christmas 1914 – a fact well demonstrated by the abundance of boxes that exist today, boxes that still contain the wartime mementos of the recipient, such as badges, cloth insignia and medals. The example here carries all its original smokers' contents. Princess Mary, aged 17 in 1914, had intended to pay for this gift from her personal allowance, but it was an impractical suggestion and instead it was suggested that a public fund be set up in her name, an idea that took shape at the Ritz Hotel on 14 October 1914. The bulk of the work in administering the fund was to be carried out by an executive committee chaired by the Duke of Devonshire. This was established to carry out the wishes of Princess Mary, that 'every sailor afloat and every soldier at the front' – 145,000 men under the command of Admiral Sir John Jellicoe, and 350,000 men commanded by Field Marshal Sir John French – should receive a gift. It was estimated that up to £60,000 would be needed in public contributions; over £162,500 was actually raised, most coming in as small gifts from ordinary people, with several high-profile publicity campaigns.

The gift itself is primarily an embossed brass box, designed by Adshead & Ramsay, with four manufacturers initially contracted to produce 498,000. The supply of the brass strip to produce the boxes was, however, a major concern, especially when in November 1914 the scheme was expanded to all those 'wearing the King's uniform on Christmas Day 1914' – over 2.6 million men. A Christmas card and photograph of the princess were also to form part of the gift. The box was to contain 1oz of pipe tobacco, twenty cigarettes, a pipe and a tinder lighter; non-smokers were to have a packet of acid drops and a khaki writing case (containing pencil, paper and envelopes). Indian troops were to receive boxes with contents varying according to religious beliefs: Gurkhas received the standard gift; Sikhs, the tin filled with sugar candies and a tin box of spices; and all other Indian troops, the packet of cigarettes, sugar candy and the tin of spices. Nurses at the front were to receive the box with a packet of chocolate. Supply of this complex list of items was a nightmare, especially as there were several manufacturers involved. The half-a-million tinder lighters required proved too much for Aspreys & Co.; substitute gifts were bought in to replace them, including the famous bullet pencil with Princess Mary's own monogram.

With the broadening of the recipients to all in uniform, three 'classes' were identified: A, including men at sea and 'at the front', those wounded, captured or interned, nurses at the front and the widows or parents of those killed; B, all other troops serving outside the UK; and C, all troops in the UK. The gifts for Class A recipients – 426,724 of them – were ready for distribution by Saturday 12 December, in time for Christmas. The remaining 1,803,147 were to be distributed in January 1915, the wide range of contents having been simplified to the box, a New Year's card bearing the date 1915, and the bullet pencil.

The Christmas truce of 1914 is one of the most celebrated happenings of the Great War; it expresses, even today, the willingness of humanity to put aside killing. It happened in Flanders, when German troops decorated their trenches with trees and sang their traditional songs. This goodwill soon spilled over into the men of both sides, and from shouts across no-man's-land led to the first handshakes that would develop into shared stories, drinks, food exchanges, and, most famously of all, impromptu football matches. Soon, the truces were frowned upon, and finally stopped, The guns would open again on 26 December; the war resumed.

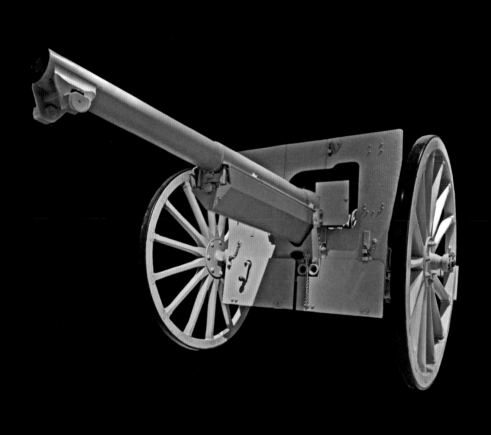

33

French 75

ARTILLERY WAS TO play the largest part in the Great War. Field guns in particular were to ensure mastery over the open battlefield, and the combatant nations all planned for pitched battles in which they could be easily brought up and deployed against the extended lines of the enemy, the gunners firing over open sights into the targets that presented themselves. Not surprisingly, field artillery was an immensely important part of the infantry divisions that went to war in 1914. But by late 1914, and into 1915, the power of the artillery piece had driven men to ground and the construction of field works, intended to be temporary, was started in earnest, the battlefields transformed into the extended siege lines that were to characterise the Western Front for the remainder of the war.

The lessons of previous conflicts had demonstrated that, with the increased firepower, range and impact of rifled weapons, there was a greater need for infantry to seek shelter. The military manuals of the day were filled with instructions on how to construct field defences – pits, redoubts, trenches and the like – all to enable the infantryman to gain respite from the 'storm of steel' that was developing due to the ascendancy of the artilleryman.

Perhaps the most famous of all field guns was the French 75, officially the *75mm gun Mle 1897*. Designed

Country of origin:
France

Date of construction:
1918

Location: *Musée de l'Armée*, Paris, France

The 75, star of the battlefield.

as a flat-trajectory field gun, it was the first quick-firing, or QF, field gun to be produced. Achieving a fire rate of at least fifteen rounds per minute in skilled hands, the gun was capable of doubling this under the right conditions. It is no wonder, then, that the 75 was revered by the French and admired by enemies and allies alike, and that post-war, the 75 should form the centre of many military museums. The *Musée de l'Armée* in Paris is no exception, and houses two examples. The example illustrated is proudly displayed in its main First World War gallery, and is restored to as-new condition. It bears the mark '22518 A.BS. 1918/Affut No. 2066 Bourges 1918', a late-war example. Such was the faith in the French 75 that production of the gun continued into the 1940s. By the end of the First World War some 17,000 examples had been built, seeing service with not only the French armies, but also the Americans and a number of other Allies besides.

The gun was rightly celebrated as the 'star of the battlefields'; it was equipped with an innovative hydropneumatic recoil system, which, together with the trail spade, meant that the gun was ready to fire almost immediately it had loosed off a round. Instead of the whole gun recoiling, it was just the barrel; the spade grip ensured that it was kept in place. With the aim maintained, all the crew had to do was reload. The breech mechanism was similarly easy to operate. The 75mm shells it fired were all equipped with time fuses. Intended to fire anti-personnel shrapnel shells that would spread a hail of spherical bullets into oncoming infantry, getting the right time-fuse setting was essential. Each fuse would normally have had to be set by hand; the 75 had an automatic fuse-setter, or *débouchoir*, that ensured the correct adjustment every time. It was no wonder that the 75, on its introduction, effectively made all other field guns obsolete. By the outbreak of war, however, friend and foe alike had made up the lost ground.

The 75 saw action in all theatres that figured French troops. Like the Adrian helmet, the 75 became an icon of French endeavour. It appeared on postcards, medals, posters and badges. Its image was engraved on the brass shell cases that held the propellant charge for the shell, destined to hold flowers on a gunner's mantelpiece. And it held the faith of the artillery generals that it could defend the country from the invading armies.

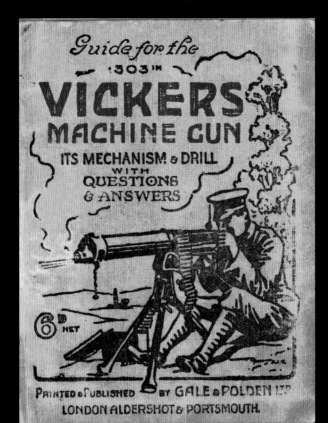

Guide for the
.303 IN
VICKERS
MACHINE GUN
ITS MECHANISM & DRILL
WITH
QUESTIONS
& ANSWERS

6D NET

PRINTED & PUBLISHED BY GALE & POLDEN LTD
LONDON ALDERSHOT & PORTSMOUTH.

34

Vickers machine gun

OF ALL THE weapons associated with the industrial battlefield of the Great War, the machine gun must be the most easily recognised. The first modern machine gun, the Maxim, invented by Sir Hiram Maxim in 1884, was the model for all subsequent heavy machine guns, including the German MG 08 and the British Vickers.

The British Army went to war with the machine gun as a specialist weapon, with two heavy Vickers (or Maxim) machine guns per infantry battalion. The Vickers .303 had been introduced in 1912 as a replacement for the earlier Maxim Mark 1 machine gun, the first machine gun in British service, introduced in 1889. The Maxim gun was a water-cooled, belt-fed machine gun, the belt made from cloth or tarpaulin. It was fired using a toggle lock action that had been invented by Hiram Maxim himself. The Vickers was an improvement on the earlier gun, though it used basically the same action as its predecessor, but improvements (and use of steel for brass parts) meant that the gun was 20lb lighter than the Maxim, at 40lb, excluding the water used for cooling and the weighty tripod. Though the Vickers became famous, and was to see service long after the war had ended, existing Maxims were also used.

The Vickers and Maxim machine guns were complex but robust, as they had to be to stand up to military service.

Country of origin:
United Kingdom

Date of manufacture:
1915

Location: Private Collection

As no one had expected the war to be a static one – with an increased role for the machine gun in both defensive (protecting a position) and offensive (creating a barrage) – this was hardly surprising. Machine gunners were to become an élite arm. The power of the British Vickers Mark 1 machine gun, and its German MG 08 Maxim equivalent, was truly frightening. Fired in short bursts of 200 rounds per minute (although both had a rate of fire of 450 rounds per minute), both guns had a maximum effective range of 2,000 yards, with the accuracy and hit rate increasing as the range decreased.

The gun illustrated is a 1915 Vickers Mark 1, set up in a reconstructed trench to provide some idea of what it would look like in action. According to the War Office manual *Infantry Training 1914*, machine guns like the Vickers operated on a frontage of 2 yards from which they could deliver a volume of fire that was equal to the effects of thirty men firing rapidly; even then, frontage required to match the effects would be some fifteen times as great. It was also calculated that even if the volume of fire could be matched by infantrymen, the effects of firing a machine gun were still twice as great. Given these facts, taken together with the knowledge that the Vickers could theoretically fire indefinitely (so long as it was cooled by a plentiful supply of water and had enough ammunition), it is not surprising that the number of machine guns in service escalated as the war progressed. The deployment of these weapons and the development of tactics became more complex as trench warfare became stalemated.

With concentrated firepower available rapidly, machine guns such as the Vickers were superb in defence, excellent both in covering the advance of infantry and in repelling attacks, and capable of traversing rapidly. The Vickers would see much action on the killing fields of France.

Developing
Trench
Warfare

35

A-frame

Country of origin:
United Kingdom
(in Belgium)

**Date of
construction:**
c. 1917

Location:
Archaeological
site, near Ieper,
Belgium

THE MILITARY MANUALS supplied to the warring nations at the outbreak of war were full of advice in the construction of trenches. Differing only in detail, these texts expected and predicted that the digging of trenches would be a temporary defensive measure only. In fact, trenches had long formed an important part of the history and science of warfare. In siege operations in particular, trenches were significant. Dug as close to the footings of castle walls as possible, they provided protection for the men who were digging shallow tunnels or saps that were to undermine and breach the defences. They would also serve to house the assaulting infantry intent on that moment when they could surge into the fray. This principle, developed in mediaeval times, would be re-enacted in unrest in the longest and largest siege operations in history, fought on the Western Front from 1914 to 1918.

The development of this type of trench warfare was an inevitable consequence of the improvement in weaponry, and in particular rifled weaponry, which could fire – with great accuracy, range and velocity – projectiles from as small as the rifle bullet to as large as the artillery shell. Unprotected, the infantryman was vulnerable to devastating firepower at longer ranges, and with the advent of quick-firing weapons such as the latest field

guns and machine guns, the only way to 'bite and hold' a position was to ensure that men got to ground as soon as possible, digging into the earth to gain the maximum protection that could be afforded. Rifled weapons had contributed to the development of trench warfare in the American Civil War of 1861–65, which had gone from Napoleonic ranks to trench operations over its five years; and its appearance in modern warfare was heralded in the Russo-Japanese War of 1904–05.

Excavations in Flanders in 2005 expose A-frames and corrugated iron revetments.

In the First World War, entrenchment of the Western Front was an inevitable consequence of the fight for position that took place during the '3' in the autumn and winter of 1914. From this point onwards the engineers of all the protagonists worked to develop and improve trench fortifications within unfavourable ground conditions, and to protect the infantry from both the attentions of the enemy and from the elements. The best positions were quickly taken and the lines set in position that would become the zone of trench warfare for some four long years.

Engineer trench design needed consideration of ground conditions. The trench illustrated was one that was excavated in the Ypres Salient in 2005 and demonstrates in some detail how these specialist soldiers coped with the difficult ground – and show how unexpected challenges of extended siege warfare became a high science in itself. Recent archaeological studies in northern France and in Flanders have allowed scientists and historians to add further dimensions to our understanding of trench warfare provided by accounts, official histories and photographs. Here, engineers have tried to combat the inevitability of water collecting in the bottom of the trench, thereby promoting 'trench feet' – a condition akin to frostbite – as men struggled through the waterlogged trench. Prefabricated wooden A-frames were sunk into the ground. The crossbar of the 'A' provides a support for an elevated walkway or duckboard. Water could accumulate below and could be drained away, if skilfully done. The rising timbers of the frame provided rigid support for the trench sides, known as slopes, which were important if the sides were not to collapse in on the trench garrison. This revetment differed from trench to trench, from army to army. In the case illustrated from the Ypres Salient, corrugated steel was used; however, sandbags, wattle hurdles, timber – all were tried according to whatever was available. Trench construction varied between nations – in many cases wattle was used as a natural revetment type.

In many cases, the depth of trenches was limited by the local geological conditions, with water-bearing layers often close to the surface. In such situations, sandbags were used to build up the trench to an acceptable height of parapet. Building up the parapet meant using the A-frame in such a way as to support construction of 'high command' trenches, or simple sandbag breastworks.

In all cases, the trench lines showed increasing sophistication as the war moved from temporary trenches to those intended to house a garrison committed to a lengthy stay. With the British and French adherence to the doctrine of the offensive – with trenches little more than a 'phase' – the development of the A-frame represents a recognition that trench warfare was here to stay.

36

Barbed wire

BARBED WIRE HAS become as much a metaphor for the suffering of the First World War as trenches and gas. As one contemporary writer, Reginald Farrer, put it in 1918: 'remember the work that every length of this wicked weed has done – the dead and dying caught in its merciless mesh, and kept hanging on its thorns for hours and days.' For the soldiers themselves, the grim humour practised in the trenches would include reference to missing soldiers 'hanging on the old barbed wire', incorporated in a popular ironic song: 'If you want to find the old battalion, I know where they are, They're hanging on the old barbed wire.'

German barbed wire.

This twisted, rusty sample of barbed wire was recovered from the fields of France, where fragments of the battles that scarred them still abound. It is German; we know this because of its peculiar form – a single wire twist with a square cross section, and a particularly fearsome set of barbs. Such wire is encountered wherever the Germans set their hand to building field defences or fortifications, or in the construction of prisoner-of-war camps. It is seen in the fields of France and Flanders, on the shores of Gallipoli, and still marking the boundary of long-gone POW camps. This specimen came from Gommecourt, a salient or bulge in the German front line on the Somme, jutting forward pugnaciously

Country of origin: Germany

Date of manufacture: c. 1915–16

Location: Private collection

135

Austrian barbed wire
entanglement.

towards the British. Gommecourt was the scene of
an ill-fated diversionary attack by the British 56th and
46th Divisions on 1 July 1916, an attack that left more
than 2,000 men dead, five times that suffered by the
German defenders. The barbed wire had played its part.

Though we often associate barbed wire with the
Great War, its origins lie in the American West, and it
is amongst the most significant inventions of the late
nineteenth century. Anyone who has visited the endless
rolling plains of Wyoming or Montana in the United

States cannot fail to be impressed by the grandeur of the landscape, and to imagine the vast herds of bison so essential to the Native American way of life. This lifestyle was to meet its end with the relentless move of American families westwards, an opportunity for 'homesteaders' to take up the US government's offer of 160 acres of free land on those very prairies. With the homesteaders came an alien concept to the native peoples: enclosure. Well known, though, is that the enclosure of this wild grassland was accomplished through a simple device – barbed wire. With huge plains to cordon off, and no hope of using natural stone walling or the split-rail fencing so common in the eastern states, a technological solution was required. And that solution was the wire that became known as 'the Devil's rope'.

Invented in 1873 – and patented a year later – by Midwest farmer J.F. Glidden, barbed wire in its earliest incarnation differed from all other types of wire for fencing. Of paramount importance were the small double-strand twists that had sharp, unforgiving barbs set in opposite directions. The intention behind these was obviously to create a barrier to movement, the barbs warning straying animals to keep to their side of the fence. But anchoring the small bunched barbs was difficult, and Glidden's approach was to bind them in place with a second piece of wire twisted over the first, locking the barbs in place. From this point barbed wire attained its fearsome reputation, and with it came a host of competitors and alternatives. It is estimated that there are at least 2,000 different types of barbed wire, and a host of collectors to boot.

With the western prairie cordoned off by fence posts and barbed wire, the possibility arose of the use of the invention in the protection of field works and the production of military obstacles, such as trench warfare itself. Military obstacles such as this had a long history prior to the opening of the Great War. Pallisades were well used, as was the mediaeval obstacle provided by stakes in the ground or reversed trees – both known as 'abates'. According to the standard British text *Military Engineering (Part 1) Field Defences* (1908), such obstacles were to be 'used in conjunction with defensive works, but may also be employed in the open to impede an advance of troops, or to increase the difficulties of a night attack'. The use of barbed wire as one of those obstacles has tentative beginnings in the latter part of the nineteenth century. Though the possibilities of trip wires or entanglements of plain wire intended to 'impede the enemy' were understood at this point, it was arguably the Russo-Japanese War of 1902–04 that saw the first thoroughgoing use of barbed wire entanglements as we know them from the Great War. Perhaps learning from this experience, the British

British barbed wire pickets.

Army was to sagely comment, in its 1908 manual, that such obstacles 'should not be liable to serious damage from the enemy's artillery', noting that 'Against entanglements and abatis, artillery fire has very little effect'. Finally, it judged, 'wire entanglement is the best of all obstacles, because it is easily and quickly made, difficult to destroy, and offers no obstruction to view'. So it was that barbed wire made its way onto the roster of military materials of the First World War.

It is possible to follow the thickening of barbed wire entanglements through the history of the war. In the opening months, barbed wire was an encumbrance to the retreating troops, retreating in the face of the German thrust through Belgium. A few strands were to be encountered here and there; a few strands more specifically associated with the protection of horse lines and the creation of warnings. But with the fixation of the trench lines in what became known as the 'Race to the Sea', as both sides tried to avoid being trapped behind their defensive positions there came the need to create obstacles to 'impede the progress of the enemy'.

Barbed wire formed a significant component of the field defences of the Great War; it was to need constant attention. Wiring parties on both sides would enter no-man's-land under the cover of darkness, in patrols of two to three men to inspect the integrity of the defences or cut paths through their own wire in preparation for a raid or in larger fatigue parties to repair and improve the front-line wire. Wire was brought up the lines by fatigue parties who, usually under the instruction of a sapper officer or NCO, would carry out the work in darkness. Such parties would be in a constant state of readiness; any noise would trigger off a flurry of star shells and Very lights intended to illuminate the inter-lopers, picking them out in stark silhouette against the night sky, an easy target for a sweeping machine gun or targeted artillery barrage. It was the invention of the screw picket – which spread like wildfire on both sides of no-man's-land – that meant complex wire barriers could be constructed relatively noiselessly, soldiers lit-erally winding them into the ground. As the defences got stronger, the barriers seemed almost impervious; the actual limit of attack often stuttered and faded at the barbed barrier. A wartime tune recalls:

> If you want to find the old battalion,
> I know where they are, I know where they are,
>> I know where they are
> If you want to find the old battalion,
>> I know where they are,
> They're hanging on the old barbed wire,
> I've seen 'em, I've seen 'em,
>> hanging on the old barbed wire.
> I've seen 'em, I've seen 'em,
>> hanging on the old barbed wire.

37

Gallipoli trench sign

THE DEVELOPMENT OF trench warfare led to the proliferation of individual trenches. There were, after all, many types – zig-zag or traversed trenches for fighting; longer trenches intended as thoroughfares to allow troops to get to the front and wounded soldiers to get away from it; trenches designed to house garrisons so that they were not in the front line; and, trenches in the rear areas to be held if the enemy broke through. From inconclusive scrapes in the ground in Flanders, trenches quickly became complex pieces of architecture that required planning and development. Trench systems soon became like subterranean towns housing thousands of people – all of them careful not to raise their heads above the parapet in daylight, for fear of having it shot off by snipers.

Country of origin:
Australia (in Ottoman Turkey)

Date of manufacture:
1915

Location:
Australian War Memorial, Canberra, Australia

With the proliferation of trenches and trench systems came the need for mapping and signage so that new occupants could get their bearings. A routine developed on the Western Front whereby battalions of men would be cycled through the trenches, typically spending up to a week on the front line, before being taken out to the reserve trenches and then finally 'out on rest' – though often such rest spells meant a return to the front line as rations carriers. It was necessary to direct soldiers through the maze of trenches, for although they were theoretically constructed in parallel lines – at least in the early stages of trench warfare on the Western Front – the re-entrants, salients and redoubts would be interconnected by communication trenches (CTs) and minor trenches intended as latrines, entrances to dugouts, trench mortar batteries, and so on. Often, these were challenging. Relief of the trench garrisons relied upon local knowledge – with guides detailed to lead men in and out, reminding them all the while to keep their heads down in the face of artillery and rifle fire.

Shell petrol tins, as used in the trenches.

Most soldiers would travel to the front line from the rear areas along crowded CTs at night – bustling, narrow thoroughfares 6ft deep, with barely enough room for men to pass. Although relieving battalions would be guided to the front by experienced soldiers from the battalion about to be relieved, sign boards would still be necessary to direct them, perhaps picked out by candlelight. Many of the long CTs had picturesque names, chosen at will and whim; these would be painted on rough and crude boards to aid in direction finding. Such boards would also exist at the front line; others, with a more urgent message, might warn of the dangers from snipers, artillery fire or the physical hazards of loose or low wires, or treacherous duckboards.

Though trench warfare is most commonly associated with the Western Front, different species of it developed in the icy mountains of the Alps, cut into the solid rocks of the high mountains that separated Italians from Austro-Hungarians, as well as in the complex terrain of Salonika, where a multinational force faced the Bulgarians across malaria-infested valleys and challenging mountain terrains. But arguably the most intense and challenging conditions were those that faced the Australian and New Zealand Army Corps (ANZAC) during their eight-month occupancy of the steep, parched and crumbling slopes above Anzac Cove in the Gallipoli Peninsula. From April 1915 to January 1916, British, Indian, French and ANZAC forces clung to small enclaves of the peninsula while they planned the opportunity to break out of their extended beachheads – an opportunity that had been squandered when they first landed. Here, with impossible routes and ever-so-close trenches, precarious saps and shallow-scraped dugouts, the ANZACs attempted to outwit their Ottoman opponents. And, through it all, finding their way to the front line was fraught with danger.

This trench sign, from the collections of the Australian War Memorial, is made from a rectangular Shell Petroleum tin adapted to make an illuminated trench marker, which was recovered from the battle-fields of Gallipoli in 1919, a silent sentinel left behind after the evacuation. The marker was found on a hill above Shell Green in the ANZAC sector. Like much of the life of the ANZACs at Gallipoli, it is extemporised; in this case, fashioned from recycled materials. The reuse of materials such as tins and wooden boxes was commonplace at Gallipoli, especially during the early stages of the campaign, when there were major diffi-culties with supplies. On the front of the tin, over the impressed 'Shell Motor Spirit' details, is punched the text 'Q5 / TO / FIRING / LINE'. Q5 was a trench or sap leading to the firing line. The text has been created by nail punch, which forms the outline of each letter and number. The side of the tin has been cut to form a rec-tangular 'door' to allow a candle to be inserted inside the tin to illuminate the text at night in order to assist sol-diers making their way in the dark. There is evidence of the war that raged around this mute bystander: there is a small shrapnel hole in the front of the tin, and another in the side 'door'.

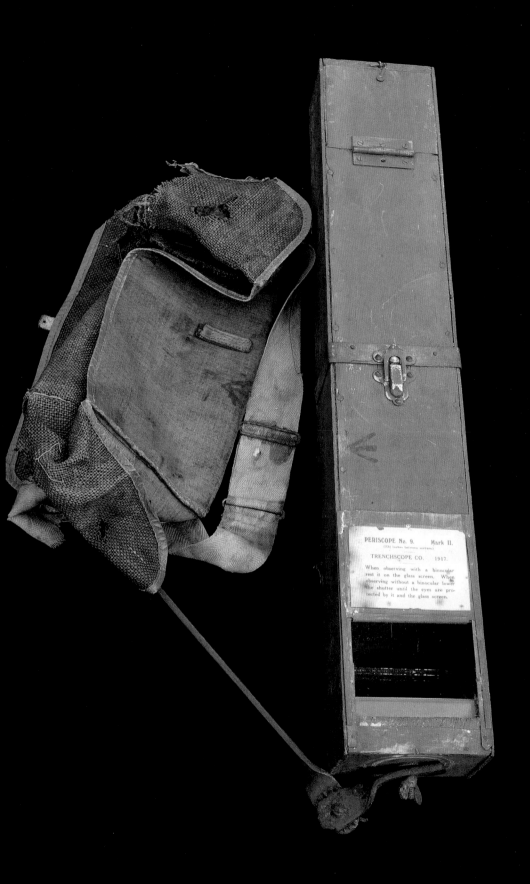

PERISCOPE No. 9.   Mark II.
(13½ inches between surfaces)
TRENCHSCOPE CO.   1917.

When observing with a binocular
rest it on the glass screen. When
observing without a binocular lower
the shutter until the eyes are protected by it and the glass screen.

38

Trench periscope

LOOKING OVER THE parapet in daylight was most unwise; snipers would have weapons fixed in position, targeted at dips in the parapet, at latrines and crossing points, and at loophole plates. There was continual loss of life on the Western Front through the actions of snipers in this way, combined with the altogether random attentions of the artillery shell. From early on, the need to be able to look over the parapet to observe activity in no-man's-land led to the production of specially designed 'trench periscopes'. Illustrated is the British No. 9 box periscope. Made by 'Trenchscope Ltd' in 1917, this is a typical issue item. This one saw service with the Australian Imperial Force (AIF) in France, and is well preserved, found together with spare mirrors and its carrying bag. Cheaply made with boxwood, it is nevertheless complete.

In an issue of *Transactions of the Optical Society* for 1915, the basic parameters were laid down for trench periscopes, the object of which, it was stated, was 'to give the soldier a view of his front whilst his head and person are sheltered'. Its author, W.A. Dixey, distilled these into four points: 1) portability; 2) degree of shelter provided; 3) field of view; and 4) camouflage to the enemy. Many patent versions were produced to try and achieve these aims; several of them were adopted

Country of origin: United Kingdom

Date of manufacture: 1917

Location: Private collection

145

THE OUTPOST

A British "Tommy" watching the enemy through his periscope

A No. 9 Box
Periscope in action

officially, others were available for private purchase. Most provided a non-magnified field of view; magnification could be gained by the use of binoculars in association with the periscope.

For portability, a simple mirror attached to a stick or bayonet was the most effective. More commonly, day sentries would be stationed next to a No. 9 Box Periscope, which provided a clear field of view sufficient for most trench duties. Spare mirrors were essential – all too often they would be spotted by the enemy and 'sniped'; shot out with a shower of glass splinters. Although portable, such periscopes were fixed at sentry posts throughout front-line trenches, effectively disguised from sniping by the use of sandbags and sacking.

Officers were drawn to more portable periscopes; the most commonly encountered periscope used by officers was the Beck's No. 25, issued from 1917, which comprises a simple small diameter brass tube, with detachable handle and a focusing eyepiece. This effective piece of equipment was not only light, durable, difficult to spot at a distance and long enough to provide the observer with sufficient protection, it was also a magnifying periscope, and popular with officers. A great many other types, many not as effective, are also known. The proliferation of 'trench' periscopes during the war matched the increasing sophistication of the enemy in providing snipers. For the Germans, equipped with the highest quality lens-making factories, and observing from the high ground, the field of view was often clear; for the Allies, restricted to their simple mirrors, observing 'over the top' was much more of a challenge.

39 *Minenwerfer*

MORTARS ARE WEAP-
ONS that are intended to
lob a heavy projectile in a
steeply arcing trajectory
over a short distance. Their
use dates back at least five
centuries, when they were
used to assist in the breaking of sieges; unlike normal
field artillery with their flat
trajectories, mortars have to
be deployed relatively close
to their ultimate targets.
Mortars are muzzle-loaded
and relatively simple; they
require just a sufficient
explosive charge to blast
their projectile towards the
enemy. Mobile, and capable
of being used by infantrymen, they were tailor-made
for trench warfare. Trench
mortars were to become

increasingly sophisticated as the war proceeded; used
as a means of destroying or reducing enemy trenches,
they were capable of killing large numbers of men in
any given trench.

The *Minenwerfer* was a German trench mortar that
was effective at both destroying sections of the front-
line trench and reducing the morale of its occupants.
Minenwerfers came in three sizes: heavy (25cm shell),
medium (17cm shell) and light (7.58cm shell). Feared in
combat, but mobile like machine guns, they were typically
captured during trench raids. The example illustrated is
a typical 25mm *schwerer Minenwerfer*, one of three different types on display at the Hill 62 Trench Museum near

Country of origin:
Germany

**Date of
construction:**
1914–18

Location: Hill 62
Sanctuary Wood
Museum, near
Ieper, Belgium

Ypres. This museum has been open since the 1920s; it is not inconceivable that this relic has been there the whole time, examined by tourists and pilgrims alike. But today, this rusting metal, industrial-looking object is difficult to translate into the snarling intensity of the weapon in combat, as it is to give physical expression to the memories of the combatants, who universally feared the power of these weapons. As described by Private Alfred M. Burrage of the Artists' Rifles: 'There is no explosion which, for sheer gut-stabbing ferocity, is quite like that of a *Minenwerfer*. The bursting of one close at hand was like one's conception of the end of the world.' As the shell could be observed in flight, sentries with whistles were placed in the front line, their duty to observe the flight of the mortar shell and alert their comrades.

The British experimented with a variety of contraptions – including catapults firing grenades – but the first effective mortars started to appear in 1915. These included the 'toffee apple' mortar: a 2in diameter tube firing an explosive charge mounted on a long shaft, but which was liable to destabilise the round in flight. More

British 'toffee apple' mortar rounds.

reliable was the Stokes mortar, a simple 3in drainpipe affair that was effectively the prototype for mortars in use today in armies across the world. Stokes bombs were dropped into the tube, a striker activating the charge and propelling the round up to 1,500 yards. Stokes mortar bombs still litter the former battlefields in out-of-the-way places; unstable still, they remain volatile, a deadly echo of a past war.

Successful as the Stokes was, it was the *Minenwerfer* that was most feared. Our rusting example is one of at least 16,500 produced and used during the war, a testimony to their value in the extended trench warfare siege.

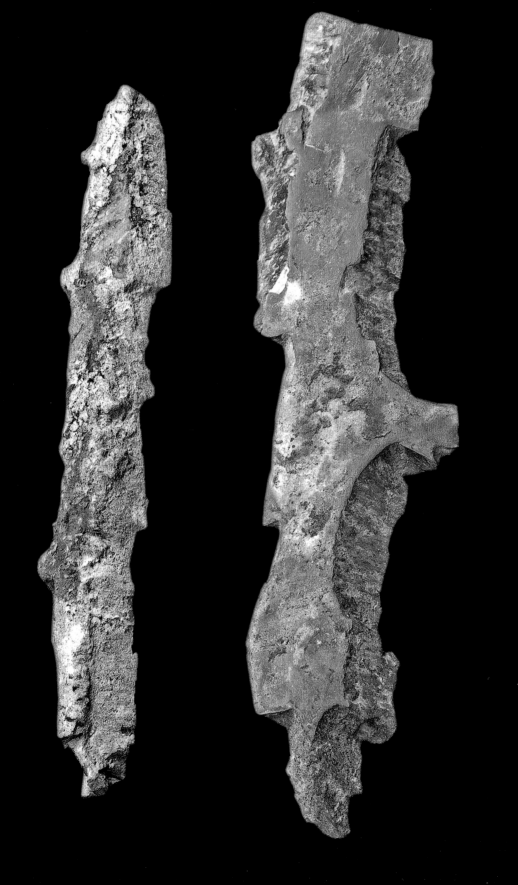

40

Shell shards

THE SCIENCE OF artillery increased in complexity throughout the war, as the gunners tried to outwit both the engineers – who had designed and built the fortifications that sheltered the infantry – and the artillerymen opposing them. But at the commencement of war, the primary role of artillery was as an anti-personnel weapon and, as a consequence, most field artillery pieces were equipped with shrapnel – explosive shells with steel bodies that were filled with around 200–300 lead or steel balls, a load that was intended to scythe down attacking armies as the shell exploded. Unlike high explosive shells, which were packed with a large amount of explosive, shrapnel was equipped with only a small charge that was sufficient to blow off the head of the shell and to liberate the bullets through the action of a disc that moved up the central tube, forcing them out. In British use, shrapnel shells were the only ones available when the Royal Field Artillery went to war with the British Expeditionary Force in 1914.

Shrapnel was an important weapon and was used to great effect as trench warfare developed in earnest. With infantry assaults committed to the deadly, shell-swept no-man's-land, it was incumbent upon the artillerymen to provide a protective shield. New techniques led to the acceptance of creeping or box barrages, protective

Country of origin:
Germany

Date of manufacture:
c. 1916–18

Location: Private collection

German large-calibre shell at La Boisselle, on the Somme battlefield.

curtains of fire that would hopefully allow the infantry to get across unmolested, the curtains lifting according to a timetable in order to allow them to advance. The same scything action that was used against men was also employed against barbed wire obstacles, but required precision to do so effectively – an ideal that was not always easy to deliver, leaving soldiers facing the uncut wire while unprotected in that grim zone between the trench lines. All too often shells failed to explode, due to faulty fuses or defective drive bands, and this meant a staggering number of 'duds' left on the battlefield.

For trench destruction, and for seeking out and destroying dugouts and other shelters, high explosive shells were more effective. The projectile delivered a huge explosive force, capable of creating huge craters and blowing in large sections of trench, while the explosively burst shell wall would create a high-velocity shower of shell splinters that were razor sharp. The most effective were those delivered by larger calibre and higher trajectory field howitzers. Such weapons would ensure that the rain of shells was as near vertical as possible. The shell fragments illustrated are from a high-velocity shell that burst above a British dugout close to the front line near to the destroyed village of Zonnebeke, in the Ypres Salient. No doubt fired from a German howitzer, its purpose was to seek out and destroy British trenches and dugout works, and, ultimately, to kill its occupants. The size and shape of each shard – over 12in long and 1in thick – is terrifying.

It has been estimated that 70 per cent of all casualties were wounded or killed by artillery fire on the Western Front. With increasing precision, artillerymen developed new ways of delivering their goods, with creeping and box barrages intended to provide a protective screen around those attacking, isolating those within from the attentions of the defenders outside the curtain of shell fire. Complex ranging techniques and increasingly complex artillery maps meant that the gunners belonged to an extremely professional and scientific corps by the end of the war. For the soldier, avoiding the attentions of the enemy's artillery fire was paramount. In the 'live and let live' system that developed in some sectors of the Western Front, maintaining the status quo was the aim, thereby avoiding anything that would bring down a barrage in suspicion of unwanted extra activity or evidence of military preparation. Soldiers soon got used to the sound of incoming fire: the 'whizz bang' of the quick-firing field gun, or the 'crump' of the explosion of the heavy howitzer – explosions that created forceful blasts and plenty of black smoke. These would also be given the names 'woolly bear', 'Jack Johnson' (after the hard-hitting black heavyweight boxer) and 'coal box'. Heavy shells would kill by the action of the high explosive that could tear apart fortifications and human flesh alike; wounds from the jagged, cruel shell fragments like those illustrated were particularly feared.

Zum Andenken im Gebete
an den tugendsamen Jüngling

Martin Bobenstetter

Bauers-Sohn in Emain
Soldat im 3. bayr. Inf.-Regt. 11. Komp.
welcher am 3. August 1916 in Russisch-
Polen durch Granatschuß im 29. Lebens-
jahre den Heldentod fürs Vaterland
gestorben ist.

Was weint ihr, Eltern, Geschwister, meine Lieben,
Weil ich nicht länger bin bei Euch geblieben?
Es ist nicht weit, blickt auf zum Stern!
Dort oben woh'n ich, gar nicht fern!
Und früh geschieden? — habt nicht bang,
Auch Euer Leben ist nicht lang,
Wie bald, wie schnell verrinnt die Zeit,
Ihr seid bei mir, ich bin bei Euch in Ewigkeit!

Mein Jesus, Barmherzigkeit!
100 Tage Ablaß.

Druck von P. März, Zöpf's Nachf., Dorfen.

Ehre dem Andenken
...endsamen Jünglings

4I

Death card

THE IMAGE OF the fresh-faced German infantryman is all too often portrayed in the issue of 'death cards', or *totenbild* – and many young men, such as Martin Bobenstetter of Bavaria, would be killed by the random and unforgiving effects of artillery fire. Relentless *trommelfeuer* (drum fire) bombardments were common from late 1914, and they only increased in intensity as the war dragged on.

Death cards are a feature of German funerary culture; from the 1840s it was a common occurrence for Catholic families to arrange for the printing of small card folders bearing religious observances, images of Christ or the Madonna and religious tracts. The issue of the cards traditionally marked the passing of family members, alerting the local population to the loss of a loved one and asking them to partake in a religious observance, the act of praying for the deceased over a mourning period of, typically, 100 days.

With the coming of war, the number of cards issued became truly staggering. Early examples often give details of the military career of the deceased, the regiment, the location and date of death – each one a witness to the slaughter of German soldiers fighting the war they had long feared: the war on two fronts. The card illustrated is typical. It tells the poignant story of

Country of origin: Germany

Date of printing: 1916

Location: Private collection

a young man who was killed on the Eastern Front by a random act of shelling in 1916 – like so many before him, and so many afterwards. The folded card has the appropriate religious observances and opens on an image of a young man in uniform:

Religious observancies on the exterior of the cards.

> To remember in prayer the virtuous youth Martin Bobenstetter

> Farmer's son in Gmain. Soldier of 3rd Bavarian Infantry Regiment, 11th company who was killed by shellfire on the 3rd of August 1916 in Russian-Poland, dying a hero's death for the Fatherland.

Martin Bobenstetter's regiment, the *Königlich Bayerisches 3, Infanterie-Regiment 'Prinz Karl von Bayern'*, had already suffered before it was transferred to the Eastern Front. In the spring of 1916 the regiment was engaged at Verdun, taking and consolidating Hill 279, the '*Termitenheugal*' at Avocourt. Suffering 70 per cent casualties, the regiment was withdrawn to the east, only to face the Russian Brusilov Offensive that was launched against the Austro-Hungarian-held front. General Aleksei Brusilov is credited with reviving the fortunes of the Imperial Russian Army by delivering a crushing blow on the Austro-Hungarians. Fought from 4 June 1916 through to September, new tactics were brought to bear with good effect: the use of lightning barrages and shock troops to gain infiltration. With the line contracting and reeling, the Austrians and their German allies had to reel back to absorb the pressure. In the firing line close to Volhynia was Martin Bobenstetter, brought from the hell of Verdun.

A Catholic, Martin was a farmhand by trade, and unmarried. Born on 13 October 1887 in Gmain, the son of Martin and Anna Bobenstetter, he joined the army on 14 August 1914 and took part in the defensive operations in Artois in 1915. By the time of his death, Martin had already been wounded at least once, in Artois in 1915. On 26 May 1915 he was hit by a piece of shrapnel on his upper thigh. Artillery accounted for the majority of wounds and deaths in the Great War; Martin was not alone in having been hit on several occasions by shell fragments. And his family were no strangers to tragedy. Already, two of his brothers had been killed: Matthäus Bobenstetter (on 28 October 1914, aged 28) and Michl Bobenstetter (on 23 May 1916, aged 21). With the loss of Martin, killed just four months after his second brother, the Bobenstetters would suffer once more; their eldest son, Georg Bobenstetter, was killed on 9 April 1917. All four brothers are commemorated in the church of Dorfen–Schwindkirchen, in Bavaria. By no means unusual, the death card records the loss of one of four brothers, and the decimation of a family by war.

42 Mills bomb

WITH ARMIES TRAINED to a high state of efficiency with their rifles in the early part of the First World War, with the advent of trench warfare, the most effective weapon was the grenade.

The British Army went to war with an extremely cumbersome example – the No. 1. The No. 1 was a 16in stick grenade with a cast iron explosive chamber and streamers to make it stable in flight. As a safety precaution, the No. 1 had a cap that was held in place by a safety pin. This cap was intended to protect the percussion fuse, which in normal circumstances was not fitted. Bombers had first to fit the fuse, the bomb being armed and ready for throwing. Streamers attached to the grenade were intended to ensure that it fell head-first – thereby exploding on impact. But, unlike its German equivalent, the *steilhandgranate*, it had a fatal flaw – the combination of a long handle and a percussion striker. The bomber had to be extremely careful not to hit the side of the trench when preparing to throw it, a difficult proposition in the confined spaces of the trench. In view of this, the No. 1 grenade was updated on 21 May 1915 with a shorter cane or turned wood handle, thereby reducing the length of the grenade to a more manageable 12½in.

Difficulties of supply, and problems with the ungainly and dangerous nature of these percussion-fused stick grenades, meant that by 1915 soldiers were making their own grenades, ignited by a slow-burning

Country of origin: United Kingdom

Date of manufacture: 1916

Location: Private collection

fuse – usually at the rate of 1in of fuse per 1.25 seconds of delay. Typical of these emergency bombs is the 'jam-tin' bomb – literally a tin filled with explosive gun cotton and shrapnel balls – that is particularly associated with the Gallipoli Campaign of 1915. They were unreliable and were to decline in popularity with the introduction of the Mills bomb in May 1915, named after its principal inventor William Mills. Illustrated is a typical example, from 1916.

Officially designated the No. 5 grenade, the secret of the Mills bomb's success lay with its ignition system, which used a striker that was activated when a pin was removed and a lever released; the lever was then ejected and a four-second fuse activated, during which time the bomber had to throw the grenade. The body of the grenade was formed of cast iron, and weighed 1lb 6½oz; its surface was divided into sections to promote fragmentation. Coloured bands indicated its fillings: red at the top to demonstrate it had been filled (like our example – now made inert), pink for ammonal, green for amatol. At the heart of the grenade was a centrepiece that contained separate cavities for the striker and the detonator. The striker was kept cocked against a spring, the striker lever holding the striker firmly in position when held against the body of the grenade, locked there by the action of the split safety pin until the bomber removed the pin and threw the grenade. On throwing the bomb, the lever flew off, thereby releasing the striker. The impact fires the cap, lighting the safety fuse, and this burns for five seconds before igniting the detonator, which then sets off the main charge.

The Mills bomb was reliable and tough; in its 1916 manual, *Notes for Infantry Officers on Trench Warfare*, the War Office was clear in its deployment as a trench weapon: '[Mills] Grenadiers will principally be employed in clearing trenches [...] and also to check and destroy hostile bombing parties.' The bomb received much use, and continued its task into a second world conflict.

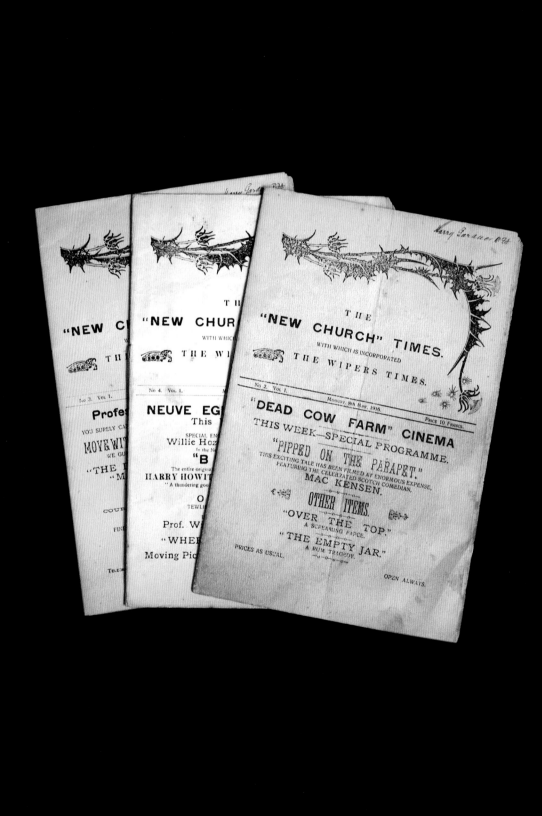

Harry Gardner 2H

THE
"NEW CHURCH" TIMES.
WITH WHICH IS INCORPORATED
THE WIPERS TIMES.

No 2. Vol 1.   Monday, 8th May, 1916.   PRICE 10 Francs.

"DEAD COW FARM" CINEMA
THIS WEEK—SPECIAL PROGRAMME.
"PIPPED ON THE PARAPET."
THIS EXCITING TALE HAS BEEN FILMED AT ENORMOUS EXPENSE.
FEATURING THE CELEBRATED SCOTCH COMEDIAN,
MAC KENSEN.

OTHER ITEMS.
"OVER THE TOP."
A SCREAMING FARCE.
"THE EMPTY JAR."
A RUM TRAGEDY.
PRICES AS USUAL.   OPEN ALWAYS.

"NEW CHURCH"
WITH WHICH
THE WIPE

No 4. Vol 1.

NEUVE EG
This
SPECIAL EN
Willie Hoz
"B
The entire origina
HARRY HOWIT
"A thundering goo
O
TEWLI
Prof. W
"WHEE
Moving Pic
TELE

"NEW C
TH
No 3. Vol 1.

Profes
YOU SURELY CA
MOVE WIT
WE GU
"THE
"M
COU
FIN

43

The Wipers Times

BY MID-1915, the war on the Western Front had settled down to the daily grind of trench warfare. Though in many sectors this meant standing on the defensive, in several hotspots there was more or less continuous action and activity, with the war prosecuted on land, underground and in the air, to varying degrees.

In some sectors, however – in parts of the Ypres Salient, towards the coast of the North Sea, or on the French front south of the St Mihiel Salient – a tacit 'live and let live' system had developed that depended upon the recognition that, despite the war, everyday military life needed to go on. Typically, the morning and evening were marked by soldiers formally 'standing to' and manning the parapet in case of enemy action. Often accompanied by a wild fusillade of fire to announce their presence and intention, once duty was done, and the enemy suitably warned, it was usual for soldiers to go about their business, cleaning their rifles, sprucing themselves up as far as was possible, cooking food and repairing trenches – whatever was necessary. This was accepted and understood by both sides.

In some cases, the system went beyond simple grudging acceptance. As the war developed, and along with it a growing sense of alienation from home in many soldiers, a level of empathy and understanding developed

New Church Times, successor to *The Wipers Times.*

Country of origin: United Kingdom (in Belgium)

Date of printing: 1916

Location: Private collection

161

between the opposing nations. This manifested itself in simple tricks, sign boards and the exchange of humorous greetings – such as machine gunners finishing off the traditional 'shave and a haircut' seven-note couplet sounding the two notes 'five bob' with their weapons, typical of the gallows humour that abounded on all sides. The possibility of trade – lobbed tins of meat or other foodstuffs – is also recorded, and this took place in closely confined locations such as the feet-apart trenches of Quinn's Post in Gallipoli. For the British on the Western Front, a mythology arose that considered some of the armies of the German nation states to be more docile than others. While the Prussians were seen to be the most aggressive, those from Saxony or Württemberg were thought to be more willing to accept the status quo of trench life.

All of this suggests that from mid-1915, trench warfare had become accepted as the norm – despite what High Command had to say to the contrary. With everyday life recalibrated to accept the peculiarity of life in the trenches, humour asserted itself. As such, trench journals were produced by all sides that tapped into this new level of consciousness. Trench journals became a phenomenon of the war; produced at a variety of levels within the army, official and unofficial, they were a means of building a unit or regional identity, and of letting off steam. Often they were produced close to the front line in battalion headquarters. The most famous is *The Wipers Times* (and its successors *New Church Times*, *Somme Times* and *BEF Times*), produced within the ruins of Ypres by officers of the Sherwood Foresters, and its stoic humour has become legendary. Three issues of the *New Church Times*, bought for the princely sum of 10 francs each by Gunner Harry Gardner of the Royal Field Artillery, are illustrated.

Many other versions were produced by individual battalions: *The 5th Glosters Gazette*, for instance, or *The Mudhook*, produced for the Royal Naval Division. Together, these masterpieces provide rare glimpses of the black humour of the trenches, and of the stoicism of the men who served there.

The War Deepens and Expands, 1915–16

44 Trench art ring

THE MANUFACTURE OF 'trench art' was fashionable both during and after the war. Trench art represents the folk art of war, reusing as it does the bullets, shell cases, copper drive bands, fragments of aircraft, pieces of wood and other detritus of war in order to manufacture objects as souvenirs.

The production of such unique objects was dependent upon the skill of the artisan, the availability of munitions and their waste products – shell brass, copper drive bands and even aluminium from fuse tops and aircraft – and the time and opportunity of the soldier to make something from it. Trench art was sometimes made by soldiers on the front line, and some rare images remain as testimony to the fact that such work was carried out, mostly by shaping and filing simple metal scraps. But more commonly 'trench art' was manufactured in rear areas, where there was more access to tools and equipment. Typical soldier items include decorated shell cases, letter openers, matchbox folds, lighters, tanks and field caps. Many pieces available today were actually made by enterprising civilians

Country of origin: Belgium

Date of manufacture: c. 1915–18

Location: Private collection

and garrison (and ancillary) troops in the battle zone, both during and after the war – especially as there was a lucrative tourism market developing post-war.

The ring illustrated is a small aluminium piece, delicate, and inscribed with the simple word 'Yser'. Symbolically important for the Belgians, the Yser/Ijser front from Nieuport to Dixmuide had been held since the opening of the floodgates at Nieuport had helped stem the tide of the German advance. With the Germans holding 95 per cent of Belgian territory, the 35km stretch of line along the Yser/Ijser River assumed mythological importance, and the Belgians held this line through to the final advance in August 1918. As early as 1915, French and British popular war magazines (*L'Illustration* and *The War Budget*) were describing the work of the Belgian soldiers in manufacturing such rings from aluminium fuse caps while holding the line along the Yser. In fact, the manufacture of such rings was common on both sides of the line, and the malleable metal and small size of the object permitted such work in the confined spaces of a front line trench. Our artisan has gone one stage further: let into the ring is the head of the British king, filed from a copper coin; perhaps a souvenir from an Allied trench visit?

With rings like these, and other trinkets, soldiers found opportunities to pledge their love to wives, sweethearts and family. The fact that this was made by a Belgian soldier, his loved one either a refugee in a foreign country or living under the yoke of occupation, makes this all the more poignant. Who made it, and how long he had before he saw his loved ones again, is difficult to perceive. But it stands as a testimony to the important watch kept by the Belgians in securing the flanks of their Allies on the Western Front.

'Yser': a soldier's inscription inside the ring.

45 War maps

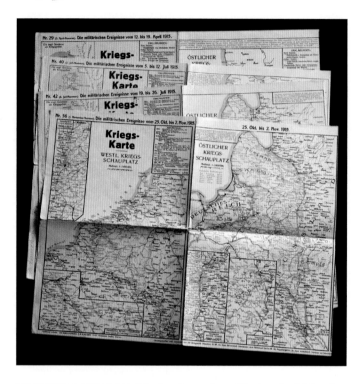

FOR THE GERMANS, the thought of being held in the deadly embrace of a war on two fronts between the strong adversaries of France and Russia had been uppermost in the minds of the pre-war military planners and had led directly to the attack on France in August 1914, in the vain hope that it could be quickly dispatched to face the formidable manpower of the Russian Empire in the east. But by 1915 the nightmare had become reality, the Schlieffen Plan had failed and the Germans were facing determined enemies. France was to be held on the defensive, and attention switched back to taking on the Russians. Men and resources were poured into the eastern theatre to exploit the weaknesses in the Russian command after the victory at Tannenberg in August 1914 – and to bolster the faltering Austrian effort in Galicia and the Austro-Hungarian loss of the fortress of Przemysl.

Country of origin: Germany

Date of printing: 1915–18

Location: Private collection

With renewed effort in the spring of 1915, the Central Powers were able to push back the Russians along a wide front, and to expel them from Poland. The Second Battle of the Masurian Lakes ensured that the German and Austro-Hungarian collaboration was efficient, so much so that the Russians, struggling to maximise their output of war materiel to support its vast armies, were pushed back in a strategic retreat that significantly reduced their threat to the German and Austro-Hungarian empires.

Maps for armchair generals have always been of interest. Despite the static nature of many of the fronts, the purchase of war situation maps, published by newspapers and map companies alike, remained a popular pursuit particularly as the fronts spread out from Europe into the Middle East and Africa. These samples, published in Germany and available to the general public from booksellers and news stands, were part of a series that was published faithfully and regularly for the whole period of the war. In 1915, with paper stocks not in doubt, the maps are strong, well-made and full of confidence. The retreat of the Russians could be plotted easily – and in schools, parlours and bars the German people could be proud that their nation was capable of sustaining two massive bulwarks against their enemies in the Triple Entente. The successive changes in the line would be eagerly awaited at this stage in the war – later, as the tide turned against the Central Powers, they would become less palatable. The war would no longer be fought on two fronts then, but the growing might of the Western Allies would prove too much. And the faltering German front was matched by the faltering quality of the maps by the end of the war: fragile, poor quality, but still proud.

By 1918 the maps had decreased in quality.

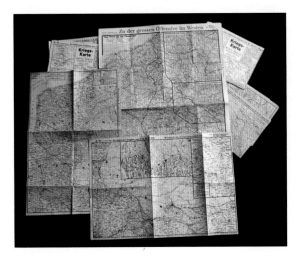

46 *Croix de Guerre*

THE OCCUPATION OF French home soil by the Germans was seen as a national disgrace by the French, and it was down to General Joffre, commander-in-chief of the French armies and hero of the Marne, to break through the German line and 'roll it up'. He selected the great dogleg salient at Noyon as the most likely point of weakness. Here the German lines in Artois and the Champagne joined; attacking this huge bulge in the line on two fronts might just succeed. In late 1914 and 1915 Joffre devised a plan that would throw the might of the French 10th Army at the Germans in Artois, close to the city of Arras, and particularly the natural stronghold of Vimy Ridge, while committing the French 4th and 2nd armies in the Champagne. In attacks that commenced

Country of origin: France

Date of manufacture: 1916

Location: Private collection

in the winter of 1914–15 he hoped that the German front would be driven in and mobile warfare resumed.

The First Battle of Artois ended in the harsh winter of January 1915, the fighting renewed in a second battle in May. The First Battle of Champagne bogged down by March 1915 – with 90,000 casualties. There would be two more offensives on these fronts in autumn. None achieved their objective of breaking the line – and the French casualties mounted to almost half a million men. These and other mass offensives would severely drain the French capacity to prosecute the war. With the bravery of the *poilu* never in question, the French authorities identified the need to publicly reward the acts of heroism of their soldiers. Though it had two awards – the *Légion d'Honneur*, granted for gallantry in war, and the *Médaille Militaire*, given to non-commissioned officers and men who distinguished themselves in action, as well as general officers in command of armies – with many acts of bravery falling below these levels, a new award was necessary.

The *Croix de Guerre* was created by a law of 2 April 1915, proposed by French deputy Émile Briant to honour the acts of his countrymen in their travails in the early offensives, creating 'a new military award, a medal for the leader to decorate his bravest soldiers on the battlefield after each case'. The sculptor Paul-André Bartholomé created the medal, a bronze cross with swords, showing the effigy of the republic. The *Croix* reinstated an older system of mentions in dispatches, with the medal representing a mention in dispatches awarded by a commanding officer, at least a regimental commander.

Our example was awarded in 1916 and, like all of these crosses, is not named to a soldier. It bears two stars that speak of untold bravery in the face of action – bravery that we will never know. Each star and other device records the level to which the acts of bravery have been identified. Our brave *poilu* received recognition at both Brigade (bronze star) and Divisional (silver star) levels. The ultimate was a silver palm leaf. Embodied in this simple device are the fierce struggles of the French soldier on the Western Front – little enough to reward him.

47 'Rising Sun' badge

THE 1ST AUSTRALIAN Imperial Force, or AIF, was raised as a volunteer army to support the mother country in its time of need. With the British declaration of war on Germany in August 1914, Australia was swift to pledge its support. And with estimates of up to 40 per cent of Australian volunteers being British by birth, it is not surpris-

ing that recruitment to the AIF would be brisk in the opening days of the war. With a population of 4 million people, 416,000 men joined the colours, representing more than 38 per cent of Australia's male population who were eligible for service. Of these, 330,000 served overseas. Almost 60,000 died in the war and 166,000 were wounded – the total casualty rate being a staggering 65 per cent.

Of these, the first contingent of soldiers were dispatched to Europe in November 1914; they were sent to Egypt for acclimatisation and further training. And it was during this training period that the Allies suffered the failure of the naval operations at the Dardanelles in March 1915, which led to the Australians and New Zealanders – brigaded together as the Australian and New Zealand Army Corps (ANZAC) – being slated for the Allied landings at Gallipoli. On 25 April 1915 ANZAC troops came ashore at a small cove that was destined to carry the name of the corps, and for five months fought with the British and French to try and overcome the Ottoman defence. They were not successful, but went on to become one of the most significant fighting forces of

Country of origin: Australia

Date of manufacture: 1914–18

Location: Private collection

the Great War, serving in France and Flanders, in Egypt and Palestine. And wherever they fought, their distinctive 'Rising Sun' badge would be evident.

This badge figured on the upturned brim of the hat that would ultimately help define the Australian soldier in two world wars, and would find its way onto the collars of the unique Australian uniform jacket. Though Aussies would stare out from under steel helmets from their arrival on the Western Front in 1916, their distinctive badges – just like those of the Canadians – would announce their presence. The example illustrated would be worn proudly by a returned veteran, or soldier's sweetheart – distinctly modified so that it bears the 'Australia' uniform shoulder title: as if it needed any further introduction.

Yet the badge has distinctly imperial origins and was adopted when Australia raised soldiers to fight in South Africa alongside the British, during the Boer War. The idea for the badge is attributed to the British commander of the forces then being raised, Major-General Sir Edward Hutton. As the story goes, Hutton had been given a gift of a 'trophy of arms' from his friend Brigadier-General Joseph Gordon. The trophy was martial in origin and comprised mounted naval swords and triangular Martini-Henry bayonets arranged in a semi-circle around a central device of the British Imperial Crown. To General Hutton, the shield was symbolic of the co-operation of the naval and military forces of the Commonwealth.

An Australian Digger in 1918.

There were several patterns of what became known as the 'Rising Sun' badge: that which was worn in the Great War carried a scroll with the words 'Australian Commonwealth Military Forces'. Proudly, this badge was worn by the vast majority of the men of the Australian Imperial Forces that served in Gallipoli and on the Western Front; with some modification, it is still worn today by the soldiers of the Australian Army.

48 'Iron Crescent'

THE OTTOMAN EMPIRE, committed to the Central Powers from 1 August 1914, originally held a defensive position, holding the Russians in the Caucasus and ensuring that the Dardanelles defences were intact and supported by the laying of minefields. With Allied pressure on both Germany and Austria-Hungary, this defensive position was itself under threat, and the Ottomans were pressed to attack the British in the Suez Canal Zone, as well as the Russians in Sarikarmish in a disastrous attack in the dead of winter. Both would be setbacks for the Ottomans.

The Ottoman forces were mobilised in August 1914 initially with three armies, growing to five in 1915. In 1914, the 1st and 2nd Armies were serving in Thrace to the west of Constantinople, facing the enemies of the Balkan Wars and, in 1915, defending both shores of the

Country of origin: Ottoman Turkey

Date of manufacture: c. 1915–18

Location: Private collection

Dardanelles and Bosphorus (the 2nd Army later serving in the Caucasus); the 3rd Army served in north-east Anatolia throughout its existence; the 4th Army, formed in September 1914, was sent to Syria and took part in the expedition against the British in the Suez Canal Zone in late 1914; and the 5th Army, formed on 25 March 1915, was to form the main defence of the Dardanelles against the Allied attacks. Three other armies, the 6th, 7th (both formed in 1915) and 8th (formed in 1917), saw service in Mesopotamia (Iraq), Palestine and Syria. All would be eligible – through the display of gallantry – for the Harp Madalyasi, also known as the 'Gallipoli Star' or, in German, *Eiserner Halbmond* – the Iron Crescent.

The *Harp Madalyasi* was an Ottoman decoration that was awarded for 'distinguished war service', ranking just below the *Liyakat* medal, itself awarded for 'military merit'. First instigated on 1 March 1915, the battered example illustrated is typical – though, as with so many decorations of the Great War, the name of the man who received this honour is unknown. Roughly produced in iron or zinc base metal, the award is a simple, five-pointed star that bears the cipher (or *toughra*) of Sultan Mehmed Reshad V, together with the date 1333 (i.e. 1915). Roughly red-painted, the award has a workmanlike feel to it – as does its robust pin, intended to fix the medal to the soldier's breast. Like the Iron Cross, the star was a decoration, not a campaign medal.

The Ottoman forces at Gallipoli were predominantly ethnic Turks, but there would be other nationalities, with at least two regiments, the 72nd and the 77th, that were derived from the Arabian peninsula. With the Ottoman Empire in an almost perpetual state of war since 1911, its troops were battle-hardened and well disciplined – factors that would play in their favour during the Allied landings. At Çannakale (Gallipoli), defenders of the Ottoman Empire were undoubtedly awarded this simple star for their bravery and dedication: Mustafa Kemal Bey – the defender of Gallipoli and the future Kemal Atatürk – was proud to wear this decoration.

49 Kukri

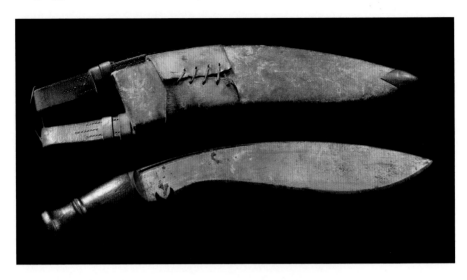

THE KUKRI (OR KHUKURI) is the traditional knife weapon of the Gurkha soldier. Intended primarily as a chopping tool, its long broad knife blade and sharp edge was feared by most adversaries. Dated 1915, this knife is typical of that carried in the Great War on all fronts. With a 13in curved blade and leather scabbard, it was manufactured in Cossipore, close to Calcutta (now Kolkata). The site of a munitions factory for over two centuries, it was the oldest factory on the Indian subcontinent. The weapon is razor sharp and is marked with the 'broad arrow' ordnance mark so characteristic of all weapons and equipment used by the British Empire. The kukri was designed primarily as a utilitarian weapon for chopping; it was well suited to close combat due to the bend in the blade – though it was just as easily used as a slashing weapon, or one used on a lunge. Either way, facing it must have been a terrifying prospect.

Gurkha soldiers are admired for their valour and bravery, as tough soldiers from the foothills of the Himalayas in the isolated mountain state of Nepal that is separate from India and direct British governance –

Country of origin: India

Date of manufacture: 1915

Location: Private collection

the Gurkha state having fiercely defended its status in border wars with the British in the early nineteenth century. Yet Gurkhas were also enlisted into the East India Company in the middle of one of these wars, in 1816, and the steadfastness of these men and their successors was valued during the mutiny that threatened British sovereignty in the region. They would fight with the British Army in other of Queen Victoria's 'small wars'.

Maharajah Chandra Shumsher Rana, the prime minister of Nepal, pledged the support of his nation, and of his Gurkha troops, to Britain at the outbreak of war. A nation of 5 million, Nepal would commit some 200,000 men to the war, 20,000 of them casualties – and 2,000 of them receiving gallantry medals. Gurkha soldiers fought on all the major fronts of the war – in France and Flanders, in Mesopotamia, at Gallipoli and in Salonika, and in Egypt and Palestine. General Sir Ian Hamilton, commander of the ill-fated force that landed in Gallipoli in April 1915, was particularly keen: 'I am very anxious, if possible, to get a Brigade of Gurkhas [...] who will, I'm certain, be most valuable on the Gallipoli Peninsula [...] just the sort of terrain where those fellows are at their brilliant best.' Three battalions of Gurkha Rifles was committed to the campaign and some 750 men were killed, twice as many wounded. Everywhere they went, their kukri went with them; this one, issued in 1915, must have seen much service.

50 Russian imperial insignia

THE RELICS ILLUSTRATED are fragments of Russian field equipment that were left behind in the Carpathian battlefields during the retreat in the summer of 1915. Avidly collected by enthusiasts in Poland, these objects are battered and worn, and their removal from the ground removes all hope that they might be properly interpreted as archaeological artefacts. But they occur in great numbers and are traded, along with other badges, buttons and pieces of field equipment that hark back to the days of Imperial Russia. These sad relics, presumably discarded by Russian troops, are adorned with the evidence of their nationality: the cap cockade that was once coloured with the orange and black colours of the Imperial family; and a button and worn belt buckle that displays the double-headed eagle of Peter the Great, the arms of Russia.

In the early summer of 1915, the Germans had targeted the Eastern Front as their main theatre of

Country of origin: Russia

Date of manufacture: c. 1914

Location: Private collection

operations. The Russians had been under pressure since their failures at Tannenberg and the First Battle of the Masurian Lakes in 1914, and the main focus of the war shifted to the Carpathians. After the seizure of the fortress of Przemysl in Galicia, the Austro-Hungarians fell back to the mountain line. With the Russian success threatening the stability of the now unified Austro–German lines, a new offensive was planned for the summer of 1915 that would once more put the Russians under pressure. With the Western Front now held on the defensive by the Germans, their manpower was available for the east to try and deal with the developing Russian threat. The Germans were able to shift an entire army, the *XI Armée* – consisting of ten infantry divisions – to the east, to work alongside the Austro-Hungarian *IV Armée*, both commanded by General August von Mackensen.

The Gorlice–Tarnów Offensive opened on 2 May 1915 and took the Russians by surprise. The strength of the Central Powers was too much; the Russian 3rd Army folded before it, its strength ebbing away to the east. With the loss of 140,000 men, the whole of Galicia was returned to Austro-Hungarian hands, and the offensive sparked a Russian withdrawal that would spread from Lithuania in the north to the Romanian border. The relics illustrated here were left behind by the soldiers in their retreat, to be preserved in the soil of Poland as an indication of the high-water mark of the Russian offensives against the Austro-Hungarians.

The Carpathians would be the scene of other Russian offensives that attempted to redress the balance; the Brusilov Offensive of 1916 recaptured much of the territory relinquished in 1915, but failed to reach the Carpathians, and ran out of steam in September. The final Russian offensive, the Kerensky Offensive, fought in July 1917 after the abdication of the tsar three months earlier, achieved little despite new tactics and artillery power. In its place came refusal to fight, rebellion and mutiny. The seeds of the October Revolution, the withdrawal of the Russians from the war and overthrow of tsarist rule were well and truly sown.

5̄1

Gas helmet

Country of origin:
United Kingdom

**Date of
manufacture:**
1915–16

Location: Private
collection

THE USE OF gas on 22 April 1915 by the Germans saw the Allies unprepared. As part of their assault at Ypres, the use of chlorine gas released from cylinders was to overcome the unprotected French troops manning the front line, with 800 to 1,400 men killed and a further 2,000 to 3,000 men injured. Chlorine gas kills by irritating the lungs so much that they are flooded, the victim actually drowning in their own body fluids. Men killed by gas show startling blueness of the lips and face, a function of the blood becoming starved of oxygen. Its first use was terrifying.

This first use of chemical weapons on the battlefield changed the face of the war; from now on, soldiers would have to be equipped to both defend themselves from the new weapon and understand how it might be used. There would be no turning back from it now. Poison gas was to be used by the British at the Battle of Loos in September 1915, when Lord Kitchener, secretary of state for war, gave instructions that retaliatory measures be prepared in order to use this weapon against the Germans.

Following the first gas attack, the British had come a long way from their quickly extemporised cloths soaked in alkaline solutions, such as bicarbonate of soda or even urine. Leading chemists quickly identified that

a mixture of sodium hyposulphite ('hypo' as used in photographic processing), sodium carbonate and glycerine was considered proof against chlorine, bromine, sulphur dioxide and other fumes, these chemical salts neutralising the poisons, and the first issue masks were made of black mourning-veil material and cotton wadding dipped in a solution of the chemicals. The mask was proven to be inadequate by scientists serving as soldiers in the British Expeditionary Force; one of them, Captain Cluny Macpherson, suggested a flannel bag soaked in the same solution that covered the head and was tucked into the top of the uniform jacket. It was also equipped with a mica window. Macpherson's 'Hypo' helmet was issued in early May, but there were still fears that the Hypo helmet would not be proof against the more lethal gases, such as phosgene or hydrogen cyanide. As such, it was replaced by a new pattern, the 'P' or 'Phenate' helmet, soaked in another counter-gas chemical, sodium phenate; the helmet was made of cotton flannelette, the mica eyepiece replaced by circular glass eyepieces, and it was fitted with an outlet valve with a tube to be gripped in the teeth. From January 1916 all 'P' helmets were dipped in hexamine – highly absorbent of phosgene gas – to become the phenate-hexamine or

The British at Loos in 1915, wearing gas hoods.

'PH' helmet. All were clammy, cloying and unpleasant to wear. These nightmarish bags were to become part of the iconography of the Great War. Illustrated is the PHG helmet – a version for gunners that ensured the goggles were kept tight to the face with elastic straps, thereby reducing fogging.

At Loos, British soldiers wore both 'Hypo' and 'P' helmets, and were supposed to carry a spare. These nightmarish creations would be famously recorded as the 'goggle-eyed bugger with the tit' by Captain Robert Graves of the Royal Welsh Fusiliers. The gas was to be dispensed from cylinders fitted with flexible pipes that connected to the business end of the affair, a ½in iron pipe up to 10ft long, and which was fitted with a jet at its end:

> Zero hour arrived at last at 5.50 am, and with a redoubled artillery bombardment the gas and smoke were released all along the front [...] the gas cloud was rolling steadily over towards the German lines [...] apart from the artillery drum-fire and the clouds of gas and smoke from eleven thousand candles, twenty-five thousand phosphorous hand-grenades were spurting out dense white fumes.

> Lt-Col C.H. Foulkes, Commanding RE
> Special (Gas) Companies

The British gas attack at Loos had mixed fortunes: the gas refused to travel in some areas, and in others the soldiers became frustrated with the clammy bags and removed them, only to become casualties themselves. Gas was to become commonplace; but with increased capability of countermeasures, its value had diminished. It remains, though, one of the most horrifying weapons ever to have been used on the battlefield.

52

Loos football

THE BATTLE OF LOOS fought in September 1915 was the first major British offensive of the war. Yet neither the British commander-in-chief, Sir John French, nor the general in charge of the attack, Sir Douglas Haig, wanted to fight at Loos. Despite Joffre's view to the contrary, the ground was poor and the strength of the German positions – holed up in fortified mining villages and slag heaps – just too great. With the Allied strategic situation in a parlous state and the Russians on the point of collapse, the need to support the French was recognised by the British secretary of state, Field Marshal Lord Kitchener. French and Haig, stuck between Joffre and Kitchener, had little choice but to attack where the British line met that of their allies, just to the north of Lens.

The men of the London Irish Rifles (1/18 battalion, London Regiment), at the left of the 47th Division line, north of the Double Crassier, would be first out of the trenches. The battalion was famous for footballing prowess, its team roundly beating others of the brigade; it was perhaps not surprising that their entry into the 'great push' would involve kicking leather footballs forwards towards the German trenches. While this was officially frowned upon, one man, Private Edwards, would nevertheless carry a deflated ball into the line;

Country of origin: United Kingdom

Date of manufacture: c. 1915

Location: London Irish Rifles Museum, London, UK

THE MAN OF LOOS

The Loos footballer;
the London Irish Rifles
monument.

inflating it before zero hour, he would launch the ball
with a goalkeeper's throw, punting it towards the line
while his colleagues followed it up:

> A boy came along the trench carrying a football under
> his arm. 'What are you going to do with that?' I asked.
> 'It's some idea this,' he said with a laugh. 'We're going to
> kick it across into the German trench.' 'It is some idea,'
> I said. 'What are our chances of victory in the game?'

Patrick MacGill, *The Great Push*, 1915

The London Irish would soon drive the Germans from
the line, the Germans streaming through Loos back
towards their second line. The football had reached its
objective; hanging on the German wire, it would eventually find its way back home to the regimental depot.

The *Man of Loos* is a bronze statue on the war memorial of the London Irish Rifles, depicting a soldier in
1915 garb, holding a football. More remarkable is the
preservation of the ball itself. Last seen by writer Patrick

MacGill as a deflated leather bag on the German wire, it survived to become a celebrated relic of the Rifles' involvement in the battle. Recently restored, the football was revered at post-war mess dinners and regimental events. Yet despite the celebrated nature of this exploit, it has been overshadowed by the use of the same motivational use of footballs, this time repeated by the East Surrey Regiment at the opening of the Battle of the Somme in July 1916.

The Battle of Loos saw the capture of this mining village – achieved on the first day – and the adjustment of the Allied line of just a few square miles. And at the end the three weeks of battle, the British had suffered 6,350 dead, including thirty-five senior officers and many more junior officers, and in total, there would be some 50,380 casualties, over 2,000 of them officers. Casualties were high in the raw New Army battalions within the 15th Division, the Scots taking a particularly high number of losses, and in the 21st and 24th Divisions that were pushed into the battle in such trying circumstances. While the territorials of the 47th Division had achieved maximum penetration in the battle, the regulars of the 2nd Division were decimated – the last numbers of an already dying breed. The British Expeditionary Force would take some time to recover. The Germans lost just under 20,000 men.

The Loos football in the London Irish Rifles' mess.

53 Alpine crampons

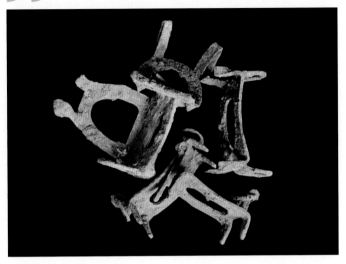

ITALY ENTERED THE war on the side of the Entente in 1915. Previously, the country had been part of the Triple Alliance that, since 1882, had bound it together with Germany and Austro-Hungary. But with the Austro-Hungarians eyeing territory in Italy, and with sensitivities over the Alpine border that defined their countries, public opinion in Italy at least was less than enthusiastic about this relationship. It was not surprising, then, that when Austro-Hungary declared war on Serbia, and Germany attacked France and Belgium, Italy took a step back from its former agreement. Italy pushed the view that it had no obligation to attack the Entente powers, and used this as a means of staying out of the war. Not surprisingly, Britain and France actively made it their business to charm Italy into joining the war on their side. With the idea of picking territorial gains from the bones of the Austro-Hungarian Empire, the Italians finally threw in their lot with the Allies, signing the Treaty of London on 26 April 1915, a treaty that guaranteed territorial gains in exchange for a declaration of war on Austria-Hungary – which was duly announced on 23 May 1915.

Country of origin: Italy

Date of manufacture: 1915–18

Location: Private collection

The Italians were now immersed in the war and the Austro-Hungarians faced enemies on three fronts. But the practical aspects of the Italian war effort were daunting. The border between Austria and Italy stretched some 400 miles from the Swiss border in the west to the Adriatic coast in the east. For the most part, the front was mountainous – and the Austro-Hungarians were in the favoured position of holding the highest points over most of it. The Italians, committed to an offensive war against the dual monarchy, had little choice but to hold the defensive along the mountains and prosecute offensive action against the Austrians along the line of the southwards-flowing Isonzo River, which divested itself into the Adriatic sea. From 1915–18 there would be twelve separate battles along this river line – the most decisive being that prosecuted by the Austro-Hungarians in October 1917, the disaster at Caporetto, which almost saw the Italians defeated.

The Alpine crampons illustrated are indicative of a completely different kind of war, one that was fought in difficult conditions of snow and ice, rock fall and avalanche. Recovered by an amateur Italian archaeologist, amongst other relics of the war from both sides, these are believed to be Italian crampons – though the Austro-Hungarian *gebirgsjäger* could just as easily have worn them. The Alpine war was another extension of the siege war that was being fought across the Western Front – except that here, the slopes were sheer, the climate difficult, the chance of death through avalanche ever-present. The crampons were there to do an important job: to maintain the grip of a man's footing, aided by ropes, ice axes and Alpine boots. Robust, the teeth of the crampon would have to bite deeply into the smooth surface of the ice, allowing whoever wore them to hold on to his footing – just as the Italian nation had to do in the wake of the German-bolstered attack at Caporetto. No doubt the soldier carried out his duty in maintaining the line before discarding these fearsome objects on the mountainside. Monte Grappa, built into an impregnable mountain fortress, would be instrumental in keeping the Austrians at bay.

54 Austrian Howitzer

THE WAR IN the mountains between Austria and Italy was a technical one: the construction of defences, the mining of tunnels through rock and glacier, the development of artillery capable of tackling the crippling altitudes and withstanding the extremes of climate. In the Tyrol, the Austrians held the high ground, but had retreated behind the ridge top in order to shield their men from barrage fire (*trommelfeuer*), the effect of constant bombardment by Italian artillery upon the Austrian positions. Each explosion brought with it the dangers of rock fragments adding to the injuries from shards of metal. In all cases, artillery was required that could fire a high trajectory round capable of falling in an arc upon the trenches below. For both sides, the use of flat trajectory weapons would be inadequate – with the Italians firing upwards towards the Austrians who, in turn, would have to fire down upon the Italians.

The howitzer illustrated is carefully preserved in the *Heeresgeschichtliches* Museum in Vienna. It is a 38cm *Belagerungshaubitze* M16 – a super-heavy howitzer that was designed for siege operations on the Italo-Austrian front. The first of their kind were given the names 'Barbara' and 'Gudrun' and were due for delivery to the Austrian front in time for the south Tyrol offensive in May 1916. A further eight heavy weapons were to see action; this one is number six, while its sister, 'Gudrun', is preserved as a war trophy in the National Military Museum of Romania (Romania having entered the war on the side of the Allies in 1916). Each gun took a considerable amount of effort and manpower to move it into position, and a 52 cubic metre pit had to be dug in order to house the weapon – and withstand the force of its discharge.

Country of origin:
Austria-Hungary

Date of construction:
c. 1916

Location:
Heeresgeschicht-liches Museum, Vienna, Austria

The total forces imme- diately available on the Austrian side of the 350km Tyrolean front were twenty-six infantry battalions, fifty-six garri- son detachments, thirty- seven fortress artillery and three engineer com- panies: 35,000 men with 146 mobile and 539 siege artillery pieces. Opposing them were the 1st and 4th Italian armies, comprising twelve infantry divisions and three specialist moun- tain Alpini groups.

Howitzers and mortars were the only effective weapons – as they were in all trench warfare battles – though the undermin- ing of trenches gave the possibility of an underground explosion. This was particularly so when the peak of the Col di Lana, a mountain affording unrivalled artil- lery observation of the Italian forces, was detonated. Occupying the peak since January 1916, a battalion of the 2nd Tyrolean *Kaiserjäger* regiment had been holding the *Gipfelstellung*, or peak position. Unknown to them, Italian engineers constructed a 52m tunnel beneath the mountain, taking four months to dig. In all, 5,020kg of explosives were in place, ready for deto- nation in April 1916. This kind of operation required time and planning; artillery preparation with how- itzers was much more the norm. In both cases, the extreme environments of the mountain warfare would challenge the fighters.

On les aura !

2^E EMPRUNT
DE
LA DÉFENSE NATIONALE
Souscrivez

DEVAMBEZ Imp PARIS

55

On Les Aura! poster

ONE OF THE most iconic images of the First World War is that used by lithographic artist Abel Faivre in a poster for the 2nd Defence National Loan for the French war effort, first produced in 1916. It depicts a French soldier, equipped with Adrian helmet and Lebel rifle, with his identity bracelet on his right wrist. The man is looking back over his right shoulder as if to summon the French public. His arm is stretched forwards, the act mirroring the soldier's excitement, and is the embodiment of the phrase '*On les aura!*' (Let's get them!). The poster was one of the most popular of the war, and was reproduced in postcard form – the object illustrated is the poster, its international icon status underlined by its presence in the collection of the Library of Congress in Washington DC.

Country of origin:
France

Date of printing:
1916

Location: Library of Congress, Washington DC, USA

The phrase '*On les aura!*' was uttered by General Philippe Pétain during the Battle of Verdun – one of the most challenging tests of the endurance of the French Army during the whole war. The fortress town of Verdun, close to the border with Germany, sat within a salient that bulged forwards into the German line. The town, strategically situated on the River Meuse, boasted a citadel that had been constructed by Vauban, as well as a range of late-nineteenth-century forts that had been built into surrounding hills in the wake of the

French defeat in 1871. The fort had held secure during the German advances of 1914 that had created the salient, and by 1915 the French had become complacent – removing most of the guns from the forts and reducing its garrison.

In February 1916, the Germans opened a massive offensive against the confined space of the Verdun salient, which would become one of the most costly of the whole war. Post-war, the German commander, Erich von Falkenhayn, claimed in his memoirs that the purpose of the offensive was simply to 'bleed the French forces to death'. According to his memoirs, no physical breakthough would be necessary – committing sufficient forces to the fray would ensure that the capability of the French Army would be stretched to breaking point. Falkenhayn's post-war writings may suffer from the need to justify an offensive that became – in frank terms used at the time – a meat grinder.

The battle commenced with a ten-hour artillery bombardment that saw 1 million shells pumped into the salient, the rain of fire felt by the men sheltering deep underground in the fortresses of Douaumont and Vaux, as well as the town of Verdun itself. This massive bombardment caused heavy losses for the French and destroyed much of the defensive system of trenches, leaving the heavily constructed fortifications to endure. New German tactics involving *sturmtruppen* (storm troops), equipped with hand grenades, were sent in to clear the defenders where they could. The French were severely tested, and when Douaumont fell to the attackers – who entered the fort along a tunnel – there were fears that the whole front would crumble.

Pétain would come to embody the French resistance to the attack. His organisational skills meant that Verdun was well supplied – despite the absence of adequate rail links. Along a road from Bar le Duc to the beleaguered city he organised a continuous flow of trucks that would bring fresh troops, more munitions, and yet more artillery to take the fight to the Germans. These trucks, travelling the *Voie Sacrée*, were essential to French effort, which finally slowed down the

The fortress at Douaumont; epicentre of the Verdun battlefield.

German offensive and created the means for a massive artillery duel that pounded Falkenhayn's positions with an estimated 15 million shells over the five months of the battle. Pétain used the phrase '*On les aura!*' in absolute confidence that the French would win out over the Germans at Verdun. Pétain's confidence meant that Verdun would not fall; his counterattack, in May 1916, stalled, and it would be to his successor in command of the 2nd Army at Verdun, General Nivelle, to finally utter the words '*Ils ne passeront pas*' (They shall not pass). The Germans did not. Pétain, hero of Verdun, would later be the disgraced collaborationist leader of the Vichy government in the Second World War, but this poster, bearing his words, still carries the power to inspire.

56

Douaumont Ossuary

THE BATTLE OF VERDUN raged from 21 February to 18 December 1916. With casualty figures of at least 700,000, it was one of the bloodiest battles in history. For the French it is seen as the defining battle of the war. The initial German offensive had severely pressed the French but it was the defenders who won, their ring of defences having held out against the mass attacks – the German mincing machine was struggling to cope in the face of the efficiency of the supply lines laid and developed by Pétain, then commander of the French 2nd Army.

Central to the defence of the city were the forts and defensive positions arranged as if in a letter H, the forts holding the high ground. Douaumont took its name from a village just to the west, which would be one of several to be wiped off the face of the earth by the battle. It was the largest of the forts, and it occupied a ridge that joined with the defence works at the *Ouvrage de Thiamont* and *Ouvrage de Froideterre*. To the south of this line was the *Fort de Vaux*, a smaller artillery fort that was nevertheless in the front line, connecting to the *Fort de Souville* in the west. Both ridges were connected by another line, through Fleury. Though *Fort Douaumont* fell early in the battle, on 24 February, the other defence works held, with Vaux the most advanced position.

Country of origin:
France

Date of construction:
1932

Location: National Monument, Douaumont, Verdun, France

The French counterattacks of May failed to recapture Douaumont; and with a renewed German offensive phase in June, Vaux was to fall on 7 June, following a harrowing battle in the confined spaces and corridors of the fort. Assaults with diphosgene or 'green-cross' gas shells on French artillery positions helped the German troops in their forward pressure, which flowed towards Souville and the defensive works at Froideterre. This was the high water mark of the German offensive, which reached Souville on 12 July 1916.

The ossuary at Douaumont.

The Douaumont Ossuary is a monument to the men who toiled in the Battle of Verdun. With ossuaries being the final resting place of human bones – a common conception in Catholic countries – it would be no surprise that such a building would be constructed on a battlefield so thickly populated with the missing bodies of the men of both nations that fought there. The job of gathering the remains started in 1918, when the Bishop of Verdun first mooted the idea of building such a monument. The first stone of the building was laid in 1920 by Marshal Pétain, and was to be built into a magnificent edifice of seventeen tombs set in a 137m-long cloister, a chapel and a tower that would look over the

Fort Douaumont today.

'murdered nature' of the Verdun battlefield. The tombs contain the remains of 130,000 soldiers who have no known grave. It is a sobering place, and can be no better remembrance of the 300,000 men who died here.

At Verdun, the tide turned in favour of the French in July. First, the Anglo-French Battle of the Somme had opened to the north, diverting German resources away from the battlefront. The Germans were exhausted in their attempts to capture Souville and the town itself; and when the French began their offensive phase under General Nivelle in October, the result was the recapture of the two forts that came to symbolise the grinding pressure of this battle: first Douaumont and then Vaux. The battle had expended the men and resources of the two enemies – and had left the battlefield strewn with so many bodies, whose bones now lie intermingled under the magnificent edifice that is the Douaumont Ossuary.

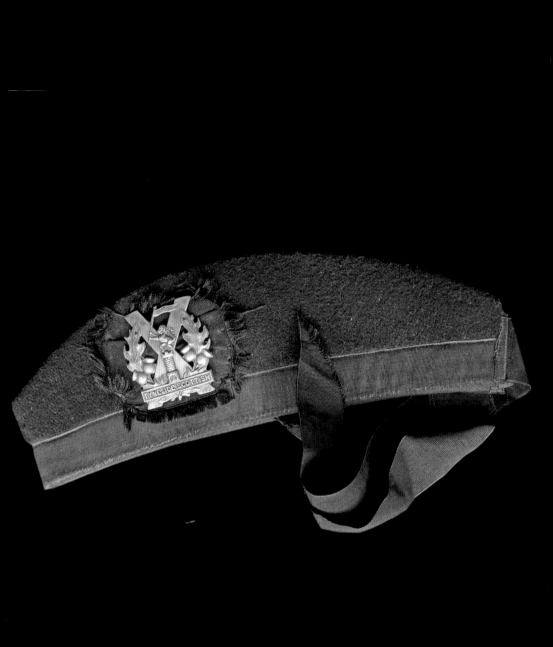

57

Tyneside Scottish cap

Country of origin:
United Kingdom

Date of manufacture:
c. 1914–16

Location: Private collection

THE RAISING OF Kitchener's Army in 1914–15 led to the creation of the 'New Army', an army of volunteers that would take some time to shape into soldiers. With the men of the regular and territorial armies fully committed to the war on the Western Front in 1914–15, it was the preferred option of the British commander-in-chief, Field Marshal Sir John French, that he should hold on until the New Army was ready to take the field. Though two divisions were allotted to the Battle of Loos in September 1915 on the Western Front – fought in support of the French at Artois – they were untried and thrown into an impossible situation. It was the Battle of the Somme, which opened on 1 July 1916, that saw the 'Pals' in action, used en masse for the first time. This day would become seared into the consciousness of the British people.

The Battle of the Somme was planned on a limited 14-mile front that straddled the River Somme; it aimed to relieve pressure on Verdun. South of the river, the French were to operate, while north of it, from Maricourt to Serre, and in front of the salient at Gommecourt, were the British. Taking over the lines from the French in July–August 1915, the British were to attack on 1 July 1916 with twenty-eight divisions, nineteen of them 'New Army', composed of Kitchener's volunteers.

Amongst the most enthusiastic volunteers were those of the north-east of England. The industrial centres of the north were all recruitment centres, and with the opportunity for men to join up together – to form 'Pals' battalions – recruitment, though variable at first, became brisk. On Tyneside, men of Irish and Scottish descent gathered to form units of Tyneside Scots or Tyneside Irish – units that would be assimilated into the much respected regiment, the Northumberland Fusiliers. Recruitment would be so successful, in fact, that there would be four battalions of Tyneside Irish – composed mostly of men of Irish extraction – and a further four battalions of Tyneside Scots. In fact the Tyneside Scottish were mostly Englishmen – over 75 per cent of them – who were lured by the possibility of wearing Highland dress. When finally assimilated by the Northumberland Fusiliers, most men were disappointed to hear that the British Army had not given them the right to wear kilts. Instead, they had to proclaim their origins through the adoption of that most Scottish of all headgear, the glengarry cap. Unusually, the Tynesiders were brigaded together, forming the 102nd (Tyneside Scottish) and 103rd (Tyneside Irish) Brigades of the 34th Division.

The cap illustrated belonged to Second Lieutenant (later Lieutenant) Gilbert Watt Sandeman of the 20th (Service) Battalion (1st Tyneside Scottish). It is dark blue, with a central red tourie, and is bound in silk, with silk tassels. Inside, it bears the initials G.W.S. – a rare example of an

Tyneside Irish in no-man's-land, La Boisselle.

attributable wartime cap. Lieutenant Sandeman was 23 in 1914, and came from a large family in Newcastle – a family wealthy enough to employ servants. Sandeman's claims for Scottish ancestry, and his identification with the Tyneside Scottish is aligned with his Scots father, John W. Sandeman, a civil engineer. It is not surprising, then, that Gilbert would join the Tyneside Scottish, and that with his position and level of education he should apply for a commission.

On the first day of the Battle of the Somme, 1 July 1916, the 102nd (Tyneside Scottish) Brigade (34th Division) were at the centre of the British line, astride the main Albert–Bapaume road and opposite the fortified village of La Boisselle. The Germans had made it their business to build up their trench defences as much as possible, and for their part, they were well dug in and held the line well. The Albert–Bapaume road was of great strategic importance, bisecting the British line, and it held the tantalising possibility that, if secured, the British and French cavalry could pass through to help unroll the line. As it was strongly held, it was decided to dislodge the German fieldworks by firing two large mines that were detonated on either side of La Boisselle village, two minutes before zero hour.

Zero hour for the attack was 7.30 a.m. Following detonation of the mine, the Tyneside Scots rose from their forward position. North of the road, the 1st Battalion were faced with crossing no-man's-land, which was 750 yards wide and caught in a valley between two strong points, the villages of Ovilliers and La Boisselle. While the valley to the south of La Boisselle was named 'Sausage', that to the north of it was 'Mash'. Completely in the open, the advancing Tyneside Scots in Mash Valley were caught in crossfire from both strong points – it was too tall an order. Some men made it across the valley to La Boisselle, but it was no use: the survivors were forced to retreat, and the Tyneside Scottish were back where they started. The 1st Tyneside Scottish lost 584 men, their battalion commander killed. Sandeman was one of the fortunate ones – he survived the war.

58

Lochnagar Crater

WITH THE DEVELOPMENT of trench warfare came
the return to ancient siege tactics, and it did not take
long before sapping and mining was tried as a viable
option. Undermining the enemy had been a respected
siege warfare tool since ancient times and military
mining was on the syllabus for most military engineer
schools prior to the Great War, though with little expectation it would be used. Trench warfare saw a revival in
the ancient art, and the armies started to undermine
opposing trench lines in late 1914; techniques progressively developed and improved throughout 1915–16.

When the British took over the Somme sector, they
inherited the mine shafts and galleries that had been
put in place by the French *Genié*, and the Germans
were equally committed to the construction of mines
and countermines to defeat their enemies. The trench
system developed by the Germans took advantage of
the terrain. With the dips and swells of chalk downland,
the trenches followed the contours and left the Allies
with the unenviable task of fighting along valleys while
facing fire on three sides. This was certainly the case at
La Boisselle. The Germans had also built into their lines
strongpoints that were intended to break up any attack;
jutting forward like self-contained trench fortresses,
they occupied ruined villages and forests. Along the

Country of origin:
United Kingdom
(in France)

Date of formation:
1916

Location:
Lochnagar Crater,
La Boisselle,
France

newly occupied Somme front these strongpoints were a serious threat to any attack – and the plan was developed to attack them from under ground. Three large mines, with around 5,000lb of explosive, were prepared – one to the north, under the Hawthorn Ridge redoubt, and two on either side of the main Albert–Bapaume road, close to La Boisselle. There were seven smaller mines laid elsewhere in the line.

In 1915, the British had suffered from shortages in artillery ammunition that had stalled the attacks in the Lens sector. With the government munitions factories struggling to cope, and with imported ammunition failing to explode, British offensives quickly lost their momentum. The British government fell in the wake of the 'shell scandal', and a new Ministry of Munitions was developed to deal with the challenge. Plans for the Somme offensive of 1916 took advantage of this change in fortune, and the bombardment unleashed by the British and French along the 14-mile front was amongst the heaviest of the war. Commencing on 24 June 1916, as many as 1,537 guns fired shells incessantly at the German positions, with one field gun for each 20 yards. A total of 1.5 million shells rained down on the Germans in just seven days, in the expectation that they would destroy the opposing trenches. But the Germans had dug deep, and dug wisely; and of those 1.5 million shells, only one-third were high explosive – the rest were shrapnel, which it was hoped would serve to cut barbed wire entanglements. With this preparation, and the explosion of the mines, the British expected to be able to rise out of the trenches unopposed, and to march at a steady pace across no-man's-land in order to occupy trenches filled with dead and dying Germans.

The Lochnagar Crater is one of the biggest craters ever formed from conflict, with an internal volume of 35,500 cubic metres. It is preserved intact as a memorial to the men who fought on the Somme and is visited annually by thousands of people per year, most notably on the anniversary of the first day of the Battle of the Somme, 1 July. The crater is deep and dry, its stable slopes cutting through the chalk. The crater stands where there was once a German redoubt in their front line. It is a remarkable sight, preserved intact within the Somme battlefields. Walking up to it, the crater still has the opportunity to take your breath away, and to allow you to wonder at the sheer power that was involved in its detonation.

The mine was commenced in November 1915, with an inclined shaft that descended some 95ft below ground. It was dug from a communication trench, Lochnagar Street, some 300ft behind the front line – and some 900ft from its intended target, the *Schwaben Höhe* strongpoint. The tunnel gallery was divided to produce two explosive chambers some 60ft apart, deep underground. In total, the chambers held 60,000 tons of the explosive ammonal. The mines at La Boisselle were detonated at 7.28 a.m., two minutes before zero hour. The crater formed was 300ft at its widest diameter and 70ft deep. It obliterated 400ft of trenches, and an unknown number of German soldiers with it.

The explosion of this mine, and the seven-day bombardment that preceded it, created a living hell for the German defenders sheltered in their trenches and within the dugouts that were excavated into the solid chalk rock of Picardy. However, the defences were too strong, the strength of the artillery explosions too weak, the mines too scattered. When the men went over the top on 1 July 1916, they were met with a maelstrom of fire that would see men lean forward as if battling against the wind. With the rattle of the machine guns and the explosions of the German artillery, the British and French infantry struggled to make headway. The first day of the Battle of the Somme was marked with losses of 57,470 men – some 19,240 of them killed in action. The Somme would be fought until November, and would peter out in the winter mud. The first day would be the 'blackest day' in British military history. For some, this marks a defining point in a long and costly 'learning curve' that would eventually lead the British Army to victory in 1918. But for many communities that had gladly waved their 'pals' on their way to France, there would be nothing but sorrow.

59 Gallantry medals

THE GREAT WAR saw the award of an unprecedented number of medals for gallantry – a fact that was not without some controversial aspects at the time, with awards of medals for distinguished service in the rear areas. Most were hard won, however. Most nations struggled to ensure that they had sufficient scope within their awards system to ensure that men (and women) were justly awarded, and many awards would be instigated during the war that would assume iconic status. That is certainly the case for the Iron Cross, resurrected in 1914 with the German Empire facing one of its toughest challenges. The Iron Cross was truly a medal that was awarded without regard for status or rank.

For the British Army, the utmost gallantry was marked by the award of the Victoria Cross (VC), first instituted in 1856 in the wake of the Crimean War. Some 628 awards were made in the First World War, granted for 'conspicuous bravery or devotion to the country in the presence of the enemy'. Clearly, to be eligible for the award, the service had to be of the highest order – one-quarter of those

Country of origin: United Kingdom

Date of manufacture: 1915–19

Location: Private collection

awarded the honour died in the act of winning it. Like the Iron Cross, the award of the Victoria Cross was not controlled by rank or status – but the other awards were. The Distinguished Service Order (DSO), first awarded in 1886, was available for officers of captain and above, for rewarding 'meritorious acts in war'. Joining this was the Distinguished Conduct Medal (DCM) for non-commissioned officers and men, instituted in 1845 for 'distinguished conduct in the field'. However, with great acts of bravery by all ranks in the early part of the war, this was clearly inadequate.

The Military Cross (MC) was initiated on 31 December 1914 for junior officers and warrant officers 'in recognition of distinguished and meritorious services in time of war'. A Greek Cross in silver, the medal incorporates elements of vertical Art Nouveau style that was popular in the run-up to the war. As the Military Cross was awarded 'in recognition of distinguished and meritorious services in time of war' it could therefore be awarded to those not in the thick of action; over 37,000 awards were made, with 3,155 bars (additional awards of the same medal) also granted. In addition, there was the Military Medal (MM) for NCOs and men instigated in March 1916.

The MC is illustrated here along with three Great War campaign medals and a DCM awarded to Second Lieutenant William Wharram of the Leeds Pals. Wharram received his DCM for actions on the Somme on 7 October 1916. Whilst serving as a private with the 11th Battalion, West Yorkshire Regiment, Wharram was awarded his medal for 'conspicuous gallantry in action', having 'bombed down an enemy trench and assisted in the capture of over 100 prisoners' on the Somme. Promoted to Second Lieutenant Wharram was awarded his Military Cross during the German offensives in 1918, the last ditch attempt at breaking through the lines. Awarded his MC 'for conspicuous gallantry', with his platoon Second Lieutenant Wharram was instrumental in 'enfilading the advance of the enemy' during a breakthrough, 'directing a very effective fire against them'. These medals were cherished and well worn by their recipient.

60

Wolseley helmet

AMONGST THE MOST iconic military headgear worn during the First World War was the Wolseley pattern cork sun helmet, or 'solar topee'. This high-domed cork helmet with wide brim was worn by British troops wherever there was a hot or tropical climate, part of a 'system' that would include the cotton uniform known as khaki drill, and coupled with a peculiar encumbrance – the spine pad. The spine pad was a quilted pad several inches wide that was literally worn strapped to the individual's spine. It was linked directly to the misguided idea that heatstroke (heat apoplexy) was caused by the sun beating down directly upon the spine – a concept that was born in the mid-nineteenth century and that lingered on into the twentieth. With heat exhaustion related directly to overheating of the body core, the provision of such items would surely exacerbate the problem.

Country of origin:
United Kingdom

Date of manufacture:
1914–18

Location: Private collection

If the spine pad was an unnecessary encumbrance, then the Wolseley helmet at least had some utility – though it could do little else than protect the wearer from the sun. Named after Sir Garnet Wolseley, a version of the helmet was worn during the Boer War, but with a narrow profile it did little to provide protection for the temples – though the standard wide-brimmed pattern was identified in dress regulations from 1900. This example is typical. It is an officer's version, its rim

Pte Robert Wheatley
of the Yorkshire
Regiment wearing a
Wolseley helmet in
Gallipoli. He was killed
in August 1915.

bound with buff leather. Ordinary soldiers were distinguished by their cloth or webbing-bound versions –
there was little otherwise to distinguish them. Both were
worn with a distinctive length of cloth, which served no
other purpose than decoration, wrapped around the
body of the helmet. Up to 24ft long, this 'puggaree' had
Indian origins, its name derived from the Hindi *pagri*,
meaning turban.

210

Khaki drill and Wolseley helmets were destined to be used in all warm-weather climates, in the Mediterranean, Middle East, Africa and India. Our helmet could have served in the trenches at Gallipoli, or during the long periods of inactivity endured by the British Army while cooped up in Salonika, facing the Bulgarians and waiting for the Greeks to join the war as active combatants (when this finally happened in 1917, the steel helmet replaced the Wolseley in combat): we will never know. In the Middle East, it would have been worn with cotton khaki drill in Palestine or Egypt. Or it could have been used in one of the most challenging campaigns of all – that of Mesopotamia.

Fought against the Ottoman Empire, facing what the British referred to as 'Johnny Turk', the British Indian Army-controlled campaign was simply to ensure that oil supplies were safeguarded and secure. But after a string of successes against the Ottomans in 1914–15, the mostly Indian forces (consisting ultimately of eight Indian divisions and one British) under General Townsend advanced from Basra towards Baghdad, some 570 miles away. Hopelessly overextended in an arid country with no roads, the British forces were repelled at the Battle of Ctesiphon, just 16 miles from the city, in 1915. Dispirited, the troops were forced to march back to Kut-el-Amara, where they suffered a five-month siege from early December 1915. As recorded by W.J. Blackledge of 6th Division: 'We never dreamt that, when we advanced towards that giant piece of broken masonry [the historic arch at Ctesiphon], that we were to be the losers, that we should find ourselves involved in a gruelling retreat of ninety of the most miserable miles imaginable.'

The garrison was marched into captivity on 29 April, 9,000 men, many of whom would die of disease and malnutrition. Fortunes would turn for the British in 1917 with the capture of Baghdad and the Berlin–Baghdad railway – part of the kaiser's wider scheme to control the region. In a campaign that saw almost 15,000 killed in action or dying of wounds, an additional 12,500 would die of disease. It is unlikely that this helmet could have helped alleviate the suffering of these men.

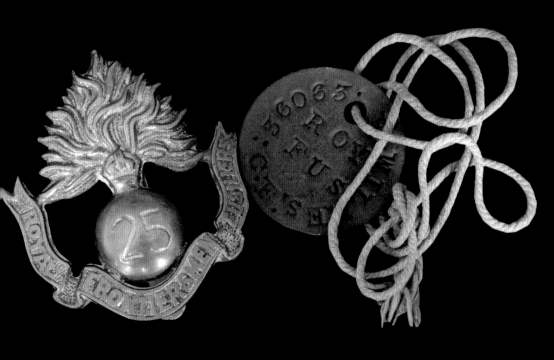

6I
Legion of Frontiersmen badge

THE 25TH (SERVICE) BATTALION, the Royal Fusiliers (City of London Regiment) (Frontiersmen) was formed from a body of men known as the Legion of Frontiersmen, an organisation raised in 1904 'to assist the state in times of need'. The legion was offered to the War Office in August 1914 to act in an irregular capacity behind the enemy lines in Belgium. It was perhaps not surprising that the War Office turned down the offer, though only after some consideration. With the press for able-bodied men still hard, the legion was finally accepted as the 25th Battalion of the Royal Fusiliers in January 1915. It was destined to serve in one of the most forgotten of all 'sideshows' – as all campaigns that diverted men away from the Western Front were called.

The campaign was initiated in 1914, in German East Africa, a country bordering Portuguese East Africa (to the south), the Belgian Congo (to the west) and British East Africa (to the north). The German commander, General Paul von Lettow-Vorbeck – and his protection force (*Schutztruppe*) of mostly African troops – was intent on draining British supplies and committing troops to the war that would otherwise be deployed in Europe. He was successful; the Germans kept the Allies on the run during a campaign that saw British troops fighting a guerrilla war against skilled opponents and

Country of origin:
British East Africa (now Kenya)

Date of manufacture:
c. 1915

Location: Private collection

travelling vast distances. Early attempts at opposing von Lettow-Vorbeck involved the ill-fated landing at Tanga in November 1914. The British were forced back into the sea and their commander, Major-General Aitken, sacked in disgrace. The Germans targeted the Uganda Railway in the British colony in 1915–16. In early 1916, the British saw Lieutenant General Smuts take charge of their campaign, with a two-pronged invasion of the German territory, supported by Belgian allies. A year later, Smuts claimed that his German adversaries were beaten – yet the campaign was fought under trying conditions to the very end.

It is not surprising, then, that the 25th Royal Fusiliers attracted men who were committed to frontier action, and not surprising that many who served in the battalion would be from the mould of the big game hunter – including the veteran F.C. Selous, who received a commission in the force despite his 64 years, and who would ultimately lose his life in the campaign. Though most of the forces that fought in East Africa were locally raised, the Frontiersmen were destined to serve there, landing in early May 1915, and were quickly engaged in the war.

The war in which the Frontiersmen served was a world apart from that on the Western Front. That this is the case is illustrated through their distinctive insignia, worn on Wolseley pattern sun helmets. Three badges are known. The first was made in a local garage, adding a hand-engraved sheet brass scroll to a Grenadier Guards badge. The second pattern, the one illustrated, was cast in Mombasa, and the third was an elaborate grenade badge carrying the distinctive enamelled Legion of Frontiersmen badge, based on the Union Flag. This example belonged to Private Edgar Wilkes (along with his identity discs), whose contribution to the war would be cut short by illness. He was discharged sick in 1916 – one of over 80 per cent who would succumb to the ravages of disease in this corner of the world.

Plumbing New Depths, 1917–18

62 Trench club

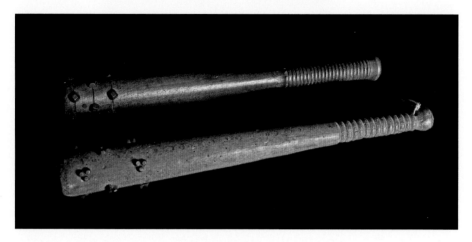

BY 1917, TRENCH warfare had become the accepted norm. Trench routine had been finely honed, with officers and men working hard to ensure that the trenches would be both strong in the defence, and comfortable enough for long-term occupation. The German *Siegfied Stellung* – known to the British as the Hindenburg Line – represented the highest art in military construction, with deep dugouts, strongly built and mutually supporting trenches, and belts of seemingly impregnable barbed wire. With the siege deepening, the restlessness of High Command was such that often costly trench raids – to demonstrate the 'offensive spirit', to wrest control of no-man's-land, to test the strength of the defenders and to capture prisoners for information – were a regular occurrence on all fronts.

Of all the items associated with trench warfare, the rediscovery of clubs and knives as weapons is identified with the descent of warfare from the ideal of open battle to the extended and stalemated nightmare of the trenches. Of these, maces or clubs have an ancestry that extends back millennia; they may represent some of the earliest weapons made by man. Their use in trench warfare equates with the need for stealth while carrying out limited assaults or trench raids; in the strict

Country of origin: United Kingdom

Date of manufacture: *c.* 1916–18

Location: Private collection

confines of the trench, rifles with fixed bayonets could not be wielded effectively. Where a modicum of surprise was needed, the club, knife, revolver and grenade found favour in night-time trench raids. In the British manual *Notes on Minor Enterprises* (1916), there was no doubting what was needed: 'Men's faces and hands should be darkened. Men should be armed according to the tasks they are to perform. Revolvers, knobkerries and daggers have been used. In addition to the grenadiers, every man should carry two grenades.'

In most cases, clubs were fashioned from whatever was to hand, though they usually had one thing in common – a long handle with a weighted end, usually garnished with some form of fearsome-looking metal. Private Stephen Graham of the Scots Guards described a typical late-war raiding party: 'The party was [...] to go out armed mainly with clubs, like savages. These clubs were made specially for them by our pioneers. They were made of the iron part of Mills hand-grenades clamped to entrenching tool handles. One sharp blow on the head from one of these and your enemy needed no more. The raiders carried no rifles.'

Typical clubs are illustrated, British examples comprising a long turned-wood handle with studs or boot cleats; other nations' efforts would look similar. Many have weighted ends, with lead or cast iron or steel mace ends constructed in workshops. Other examples of these have nails instead of cleats, with at least one known to be from the archaeological excavation of front-line trenches in the Ypres Salient. These types may well have been manufactured in army workshops. Other versions were probably extemporised in the trenches, or even at home, and sent to the front line. Carved wood knobkerries are also known. The short-handled spades used by Germany and France as entrenching tools were also popular, especially with the spade sharpened to lethal effect.

Clubs were used by all the combatant nations, and were found on all fronts. As one commentator has put it: 'this medieval weapon, which in times past had come to signify authority and status, now represented the brutality of trench warfare.'

63 *Grabendolch*

WITH THE CLUB or knobkerrie making its appearance in trench warfare, it is not surprising that the dagger would join it as a weapon of choice of many soldiers – especially as, in most cases, the issue bayonet was too long to be of any effective use in trench raids. The acceptance that knives were an essential part of trench life came about through the German tradition for hunting knives.

In the early part of the war, companies in the traditional knife-producing areas of Solingen in the industrial heart of Germany produced a range of knives for sale to hunters, which became popular as gifts for 'the man at the front'. Often these were engraved with patriotic phrases: *Mitt Gott für Kaiser und Reich* (With God for Kaiser and Empire) was typical. A great many types are known. Their blades are short, their handles variable in design and form – from deers' feet and bone through to ebony. Housed in simple leather scabbards (sometimes replaced by steel examples), they are commonly seen worn on the belt of the German soldier.

Country of origin: Germany

Date of manufacture: *c.* 1915–18

Location: Private collection

But by March 1915, the *Grabendolch* (trench dagger), *Nahkampfdolch* (close-quarter dagger), *Armee-Dolch* (army dagger) or simply *Dolch* (dagger) became official issue to German troops. According to Robert Graves, writing in his 1929 classic *Goodbye to All That*: 'The bowie-knife was a favourite patrol weapon because of its silence.' Stealth, then, was everything once the soldier had left the confines of his trench and ventured out into no-man's-land.

The *Grabendolch* illustrated is typical of the official issue made to German troops from 1915. Each state ordered examples from the knife manufacturers for issue to its troops. The fancy handles and engraved blades so typical of the pre-war knife have disappeared. In their place was a 13cm blade and long handle extension, or tang – riveted to which are two wooden grips, each with nine wooden oblique grooves. This example has been taken from a German captive by a British soldier and is marked 'Sambre, 1918' – one of the last offensives fought by the Allies, the Germans being in full retreat. The *Grabendolch* was no longer capable of carrying out its grim purpose.

As no official knives were to be issued to British troops, captured examples like this were used, while privately purchased examples such as the Pritchard 'push dagger', or even home-made examples, were actively employed. Typical was the use of cut-down bayonets, such as the 1907 pattern Lee–Enfield bayonet, or the obsolete French Chassepot sword rifle, cut down and shaped into a more manageable blade. The Canadian Ross bayonet (for the ill-fated Ross rifle, withdrawn as being unfit for front-line service in late 1916), already relatively short, was another to be modified. Any other suitable piece of metal that would carry a blade was also to be pressed into service. Together with trench clubs, these crudely fashioned knives are gruesome reminders of a terrible war.

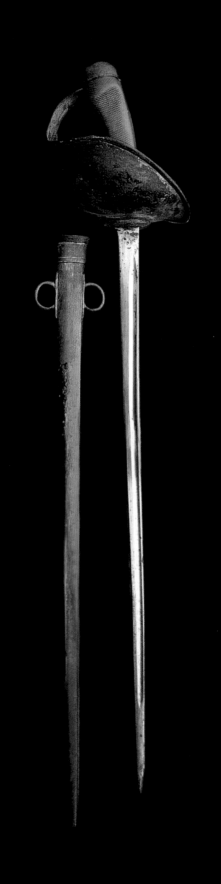

64

Cavalry sword

Country of origin:
United Kingdom

Date of manufacture:
1915

Location: Private collection

AT THE OUTBREAK of war, cavalry – still seen as an élite arm by most nations – was actively deployed on all fronts. Ultimately the purpose of cavalry was to create a highly mobile force that could be deployed en masse as a shock weapon, or in an advanced reconnaissance role. The war opened with both France and Germany fielding ten cavalry divisions each; but for the invaders there were missed opportunities to deploy against the Allied troops while they were retreating in the wake of German pressure, and with trenches stretching from the Swiss frontier to the North Sea, the opportunity for cavalry deployment on the Western Front was effectively lost, the open door slammed firmly shut. In France and Flanders, the dream of 'sending the cavalry through' was often repeated. With trenches breached, the aim was one that would eventually become the motto of the Tank Corps – 'through mud and blood to the Green Fields Beyond'. Though the dream was a reality in the Battle of Amiens in 1918, with cavalry deployed alongside medium tanks, for the most part cavalrymen would be underemployed. On the Eastern Front there were much greater opportunities for action, but even here cavalry actions were fitful affairs, and great resources were expended in keeping men and horses in action.

The British 1908 pattern cavalry sword was designed for thrusting – it was a weapon to be used in the charge, arm outstretched, the horse at full gallop. While earlier swords had been curved, designed for both 'cut and thrust' action, the new sword was skewer-like, with a 't' section that would resist breakage. Though having an overall blade length of some 35in with its primary purpose being for thrusting, only half of this was sharpened. The sword was long, gruesome in its intent and devoid of frills. The steel basket was designed to protect the cavalryman's hand, which was supported by the shaped grip and large pommel to give balance. In an outstretched arm, the sword could counter infantrymen armed with bayonets, or even the possibility of the lance, still used by some regiments early in the conflict. This sword was the last to be approved in British service; though our example has seen better days, it is typical of the weapon, and was issued for service in April 1916. For the most part, though, the cavalryman would get little opportunity to use his weapon – and would instead rely upon the SMLE rifle, deployed as mounted infantry, or, ultimately, dismounted cavalry.

With the lights dimming on the cavalry arm in Europe, its last swan song was in the Middle East. The 1927 British treatise *Where Cavalry Stands Today*, written by an officer of the 12th Lancers, expresses why: 'As an arm of assault, cavalry attains its maximum power when operating mounted, covered by the fire of its own automatic rifles, machine guns and artillery. In [Palestine and Mesopotamia] there were seldom any impassable obstacles to a mounted assault.' With hope for the future, it continues:

> The finest example of an indirect pursuit by cavalry is [...] General Allenby's final offensive in Palestine in September 1918. With able assistance from their own aircraft and unhampered by air attacks from the enemy, they covered seventy miles within the first thirty-six hours, and within fourteen days the whole of the Turkish forces in this theatre of war had been destroyed, over 100,000 prisoners and 500 guns being taken.

Yeomanry trooper equipped with 1908 pattern cavalry sword.

It is in this theatre that our sword would have seen most of its action. The price was heavy, though. With most horses used as beasts of burden, casualties were high. The British alone lost just under 500,000 horses in the Great War, and 2.5 million were sick or wounded; German horse mortality was around 900,000.

65 Tank mask

IF THE GERMANS had pinned their hopes on gas being a breakthrough weapon in 1915, then it was the introduction of tanks that was to be the miracle weapon of 1916; in 1917, the success of 'the tanks', used en masse for the first time at Cambrai, was a source of rejoicing – and though the mechanical weapon suffered badly in the quagmire of the Third Battle of Ypres, it would re-emerge as a major part of the all-arms battlefield of 1918.

The tank, a British invention of 1915, was designed to cross trenches of at least 8ft 6in wide (and climb obstacles of 4ft 6in high), thereby puncturing the German lines, and was to participate in the latter stages of the Battle of the Somme. Its characteristic rhombic shape – destined to become an icon used by souvenir manufacturers, trench artists and savings schemes – was designed to give as great a surface area as possible to the tracks in order that they might both cross open trenches and climb gradients. The Mark I was deployed for the first time in the latter stages of the Somme. The tank was to evolve during the war, increasing its reliability, the Mark IV being the main battle tank of the later war period. It was to be deployed in two basic forms, with 6in guns (male) and with Lewis

Country of origin: United Kingdom

Date of manufacture: c. 1915–18

Location: Private collection

or Hotchkiss machine guns (female) arming their side-mounted sponsons. Both forms, travelling at an average speed of 4 miles per hour, would be vulnerable to shell fire. They were operated at first by men of the Machine Gun Corps (Heavy Section), but by July 1917 a new unit had evolved, the Tank Corps.

Each tank had a crew of eight: commander and driver, two gunners and four men to command the complex gears that were required to drive what was essentially a steel box across the rough terrain of the battlefield. The tanks were hot, crowded and dangerous at the best of times – with plenty of protruding metalwork that could lead to a man knocking himself unconscious in action. To combat this, tank crews were issued with leather helmets to protect their cranium, and chain mail masks to protect their faces and eyes. A rare set is illustrated. The chain mail mask was tied around the face, the metal and leather visor (this one has a replacement leather face piece) bent into position to protect the eyes and nose, and the chain mail hanging from it to protect the cheeks and face. The purpose of the mask was to prevent shards of metal flying into the face, these shards being an inevitable consequence of bullet strikes on the outside of the tank leading to the spalling of hot metal 'splash' inside the tank.

Neither the helmet nor the mask were particularly welcomed by the crews themselves: wearing them must have been uncomfortable in the hot, cramped compartment. Central to the tank was its engine; the action of its 6-pounder guns (or machine guns) adding to the heat and smoke inside the machine. Though the use of the mask lingered on, the helmet was abandoned early on: its shape was rather too close for comfort to the German *stahlhelm*. Personal armour became a minor feature of the war as it developed. Breast-plates and helmets were worn by sentries and static guards on the western and Italo-Austrian fronts, mirroring those of ancient wars – and this was no different in concept from that worn by the men in the interior of the tank, that technological marvel.

66 *Karl Truppenkreuz*

ITALY HAD ENTERED the war in 1915 with high hopes of success against the Austro-Hungarian Empire, which was hard-pressed facing the Serbs, and on its Eastern Front the Russians. Though mountainous warfare developed along most of the northern border, it was the offensives along the Isonzo River that expended much of the Italian efforts. Here, in eleven successive attacks between 23 June 1915 and 12 September 1917, the Italian commander, General Cadorna, pushed his men forward with often ill-conceived mass frontal attacks and poorly planned artillery preparations. Viewed by most commentators as a martinet who commanded the Italian troops through iron discipline, Cadorna had absolute faith that his offensives would drive the Austrians sufficiently to suffer a defeat.

For the Austrians, the entry of their former allies into the war was seen as a betrayal of the Triple Alliance, and they were prepared to resist the Italian offensives. Their battle lines were drawn along the line of the river, and extended back into Slovenia and the mountainous area that contained the Carso Plateau. With Cadorna using an unwaivering recipe of mass frontal attacks, the attrition rate of the Italians and their Austrian defenders was staggering. In the severe mountain climate, there was a winter lull in the fighting after the ninth battle of the Isonzo (31 October–4 November 1916). The Italians had made some progress after bruising encounters, and were pushing the Austrians hard – though with limited gains.

Country of origin: Austria-Hungary

Date of manufacture: 1916

Location: Private collection

In Austria, there were great changes. The old emperor, Franz Josef, died on 21 November and was replaced by his nephew, Karl, who had been elevated to next in line to the throne after the death of Franz Ferdinand in Sarajevo in 1914. As Emperor Karl I, he assumed command of the army. One of his first acts was to institute a new medal in recognition of the trials his men had suffered in facing the Italians, Russians and Serbs on all fronts. The *Karl Truppenkreuz* was instituted on 13 December and was awarded to all soldiers of the Austro-Hungarian Army who had seen twelve weeks' service on the front line, and who had participated in a battle. With the Isonzo battles, and the initially successful Brusilov Offensive of June 1916, this was a major proposition.

Our example is typical of the 651,000 that were awarded. Symbolically, it is made from zinc – that most simple of metals – and bears the inscription *Grati Princeps et Patria, Carolvs Imp. et Rex* (A grateful prince and country, Karl emperor and king). Bearing the imperial crowns of the dual monarchy, it bears the legend *Vitam et Sangvinem* (With life and blood) and the date 1916. Simple and heartfelt, this medal was later joined by another for sick and wounded troops, in August 1917. It was typical of Karl that his thoughts were with his men. It is impossible to say now who wore this medal, or if it was ever taken from its paper wrapping.

In eleven successive battles on the Isonzo, the Italians had lost a staggering 605,000 men, either killed, wounded or missing; the Austrians had suffered losses of almost 425,000. Both nations would need the support of their allies in the battles to come. And, at Caporetto on 24 October 1917, the Austrians, bolstered by their German allies, came closest to breaking through, losing a further 300,000 men. The Italians were forced back in retreat to the line of the Piave River – and the Italian line held, just; Italian losses were backed by the arrival of British and French divisions, withdrawn from the Western Front. With the line stabilised, and ethnic tensions growing, Karl would face mounting difficulties that would lead to the defeat of his troops at Vittorio Veneto in October–November 1918, and ultimately see him sue for peace.

67

Chinese Labour Corps badge

THE PROVISION OF adequate labour to serve the fighting men was a major question during the Great War. For the British, the options were the creation of a Labour Corps formed in April 1917 of medically downgraded soldiers, or of recruits not otherwise suited to front line life. The Non Combatant Corps – formed of conscientious objectors and led by officers and NCOs from the military prison service – was another. In the rear areas, prisoners of war were also employed, though it was forbidden to use them in areas of danger or on projects of obvious military application, such as loading munitions. On the other side of no-man's-land, the Germans used a similar system, with men who were older or medically downgraded serving in the *Landsturm ohne waffen* (the *Landsturm* 'without arms'). These men were committed to labour employment only (*Arbeitsverwendungsfähige*), and in 1917 formed labour battalions, road construction companies and other auxiliary units. The Germans also used civilian labour in the occupied countries; labour gangs were raised, often forcibly, and made to work on military labour projects. With the British and French unable to force labour in this way, they sought labour corps from across their empires in order to bolster their activities at the front.

The Chinese Labour Corps (CLC) was a means of the British accessing the country's vast human resource.

Country of origin:
United Kingdom

Date of manufacture:
1917–18

Location: Private collection

Though China was then not at war with Germany, the idea for the CLC came from Liang Shiyi, acting finance minister of the Chinese government in 1915, who suggested raising an army to be sent to Europe for training and service with the Allies – his eyes set on future rewards that might come China's way in the wake of the war. It would take a year before Chinese nationals would enter the war. Chinese labourers was sought by both allies, the French being the first to contract civilians in May 1916. The British followed suit and, in early 1917, the first contingent of some 1,000 workers set sail for Europe.

Chinese Labour Corps.

The men of the CLC were mostly farmers from Shandong and Zhili, and reported to the port of Weihai Wei before undergoing a medical – 60 per cent were rejected as unfit. The recruits were given a serial number and, gathered in groups of fifteen, they selected their leaders, or 'gangers'. Transported to France, the Chinese worked in companies of 500 men, 476 of them labourers, the rest officers, NCOs and Chinese 'gangers'. Housed behind the lines in camps, they worked some ten hours per day, seven days per week. They worked in ports, in the construction of roads, camps and aerodromes. They maintained heavy equipment and, at the end of the war, they were employed in filling shell holes and searching for and burying casualties.

The cap badge illustrated is a rare survivor from the CLC – a chapter of life on the Western Front that is little known. Cheaply made and stamped 'CLC', the badge would have been attached to one of many different types of headgear that was available to the Chinese. In this case, the badge has been reused after its simple fixings had dropped off; holes have been punched to allow it to be sewn to the cap. In fact, no official uniforms were issued to the Chinese workers as non-combatants – though their European officers and NCOs wore stand-ard British uniform. Most wore some form of military style clothing, however. Reused, the badge was a valua-ble commodity undoubtedly passed from one worker to another. All men were there for the chance to gain extra money: workers in France received as little as 1 franc per day; 'gangers' were given more. Rations per man were, not surprisingly, mostly rice – up to 24oz per man, plus meat, vegetables, flour and margarine.

The British employed a range of personnel of other nationalities in their own dedicated Labour Corps: Egyptians, Indians, Maltese, Fijian, people from Mauritius and the Seychelles, South Africa and the West Indies, all falling under the Directorate of Labour of the British Expeditionary Force. Some 94,500 Chinese served in France, 2,000 of them never to return home. Their gravestones record their contribution: 'Faithful unto death'; 'A good reputation endures forever'.

68 Canadian identity bracelet

IT WAS OFTEN the case that soldiers were unhappy with their simple identity discs. Would the simple disc be enough to identify them if killed? To maximise their chances, it was common practice for men to buy engraved or stamped discs from local entrepreneurs in the rear areas and base camps. Typical examples include functional aluminium or finer silver versions of identity bracelets. And soldiers made their own

versions from the scrap materials that abounded: foreign coins smoothed, pierced and stamped for use, or simple bracelets made from scrap shell brass or copper. The bracelet illustrated, just 2½in across, belonged to Private John Stevenson of the Canadian Army Medical Corps. It is made from the brass of a shell case that has been cut, smoothed and stamped to form a simple clasp. Stevenson was a native Scot, born in Hamilton, Lanarkshire. He joined the Canadian Expeditionary Force (CEF) on 21 November 1914.

In addition to Stevenson's name, regimental number and unit, he proudly engraved the name of his adopted country – Canada – on this simple shell-brass band. Also punched into the band was one of the most significant dates in Canadian history, 9 April 1917, and one of the

Country of origin:
Canada (in France)

Date of manufacture:
1917

Location: Private collection

most significant places – 'Vimy Ridge'. John Stevenson was a private in the 6th Canadian Field Ambulance, based at Fresnicourt, about 12 miles from Vimy. Its war diary for 9 April 1917 – the opening day of the Battle of Arras, and the assault of the Canadian Corps at Vimy Ridge – records the actions of Stevenson and men like him that day:

> This is the day of our advance and we hear that we have been successful in taking VIMY RIDGE and THÉLUS, capturing a few thousand prisoners with very few casualties for such an action. Six of our bearers were wounded [...] 'A' Section cleared from POST CENTRALE with 'B' and 'C' sections clearing the field to the R.A.P's [regimental aid posts]. We had bearer squads of prisoners, in charge of our bearers, eagerly assisting us to clear. We searched the field, shell holes and dugouts and by 6.00 had all cleared.

The attack at Vimy was, as already mentioned, part of the Battle of Arras, which in turn was to support a French offensive on the Aisne under the hero of Verdun, General Nivelle. Vimy Ridge was significant, it had a commanding position overlooking the low Flanders plain, and the French had attempted to wrest its control from the grasp of the Germans on several occasions in 1914–15. The co-ordinated and well-prepared attack by the Canadians involved the use of tunnels and intelligent use of artillery bombardment – by 12 April the ridge was firmly in Canadian hands. The attack was significant in other ways: it was the first time that the four divisions of the Canadian Corps had acted together, serving under Canadian command. To many, it represented the emergence of the nation from under the wings of the mother country. But Private Stevenson, survivor of the attack on Vimy Ridge, would never see his adopted country again. He would die from wounds received in November 1918, eighteen days after the Armistice was signed that ended the war.

69

Lemon squeezer hat

NEW ZEALAND, ON the other side of the globe from its mother country of Britain, was to hear of the outbreak of war one day after it had spread through Europe. On 5 August 1914, the announcement was read in public to the people of this small dominion, who reacted positively to support Britain. Matters moved quickly: on 6 August the British government requested that the New Zealanders act to capture and occupy the colony of German Samoa, which it achieved on 29 August – only the second piece of German territory to fall at this stage of the war, after Togoland.

With New Zealand committed to the conflict, its main contributions would be the supply of military manpower and agricultural products for the remainder of the empire. Quickly raising a volunteer expeditionary force, New Zealand immediately committed a force of two brigades, a total of 8,500 men that was dispatched to Europe within two months of the opening of the war. The New Zealanders were to join the men of the Australian Imperial Force (AIF) in convoy in October 1914, but were diverted from their original destination; instead they would land in Egypt for training, before being sent – as the Australian and New Zealand Army Corps (ANZAC) – to Gallipoli. Pivotal in this campaign, New Zealanders would be credited with reaching

Country of origin:
New Zealand

Date of manufacture:
c. 1916–18

Location: Private collection

the summit of the dominating peak in the peninsula, Chunuk Bahr, in August 1915 – only to be swept off it by naval gunfire. In all, some 2,700 New Zealand men were killed, with some 4,850 sick or wounded.

Evacuated with the rest of the forces at Gallipoli by January 1916, the New Zealanders were transferred to Britain, and would then be destined to serve in some of the most significant battles to be fought along the British sector of the front line. Although by 1918 men from across the empire would be dressed in uniformity with the British, in the early stages of the war there were significant differences between the dress of the British soldier and that of his comrades in arms. Headdress was one way of distinguishing the 'colonial' soldier; the 'lemon squeezer' hat distinguished the New Zealand soldier and the characteristic 'slouch hat', adopted widely in 1916, the Australian.

The New Zealand lemon squeezer hat was first used by the Wellington Regiment. Some stories relating to the hat suggest that it was adopted in recognition of the outline of Mount Taranaki, a New Zealand scenic landmark, or due to the practical possibilities of promoting rain run-off. And though there is debate over the date of the hat's first acceptance, it is known that the regiment wore it before they sailed for Europe in August 1914, and by early 1916 its use had spread to most other branches and components of the army – with the exception of the mounted rifles. The hat illustrated is well used and bears the badge of the Auckland Regiment. Its 'puggaree', or cloth hatband, is distinguished by the strip of red running through it – indicating infantry usage. Other branches had different colours. The Auckland Regiment served in all the main theatres and battles of the New Zealand Expeditionary Force (NZEF), from Gallipoli to the Western Front.

At the Battle of Messines (1917) in the Ypres Salient, the New Zealanders formed part of the British thrust to wrest a prominent feature, the Messines–Wytschaete ridge, from German hands. With intricate preparation, British and ANZAC tunnellers had constructed a labyrinth of tunnels beneath the German lines that were

A soldier of the New Zealand Rifle Brigade wears the lemon squeezer hat.

packed with explosives. At zero hour on 7 June 1917, nineteen mines were detonated under the ridge, accompanied by a fierce artillery bombardment. The men of the Auckland Regiment witnessed the moment, as described in its official history:

At 3.10 a.m. there was a shaking of the earth, a column of leaping flame quickly obscured by smoke and debris, and then a muffled roar. The mines had gone up. A brief pause. The sudden rattle of thousands of machine-guns, a flash round the horizon, and then with a thunderblast of sound the great barrage fell on the German line.

The New Zealanders had been given the objective of the fortified position of the village of Messines itself; the Aucklander's were in the thick of the fighting, with 671 killed or wounded before they consolidated their lines. A monument stands at Messines in honour of their achievement.

New Zealand's part in the Great War was disproportionate to its size, with some 10 per cent of its population serving overseas, some 100,000 men and women. In all, 42 per cent of the men eligible to serve did so; some 16,697 men were killed, 41,317 wounded and some 1,500 others died on active service. At 58 per cent, New Zealand had one of the highest casualty rates of all nations in the war. Other than Britain, New Zealand alone introduced conscription to the armed forces in 1916; the commitment of the country to the war effort was total.

70

Pillbox

AFTER THE 'RACE for the Sea' and the jostling for position that took place in the early part of 1915, the Germans – early in the war on their Western Front – shifted their attention to the east. The battles of Tannenberg and the Masurian Lakes at the close of 1914 had been catastrophic failures for the Russians, who moved on to the offensive in the south of their line – against the weaker Austro-Hungarians. By 1916, the Russians were inflicting casualties on the Austrians in the Brusilov Offensive in Galicia. The Germans, with their line stabilised in strong defensive positions, shifted men and divisions eastwards in an attempt to dispatch the Russians once and for all. But it would not be easy.

Country of origin: Germany (in Belgium)

Date of construction: 1915–17

Location: Tyne Cott Cemetery, Passchendaele, Belgium

With the Germans committed in the east, they had no choice but to ensure their front line in the west was the strongest it could be. The huge costs in lives and materiel of prosecuting the offensive against Verdun in February–September 1916, and the effects of the Anglo-French Somme Offensive of July–November of the same year, determined that the German line should be capable of resisting the strength of the Allied armies in the west. To this end, the Germans created a number of fortifications that were designed as the border of the Greater German Reich. The *Siegfried Stellung*, known as the Hindenburg Line by the Allies, which ran from near Arras and on to the Chemin des Dames, was constructed to provide the strongest defensive positions; retiring to these positions, the Germans made their front line shorter, their defences more intense.

In the Ypres Salient, the *Flandernstellung*, the Germans had long held the upper hand. Taking the ridge tops had meant that the British and their allies were under continuous observation, shelled on three sides. Removing the Germans from their vantage points was always a dream of the Allies, so ensuring that they would have to advance over long forward slopes under direct observation was essential. But the ground here was very different from that held down in Artois and Picardy. There the Germans held free-draining chalk soils, capable of supporting deep dugouts and comfortable trenches. For the Germans on top of the ridges in Flanders, the topographical advantage was compromised by the fact that the soils beneath their feet were water saturated – even more so, if that could be possible, than those experienced by the British on the clay plain below. It was all to do with the way that the rain soaked away into the ridge tops – it had nowhere to go.

Our objects are unprepossessing concrete boxes that sit amongst the gravestones in the biggest Commonwealth War Graves Commission Cemetery in the world – Tyne Cot Cemetery, near the village of Passchendaele. These 'pillboxes' – known as MEBU, or *Mannschafts Eisenbeton Unterstände* – were built in mutually supporting waves across the ridge tops. If the Germans could not dig downwards to safety, then they would construct surface concrete shelters that were capable of withstanding the fierce artillery bombardment – though more often than not their occupants would suffer from the concussive force.

MEBU became celebrated as strong works of the enemy. One local New Zealand daily, *The North Otago Times*, gives a good description in its issue for 10 October 1917 – while Third Ypres was still raging:

> The last word in military engineering is known as the 'mebu' [...] In the subterranean chamber the Germans keep their stores and ammunition, and also seek shelter when the artillery fire of the attacking forces compels

Cross of Sacrifice erected on a MEBU pillbox in Tyne Cott Cemetery.

them to do so [...] While the concrete defences of the Germans appear to be proof against field artillery fire, the fact remains that they rapidly crumble before the drum-fire of the British and French heavy artillery.

The pillboxes in Tyne Cot were part of the *Flandernstellung*. They would be taken by direct assault from the 40th (Tasmanian) Battalion, 3rd Division AIF, during the Battle of Broodseinde – part of the Third Battle of Ypres, Haig's offensive that, it was hoped, would break though the German line.

The Third Battle of Ypres was a hard slog, against both the elements – with heavy rains causing the shell-cratered landscape to become waterlogged – and the strength of the pillbox fortifications of the *Flandernstellung*. Fought as a series of 'bite and hold' battles, the costs of moving forwards were heavy. At Tyne Cot, the men of the 40th Battalion assaulted the pillboxes on 4 October 1917. With one VC, two MCs, one DCM and nine MMs awarded for this action, the fighting was intense. The MEBU fell – they would be incorporated into the Allied line, hard fought. In peacetime, and at the centre of the cemetery, King George V recommended that the Cross of Sacrifice be constructed on top of the central pillbox there; a fitting memorial to its captors.

71

Mark IV tank

THE TANK HAD been introduced to the world in 1916, when it was deployed at the Battle of Flers, during the Somme campaign in 1916. This metal monster was a relevation: it was capable of crossing trenches and flattening barbed wire, and it was capable of protecting its occupants from both rifle and machine gun fire – though it could be stopped in its tracks by field guns. The German response was initially to develop a large calibre 'anti-tank' rifle that was capable of propelling a high-velocity round at the armour of the tank, with the hope that it could be disabled. They also built their own tank, the A7, which was a top-heavy and unwieldy machine, mostly unsuited to its task. The Germans instead resorted to capturing British machines and deploying them against their former owners.

Country of origin: United Kingdom

Date of construction: c. 1917 (donated 1919)

Location: Ashford town centre, Ashford, UK

The effectiveness of the tank used en masse was first proven at the Battle of Cambrai. Here, in November 1917, the British deployed some 379 tanks in a surprise attack on the German Hindenburg Line, a formidable defence works that had been developed along prepared positions in the wake of the Battle of the Somme a year earlier. Here, the Germans had constructed deep trenches, even deeper dugouts for the trench garrison and wide belts of barbed wire. New techniques and weapons were deployed in the battle, including

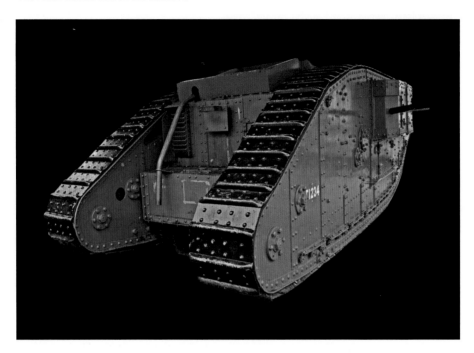

anti-battery fire registered by sound-ranging, an acoustic method of locating guns, and an unregistered, creeping barrage. Artillery was the key, supporting the six infantry divisions, and tanks were deployed in order to crush the barbed wire defensives and support the infantry. The main tank deployed was the Mark IV.

The 28-ton Mark IV tank was introduced in 1917 and was the most numerous of all battle tanks deployed in the war. It possessed the typical rhombohedral shape designed to give the vehicle capability to cross trenches, its tracks capable of pulling the tank from the ditch-like structures – though it was only capable of running at 3–4mph. There were two basic forms: the 'male' tank, equipped with two 6-pounder guns, side-mounted in sponsons, and three Lewis guns; and the 'female', equipped with six Lewis guns.

Prosecuting a world war was costly, and ensuring that there were sufficient funds in the coffers led the government to appeal for war savings from the public. Purchase of National War Bonds and War Savings Certificates was portrayed as a patriotic duty, allowing the money to be used in the development and construction of the materiel of war. Women were appealed to directly; in a poster by Bert Thomas likens the investment in war savings to the actions of Joan of Arc in 'Saving her Country' many centuries before. As in the Second World War, many novel approaches were taken to promote war savings, none more so than the 'Tank Banks' that toured Britain in 1917. Following the debut of two Mark IV tanks at the Lord Mayor's Show in London during November 1917, the government mobilised examples of these new 'wonder machines' in order to raise money and support from the sale of War Bonds and War Savings Certificates. While the cost of the war was estimated at £1 million per day in 1914, by its end this would increase to around £5.7 million. Six Mark IV male tanks – Egbert (No. 141), Nelson (No. 130), Julian (No. 113), Old Bill (No. 119), Drake (No. 137) and Iron Rations (No. 142) – were to tour Britain in 1918, raising millions of pounds through 'Tank Bank Weeks'. Each tank became the focal point for donation. Postcards, tank moneyboxes and other memorabilia were produced in commemoration. With the war's end, those boroughs that had raised the most money received a full-sized tank, usually displayed in parks and squares – the last survivor, our object, now stands in Ashford, Kent, as it has done since 1919.

One of the touring 'tank banks' in 1917–18.

Copyright No. 3562.

OUR TANK-BANK.
THE TANK WILL BRING US VICTORY.

Passed by Censor.

72

Wound Badge

WOUNDING IN ACTION formed the vast majority of casualties in the Great War, and while it was uncommon for soldiers to escape wounding, it is significant that others might be wounded on several occasions. The recognition of wounding in some form or other – either as a distinction to be worn on a uniform, or as a medal – was slow in coming.

For the French and British, occasions of wounding were first recognised by the award of uniform distinctions in 1916. The French *Insigne des blessés militaires* was issued in the form of a medal ribbon, while the British were granted a distinctive 'wounding stripe', a distinction first suggested to General W.R. Roberston by influential British writer Sir Arthur Conan Doyle. This strip of braid (or brass equivalent) was worn on the lower left sleeve for each incident of wounding – though not necessarily for each wound.

The Austro-Hungarian approach was to award a simple medal to their wounded soldiers, a large 37mm disc in 'war metal', marked *Laeso Militi*, meaning 'to wounded warriors'. First awarded in August 1917, the number of wounds were demoted by stripes on the ribbon, up to a maximum of five. Arguably the most famous decoration for an incidence of wounding, the American Purple Heart, was not instigated for solders wounded in the war

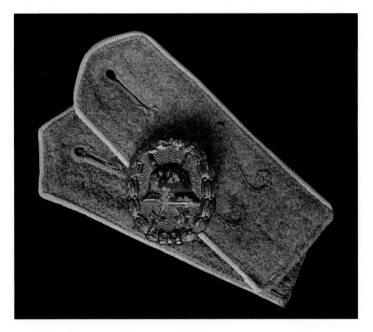

Wound Badge and German shoulder straps.

until much later on. Though some 320,000 were eventually awarded to those who had been wounded in the conflict, it was not until 1932, on the 200th anniversary of George Washington's birth, that the award was first made.

Illustrated, though, is the German approach – in this case a battered and well-worn badge that was designed to be worn attached to the soldier's uniform jacket, on its left-hand breast – the issue of war badges made on the command of the kaiser in 1918.

> Recognising those who were wounded in service of the Fatherland I want to bestow them with an award. The award shall be given to those who shed blood for the Fatherland or who lost their health due to enemy action and have become unfit for duty.
>
> Kaiser Wilhelm II, extract from the donation deed of the Wound Badge, 3 March 1918

Up to 11 March 1918 the Wound Badge was bestowed to Prussian troops only; after that date Bavarians and 'other Germans' could earn it as well. On 3 June 1918, the Bavarian War Ministry declared that the Wound Badge was

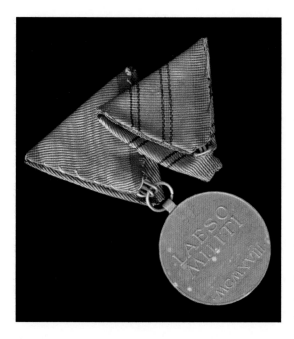

Austrian wound medal.

an 'award', not a 'decoration', and on 24 June the kaiser recognised the contribution of the navy through the Naval Wound Badge, which was to be awarded in the same grades as the army and under the same regulations.

In all cases, the badge was awarded in three grades: *schwarz* (black); *silber* or *mattweiß* (silver or tarnished white); and gold or *mattgelb* (gold or tarnished yellow). The colour of the badge indicated the degree of wounding: black for one to two wounds, silver for three to four wounds and gold for five wounds or more. The badge depicted the adopted symbol of strength, the *stahlhelm* steel helmet.

It was awarded by regimental staff and regional commands. From 30 January 1933 the Wound Badge award document could be handed in at the pension office to prove that the holder was eligible for a disability pension. Due to the late nature of the creation of the award in relation to the war, many soldiers who were wounded never received their badges, a situation that was not fully remedied until after the collapse of the Weimar Republic, so the last awards of this type were handed out as late as the early 1940s. In fact, from 30 January 1936 onwards, the badge could be awarded regardless of the number of wounds received: in silver (*mattweiß*) for loss of a hand, foot, eyeball, loss of hearing in both ears, severe brain damage or massive disfigurement of the face; in gold (*mattgelb*) for blindness or anyone who had to be permanently cared for in a nursing home. If nothing else, the issue of the badge at this late stage was a recognition of the fact that most old soldiers lived with the effects of the Great War for decades after it had finished, a legacy shared by all combatants.

73

Stahlhelm

THE *STAHLHELM* WAS the German answer to the French Adrian and the British War Office pattern ('Brodie') helmet. It replaced the purely ceremonial *pickelhaube* in 1916, and was first used in action in the battles for Verdun. Though the Germans had experimented with facial shields and crown plates in certain parts of the line, the need for the *stahlhelm* grew out of the increasing number of preventable head injuries in the trenches, often from spent bullets. Developed by Captain Frederick Schwerd of the Technical Institute in Hannover, and Professor August Bier, naval doctor-general, the helmet was made of 1mm thick chromium-nickel steel stamped from circular sheets. Ventilation holes were marked by distinctive lugs; these were also used for the fixture of an additional armoured plate, the *stirnpanzer*, an additional defensive tool used by static guards. By the end of July 1916 some 261,000 helmets had been distributed, and by the end of the war, some 7.5 million had been produced.

Our example is typical of the many that saw action in the war. Finished in simple field-grey paint, it is of normal size: larger and smaller versions were produced. It is typical of many take-home souvenirs taken by Allied troops. Fitted with the simple leather pads that made up the liner, it differs from later helmets in simple details –

Country of origin:
Germany

Date of manufacture:
1915–18

Location: Private collection

Sturmtruppen.

and by its simple paint scheme. From July 1918 General Ludendorff, chief of the General Staff, had ordered that the *stahlhelm* be painted in camouflage colours of green, yellow, ochre, rust and brown in a pattern of angular patches separated by thick black lines. Ludendorff had been impressed with the helmet when he first saw it, in autumn 1916: 'A company of the famous Rohr Storm battalion formed the guard of honour for the Field Marshal. For the first time, I saw a formation in full storming kit, with the steel helmets which had proved so extraordinarily useful.'

Sturmtruppen were assault troops that had been so successfully used at Verdun. The Rohr Storm Battalion was developed by Captain Rohr, and depended upon soldiers infiltrating the front line after it had been bombarded by heavy artillery fire. Stormtroopers were well equipped, not just with the *stahlhelm* (which was common issue amongst other troops) but also with bags for stick grenades, as well as trench clubs, knives and short assault weapons, including light machine guns. Rohr's men were an élite and the tactics evolved would be tried and feared. And in 1918, the Germans were able to pierce the Allied lines by their use, by-passing strong points and advancing rapidly – so rapidly in fact that they were left unsupported. They were victims of their own success – and in 1918 this was not something the Germans could afford.

The strength of the imagery of the *stahlhelm* was such that it led, post-war, to the formation of a German 'League of Front Line Soldiers', *Der Stahlhelm*, founded in December 1918. This nationalistic group promoted the view that the front-line soldier had been 'stabbed in the back' – a fervent belief of von Ludendorff himself:

> After our great downfall, let us, in memory of the heroes who have fallen believing in Germany's greatness, the heroes whom the country now so badly needs, learn once again to be Germans, and to be proud that we are Germans.

Der Stahlhelm.

74 Demarcation stone

WITH THE FAILURE of the last Russian offensive in July 1917 and the collapse of the Russian Provisional Government, the situation on the Eastern Front had reached a parlous state for the Allies. With their focus still on the east, the Germans continued to push: they captured the Russian city of Riga in September 1917, and by October were only 500km away from St Petersburg. With revolution in Russia, Lenin's Bolsheviks took control and within a month had negotiated a ceasefire with Germany – a ceasefire that did not last but which was replaced with Operation *Faustschlag*, the last Austro-German offensive in the east. The Bolsheviks could not procrastinate any more; after huge gains, the Russians were forced to sign the Treaty of Brest-Litovsk in March 1918, which put them out of the war. For the Central Powers, Germany in particular, this marked the possibility of returning to the offensive in the west. According to General Ludendorff: 'Owing to the break-down in Russia, the military situation was more favourable to us at New Year, 1918, than one could ever have expected. As in 1914 and 1915, we could think of deciding the war by an attack on land. Numerically, we had never been so strong in comparison with our enemies.'

If they were to act, they had to do so before the Americans, brought into the war in 1917, could arrive in any strength. With this in mind, the German High

Country of origin: France

Date of construction: 1921–27

Location: Souain, Marne, France

Command moved some fifty divisions westwards and planned a series of offensives, the *Kaiserschlacht*, for the spring of 1918. On 21 March 1918 the first of these, Operation Michael, pierced through the British lines at its weakest point, the location of the 5th Army on the Somme. A five-hour artillery bombardment, followed by the movement of German stormtroops, led to the retirement of the British – a retirement that slowed as German casualties mounted. Other offensives followed, testing the weakest parts of the line: against the Portuguese Expeditionary Force in the north, in early April; on the Aisne and at Noyon in May–June; and finally on the Marne in July. Though the Germans had returned the war to open fields, each of these drives lost their head of steam, and it was up to the Allies to turn to the offensive.

Along the line of the maximum German advance across France and Belgium in 1918 are 'demarcation stones' (*Bornes du Front* or *Demarcatiepalen*). Originally intended to be placed at every kilometre along the 650km Western Front – 28 in Belgium, 212 in France – the stones were conceived and designed by the French sculptor Paul Moreau-Vauthier in 1920, who enlisted the support of three organisations in funding the project: the *Touring Club de France*, the *Touring Club de Belgique*, and the Ypres League. It was an ambitious project, but by 1930 the funding had dried up – 119 of the stones remain today.

German soldiers released from the Eastern Front.

Each stone is sculpted from granite 1m high and is equipped with the steel helmet and equipment of the nation that held the German advance in 1918. The stone illustrated is from the Department of the Marne, at Souain. Equipped with French helmet and equipment and exploding grenades, it is named to its location and carries the phrase '*Ici fut repoussé l'envahisseur*' (From here the invader was pushed back).

75

Glade of the Armistice

ON 8 AUGUST 1918, the Allies commenced an offensive that would see the Germans pushed back continuously for 100 days. Under attack from ten infantry divisions at Amiens, and exhausted after the failure of their own offensives in the spring and early summer, the German Army would lose some 30,000 men on what General von Ludendorff would christen as 'the black day of the German Army'. At Amiens, on dry chalky ground that was good for tanks and at the junction of British and French troops, the surprise was total, the Canadian and Australian spearhead being driven deeply into the German front, piercing it and forcing the Germans back. With the front widening away from this incision, the united Allied armies under Marshal Foch piled on the pressure. The Germans lost Noyon to the French on 17 August, and Bapaume to the British on 29 August. The Hindenburg Line – the *Siegfried Stellung* – was the only thing left in the way of Allied victory. In the first of a number of Allied assaults of the 'Grand Offensive', the French and Americans attacked in the Meuse-Argonne on 26 September, and a number of attacks followed. But it was on 8 October 1918 that the Hindenburg Line was breached by the British 1st and 3rd Armies. There was nothing left to the Germans other than to sue for peace.

Country of origin:
France

Date of construction:
1922

Location: Glade of the Armistice, Compiegne, France

The imperial chancellor, Prince Max of Baden, had already indicated that Germany was seeking peace, two days before. Germany's main allies, the Austro-Hungarians and Ottomans, were already weakening; Bulgaria, joining the Central Powers in 1915, and faced with a multinational force on the Macedonian front, was forced into submission on 29 September after an Allied offensive. The Ottomans capitulated on 30 October 1918 in the wake of British-led attacks in Palestine, and the Austro-Hungarians sued for peace under Emperor Karl, signing the Armistice on 4 November. But in early October, Prince Max had approached the Allies (via the Swiss government) with the proposal that it would accept President Woodrow Wilson's diplomatic solution – his Fourteen Points, guaranteeing free trade, open agreements between nations and self-determination of sovereignty. Germany was in a parlous state. Its armies were now being pushed back to their start points by the aggressive attacks of their enemies. Casualties continued to rack up, and at home the effects of the Allied naval blockade were having a material effect on the population. It had no choice but to seek surrender.

The Glade of the Armistice is in the Forest of Compiègne, to the east of Paris. Laid out in grand style in 1922, a clearing of 100m in diameter was created in the thick forest and made to resemble the *Place de l'Étoile* in Paris. Today, the clearing is populated with stone monuments, as it was on its construction. Low granite stones record the positioning of two railway carriages on what was then a quiet railway siding; one of them Marshal Foch's, the other the German delegation. Between them is a central slab, which on its completion contained the words (in French): 'Here, on the 11th November 1918, the criminal arrogance of the German Empire was overcome, defeated by the free nations it set out to enslave.' Looking on is a granite statue of Foch himself. And in a building set back from the glade was preserved the railway carriage in which the German delegation signed the Armistice with the Allies, at 5.10 a.m. on 11 November 1918, in the special Wagons-Lits carriage that was fitted out as Marshal Foch's office. Hostilities would end at 11.00 a.m. that morning.

War at Sea, in the Air

76

USS *Texas*

USS *Texas* in 1914,
and preserved today.

Country of origin:
USA

**Date of
construction:**
1914

Location:
Battleship *Texas*
State Historic Site,
Texas, USA

IN 1907 HMS *Dreadnought*, the first of a kind, was launched. Whereas the battleships of the late nineteenth century were distinguished by their dedication to a variety of gun calibres, HMS *Dreadnought* was distinctly different. Naval doctrines at the close of the old century were predicated on the idea that while ships' initial engagements would be at long range – therefore requiring large guns, typically 12in – much of the fighting would take place at relatively close range; and here the obvious choice for gunnery were smaller calibre quick-firing weapons that could finish off a beleaguered enemy. With HMS *Dreadnought*, this panoply of guns of varied calibre was destined to become a dead concept.

One of the many outcomes of the Russo-Japanese War – which also saw the extension and development of trench warfare and siege tactics – was the acceptance that long-range gunnery could be effective. The Battle of the Yellow Sea, fought on 10 August 1904, was destined to be the world's first battle between modern steel ships, and the first to really test the concept of long-range gunnery, engaging at ranges of 8 miles. Already moves were afoot to plan for ships capable of engaging each other at distance – 'all-big-gun' ships with thicker armour. The birth of the dreadnought class came from the appointment of Admiral John 'Jacky' Fisher as First

Sea Lord in October 1904. Fisher, an innovative naval thinker, had proposed 'all-big-gun' ships and, on his appointment, he set up a committee to consider ship design that was influenced, at least in part, by the sea battles of the Russo-Japanese War – and other countries, Japan and the United States amongst them, were actively pursuing the idea. But with HMS *Dreadnought* came the physical embodiment of the ideal. Laid down on 2 October 1905, it was launched four months later. Equipped with ten 12in guns paired in rotating turrets, and 11in belt armour, the *Dreadnought* was capable of speeds of 21 knots, its steam turbine engines powered by oil. It had considerable armour, even though Fisher himself preferred lighter armour traded off by greater speed as battlecruisers – an extension of the all-big-gun concept.

The big guns of the first 'all-big-gun' ship HMS *Dreadnought*.

When finally the European conflict erupted, the dreadnought class was the mainstay of the battle fleets. From 1906 to 1914, ninety all-big-gun ships were constructed. Britain, with its traditional commitment to the navy, built the most – thirty-four in total; its rival, Germany, mustered twenty-four. Japan and the United States managed eight each; Austria, France, Russia and Italy four each. Of these, the only survivor is the USS *Texas*, completed in 1914. The building of the *Texas* was authorised by the US Congress in 1910 but was amongst the last dreadnoughts to be built. Equipped with ten 14in guns and 12in belt armour, it saw action in both wars. First used in punitive operations against the Mexicans in the summer of 1914, the *Texas* was assigned to the US Atlantic Fleet. But with the US entry into the world war in 1917, the American dreadnought was assigned to serve with the 6th Battle Squadron of the British Grand Fleet. Arriving at Scapa Flow on 11 February 1918, the *Texas* was involved in convoy protection duties and in supporting the British blockade of Germany – with very little hope of engaging in the 'dreadnought-to-dreadnought' actions it was built for. With HMS *Dreadnought* decommissioned and sold for scrap in 1923, the *Texas* is the last wartime example of a type of ship that helped precipitate the world into an arms race that ultimately led to the world conflict. Today, the *Texas* is preserved by the state that gave the ship its name.

USS *Texas* in New York, 1914.

77

Naval *Reichskriegsflagge*

WITH THE BRITISH EMPIRE spread across the globe, and with school textbooks and atlases showing British possessions, dominions, colonies and protectorates as a splash of red across five continents, the British Royal Navy was pre-eminent in the run-up to the Great War. The maintenance of this powerbase was of the greatest importance to the British, and any challenges to its supremacy at sea were viewed with great suspicion. With the launching of the game-changing HMS *Dreadnought* in 1906, all other large naval ships were effectively made obsolete, and navies across the world commenced retooling their fleets with the large gun battleships.

When Kaiser Wilhelm II came to the throne of the *Deutches Reich* in 1888 he was keen to emulate the naval prowess of Britain and France, and to extend the reach of the empire such that Germany could be ranked as a global power. In 1897, the expansion of naval power was ramped up when Rear Admiral Alfred von Tirpitz was appointed Secretary of State for the Navy. With Tirpitz focused on surpassing British naval power, expansion commenced in earnest. Two naval bills, in 1898 and 1904, charted the construction of thirty-eight battleships and fifty-eight cruisers – with Tirpitz focused on adding at least ten more major ships to the roster. With the launch of HMS *Dreadnought*, the Germans were

Country of origin:
Germany

Date of manufacture:
1914–18

Location: Private collection

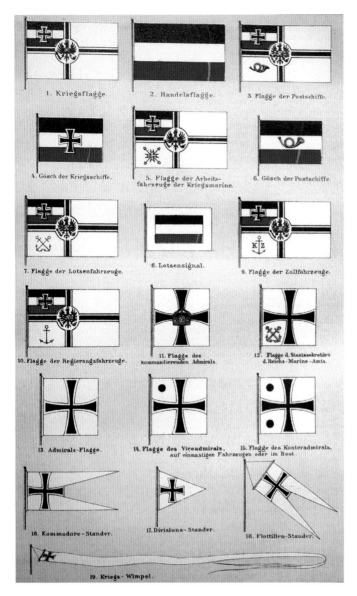

1. Kriegsflagge.

2. Handelsflagge.

3. Flagge der Postschiffe.

4. Gösch der Kriegsschiffe.

5. Flagge der Arbeits-fahrzeuge der Kriegsmarine.

6. Gösch der Postschiffe.

7. Flagge der Lotsenfahrzeuge.

8. Lotsensignal.

9. Flagge der Zollfahrzeuge.

10. Flagge der Regierungsfahrzeuge.

11. Flagge des kommandierenden Admirals.

12. Flagge d. Staatssekretärs d. Reichs-Marine-Amts.

13. Admirals-Flagge.

14. Flagge des Viceadmirals, auf einmastigen Fahrzeugen oder im Boot.

15. Flagge des Konteradmirals,

16. Kommodore-Stander.

17. Divisions-Stander.

18. Flottillen-Stander.

19. Kriegs-Wimpel.

Kaiserliche Marine flags.

faced with abandoning the expansion, or building their own. They were not swayed from the path; the German dreadnoughts were laid down in 1907.

The growth of the German Navy, the only German imperial force (the 'German Army' was actually composed of an amalgam of many state armies) was perceived as a direct threat to the largest naval power, Britain. In an escalating arms race, the delicate power balance between the strongest European nations – Britain, Germany, France, Austro-Hungary and Italy – was shifted. Traditionally isolated, Britain sought to clarify its relationships with France and Russia, and the stage was set for the alliances that would propel the continent of Europe to war.

Each German ship carried and flew an Imperial War Ensign, or *Reichskriegsflagge*, like that illustrated, which was used by the Imperial German Navy up to 1919. This flag, first developed for the North German Federation prior to the Franco-Prussian war in 1867, consisted of a white field, an offset black cross with a central white disc bearing the Prussian eagle and a black-white-red flag. In the top left-hand corner, the canton, was a black Iron Cross. The flag was modified twice in its long life, with minor changes to the eagle and to the general design: the changes made in September 1903 were because of an incident in which a Russian warship mistakenly raised the British white ensign to salute a German squadron. The 1903 pattern was introduced on 26 September 1903 (changing the previous ensign and jack, or *Gösch*). The changes increased the thickness of the cross as well as the border of the central disc, in order to distinguish it from the white ensign with its central red cross and union flag in its top right corner – a symbolic distancing of the two navies at the time of increasing suspicions.

With the German fleet symbolically scuttled at Scapa Flow in an open act of defiance against the British in 1919, the kaiser's war flag was consigned to history. This example, made by Bonner Fahnenfabrik, bears no *Kammerstempel* (office stamp) – indicating that it was not an official flag drawn from naval stores but rather a later example dating to the 1920s and 1930s. These flags were still flown by German warships on special occasions – such as the anniversary of the Battle of Jutland, a battle that both sides claimed as a victory.

78 Royal Naval Division badges

DEFYING ANY ATTEMPT at military categorisation is the Royal Naval Division (RND). Formed in August 1914 from Royal Navy reservists, the RND was the brainchild of the First Lord of the Admiralty, Winston Churchill. With mobilisation on the outbreak of war, it soon became apparent that there would be too many reservists called to the navy on the outbreak of war, and not enough ships to house them. As such, the RND was raised from these men to serve as soldiers – though retaining their naval distinctions and ranks. The Royal Naval Division had a shore establishment in Crystal Palace Park in south-east London – officially Royal Naval Shore Station HMS *Victory* IV, but very soon developing its own identity as 'HMS Crystal Palace'. The RND was an essential addition to the war machine. With the navy revered by most people in the island nations of Britain, the fact that the Grand Fleet had not yet met the German High Seas Fleet in battle was perplexing. The

Country of origin:
United Kingdom

Date of manufacture:
1915–18

Location: Private collection

raising of the RND perhaps indicates above all things the difficulty that the admiralty faced – it could not keep able-bodied men away from the front line while the army was actively seeking more men.

Originally, there were eight battalions raised, each named after famous admirals, organised into two brigades: Benbow, Collingwood, Hawke and Drake battalions (1st Brigade); Howe, Hood, Anson and Nelson (2nd Brigade). Four battalions of Royal Marines were also to serve alongside their blue-jacketted colleagues. The division was to serve with distinction at Antwerp in 1914, at Gallipoli in 1915 and, later, as the 63rd (Royal Naval) Division on the Western Front. The RND was at first to wear naval blue and 'Nelson' caps with distinctive cap tallies – it was in this garb that the men of the RND were sent to the defence of Antwerp by the volatile First Lord of the Admiralty. The division remained under admiralty control throughout the war. Khaki uniforms replaced naval blue in 1915 as the division was sent to the Dardanelles; on their return, two of the battalions were so heavily depleted – Benbow and Collingwood – that they were disbanded.

The cap badges illustrated were worn by men of the RND from late 1916. The badge worn by the Drake Battalion took Sir Francis Drake's ship and his personal motto *Auxilio divino* ('By divine aid'); Hood Battalion took a Cornish chough bird from the arms of Admiral Hood, hero of the American Revolutionary War; the coronet, spear and 'Never Despair' (*Nil desperandum*) motto is from the family arms of Admiral Anson, who circumnavigated the globe; while the Nelson Battalion took a depiction of HMS *Victory*. Each of these screams out their naval connections, yet these men's boots were firmly rooted in the ground. Despite this, attempts to transform the division into fully fledged soldiers was resisted throughout the war. And as the war claimed more lives, so the unique nature of this naval unit was changed as soldiers replaced the sailors who were rapidly falling in battle on the Western Front. The division was disbanded in 1919, the graves of its sailor-soldiers in peace in France, Belgium and Gallipoli.

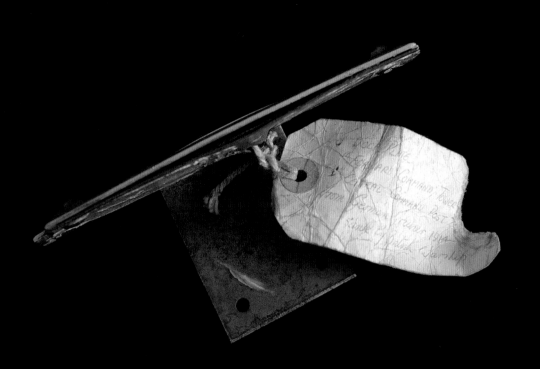

79

SMS *Emden* relic

THE NAVAL WAR in 1914 was full of frustrations for the British Royal Navy, the most powerful navy in the world. The British had suffered badly at the hands of the *Kaiserliche Marine*; in September 1914, the U-9 shocked the British press by sinking three aged British cruisers in quick succession. With HMS *Aboukir* torpedoed and sinking, the other two cruisers came to support it. HMS *Hogue* was rapidly targeted and in trouble; while it sank, HMS *Cressy*, weaving to avoid its own fate, was soon heeling over too. The loss of this small group of ships, soon to be known as 'the live bait squadron', rocked the nation, and left 1,459 men dead. Though the balance of power remained with the immensely powerful British Grand Fleet, cracks were appearing. And this was not helped by the Battle of Coronel, fought in the South Atlantic on 1 November 1914. Here Admiral Maximillian von Spee took on the British off the coast of Chile, sinking two British cruisers with the loss of 1,570 men. The First Sea Lord, Admiral John 'Jacky' Fisher, was incensed; he assembled a force of battlecruisers and cruisers under Admiral Sturdee to the South Atlantic in order to track down and destroy the upstart Germans. This he did, at the Battle of the Falkland Islands, fought a month later; von Spee and six of his ships were lost in this battle.

Country of origin: Germany

Date of manufacture: 1908

Location: Private collection

THE NOTORIOUS GERMAN CRUISER "EMDEN" SUNK BY H.M.A.S. "SYDNEY" OFF COCOS ISLAND,
9TH NOVEMBER, 1914.

ABRAHAMS & SONS, DEVONPORT, 673.

Though these actions grabbed British headlines, the fact remained that the British still controlled the most important part of the coastal waters and seaways that dominated Germany, the German fleet bottled up in Wilhelmshaven. The Indian Ocean, surrounding the imperial jewel of India and stretching down towards Australasia, was another focus for attention. Here, the German East Asiatic Squadron was roaming, which would lead to the actions of one of the most charismatic naval commanders of the war, Captain von Müller of the SMS *Emden*. Our illustrated object is a rare fragment of the naval war, presumed to be a piece of one of the most notoriously successful of all *Kaiserliche Marine* ships, a ship that operated well away from the spotlight focused on the 'will-it-or-won't-it' world of the High Seas Fleet. With the *Emden* run aground after the Battle of Cocos on 9 November 1914, fragments of this light cruiser were recovered as trophies. There is an armoured turret and other guns in Australia, removed and on display in Sydney, from at least 1916. The reason? Australia was to figure largely in the sinking of this ship, with the nation's first naval battle that saw the Australian cruiser HMAS *Sydney* force the German vessel to ground at the Keeling Islands. Fragments from the wreck were gradually salvaged until its remains were pushed out into

SMS *Emden*, the 'notorious cruiser'.

deeper waters. This fragment, a sign from the control tower, was easily removable.

The *Emden* had been on station in Asiatic waters since commissioning. It had served alongside British ships during the Boxer Rebellion, and was based at the German colonial station of Tsingtao – though Müller was quick to move his ship as war seemed imminent; just as well, as Tsingtao was to be captured by an Anglo-Japanese force in November 1914. Joining von Spee's Asiatic squadron, the *Emden* set off on a course that saw it take several prizes in the Indian Ocean. Steering north-westwards after rounding Sumatra, von Müller was to set out on a spree that saw him take twenty-six merchantmen and naval vessels in four weeks during September–October 1914, in the seas between Burma and India, and surrounding Ceylon (now Sri Lanka) and the Maldives. Müller ensured that the crews of the ships were taken off before destroying his prizes; he was also to ensure that neutral ships were left to pass on their way. In a war that increasingly saw few echoes of a chivalric past, Müller did his best to emulate this. His dash and daring also led to the *Emden* bombarding the Indian city of Madras, causing panic in British India. In just a few months, the German cruiser was to create havoc. It was no wonder that it would be hunted down by the Allied naval forces.

In November 1914, von Müller turned his attentions to the destruction of the telegraph station on Direction Island, in the Cocos Islands. It was a fatal mistake. With the commander of the telegraph station aware of the German vessel, he sent out a warning signal. And with the ANZAC troop convoy on its way to Europe, one of its escorts, the Australian cruiser HMAS *Sydney*, was dispatched to deal with von Müller and the *Emden*. The *Sydney* poured fire into the German ship, hitting it over 100 times; von Müller had little choice but to beach the stricken ship. The captain of the *Sydney* had to fire once more before the Germans surrendered. But for the charismatic German captain this would not be the end of the story. Commandeering a British schooner, he escaped with much of his surviving crew, a true adventurer.

8o

RFC cap

WITH ADVANCES IN aviation proceeding apace, the Royal Flying Corps (RFC) was officially created on 13 April 1913 in order to answer the military need for aircraft. The value of aerial reconnaissance of a sort was first demonstrated in the late nineteenth century with the use of captive balloons – so it was a logical step forward that when the first powered flight aircraft staggered into the air, its potential to observe and report movements of men and materiel on the ground was large. The RFC had grown out of the versatile Corps of Royal Engineers, but was unusual – in the first year or so of its life it would be a shared entity, with both military and naval wings. This marriage was not destined to work; on 1 July 1914 the Royal Navy claimed rights to the 'naval wing' of the Flying Corps, and renamed it the Royal Naval Air Service. From this point onwards the two air services would operate in tandem.

Country of origin:
United Kingdom

Date of manufacture:
c. 1914–18

Location: Private collection

The cap illustrated belonged to an unidentified officer of the Royal Flying Corps. The uniform style adopted by the new corps was distinctive; officers and men alike wore a double-fronted jacket with no buttons showing, so simple that it was referred to as a 'maternity jacket' (someone must have drawn a parallel with women's maternity clothing at some point, but who and when is not recorded). With pilots wearing 'wings' indicating their status, and bronze RFC badges on their high collars, the uniform cut a dash – especially as it was topped off with the khaki serge 'Austrian pattern' cap, worn distinctively upon the side of the head. With a bronze cap badge and tailor's label, this cap belonged to an officer – unidentified: a pilot who never came home? Possibly, but just as likely a ground-based officer.

The work of the Royal Flying Corps was predominantly that of observation of ground activities, reporting on enemy dispositions, troop movements, or the development of new defences – where possible taking photographs in order that detailed trench maps could be drawn up that would aid the infantry in their attacks, and the artillery in destroying their opposing batteries of guns. In the early days of the war, aircraft such as the Royal Aircraft Factory BE2c were designed to be a stable platform for such work. But this activity invited enemy opposition, and very soon aircraft and pilots appeared on the scene whose sole purpose it was to shoot down their enemies out of the sky.

The average life expectancy of a pilot in the Royal Flying Corps is difficult to evaluate. In the air, manoeuvrability, rate of climb, speed and armament were factors that changed the face of aerial battles. In April 1917 – Bloody April – pilots with few operational hours and obsolete aircraft were pitted against German aces flying sleek aircraft such as the Albatross, and life expectancy was very low indeed. With the arrival of new machines, things improved.

Second Lieutenant Medlen was typical. A grainy photograph reveals him as a bright young man proudly wearing his RFC cap. Just 21, he was a promising engineer at the Woolwich Arsenal. He joined the RFC in June 1917 and was examined in order to become a pilot on 30 August. He was found to be unfit as a pilot, but having perfect vision he was accepted as an observer. A copy of the telegram to his father announcing his death in action on 22 December 1917 is present in his records. Poignantly, Leslie Medlen had only been confirmed as a Pilot Officer Observer the day before his death on the Western Front. His local newspaper, the

BE2C reconnaissance aircraft in India, 1917.

Kentish Independent and Kentish Mail, reported his death in two articles on 4 January 1918: 'He and his pilot were shot down by a German machine that they had gallantly attacked [...] [he] was killed instantly by a bullet through his head.'

Second Lieutenant Medlen is buried in Aubigny Communal Cemetery Extension, Aubigny-en-Artois, France, a cemetery that contains a great many airmen, the majority of whom are officers and aircrew presumably shot down in combat. Second Lieutenant Medlen's grave bears the personal epitaph:

> In loving remembrance
> Of a brave and noble
> Son and brother

81
Aerial photographs

THE PRIMARY FUNCTION of the aviation services of all countries in the First World War was reconnaissance and, from the beginning, photo-reconnaissance was the ideal. In the first stages of the war, the military air services employed unarmed aircraft that were stable platforms for cameras, which were hand-held over the side of the aircraft. Though some adventurers took pistols into the air in case they encountered the enemy, for the most part the business of snooping on the troops below was only as dangerous as the quality of the aircraft, its ability to stay airborne, and the capability of the engine to keep it in the air. With the war developing rapidly into a static one of positional warfare, keeping a regular check on the developing trench systems was essential if attacks were to be successful, or artillery bombardments were to be on target. And while reconnaissance aircraft were plying their trade, 'scouts' were sent up – aircraft equipped with machine guns intent on only one thing: knocking out the eyes of the armies by sending aircraft crashing to the ground. It was with this task in mind that aces such as Manfred von Richthofen targeted patrol and reconnaissance aircraft: at least fifty of his eighty confirmed victories were of this type.

The aerial photographs illustrated were taken by the aircrew of German *Flieger-Abteilung* 33, formed on

Country of origin:
Germany (in Belgium)

Date of printing:
1917

Location: Private collection

279

11 January 1917 from personnel of *Flieger-Bataillon* 1. Based at Moorsele, the squadron was equipped with DFW CV, a well-respected reconnaissance aircraft first introduced in 1916. It was well able to defend itself in combat, as British fighter ace James McCudden recorded in 1917: 'As I dived down I went quite close to the Hun and opened fire [...] For the next five minutes I fought that DFW [...] at last I broke off combat, for the Hun was too good for me and had shot me about a lot.' *Flieger-Abteilung* 33 was no stranger to McCudden, with two of its pilots – lieutenants Georg Müller and Walther Dern – shot down by him on 19 December 1917.

These photographs were all taken in January 1917, and depict the Ypres Salient, spying on the British rear areas at Dickebusch and examining the ground at Passchendaele. The top one shows fields and some trenches, and is signed by pilot Lieutenant Eugen Röcker. A student of theology, Röcker started the war as an infantryman, facing the French attacks in the Champagne region and experiencing the great changes in trench warfare. He wrote of his experiences on 3 November 1915:

DFW CV aircraft engaged in ground reconnaissance.

I have witnessed the development of trench-warfare for more than a year. One year ago the art of building trenches was still in its infancy. Today it is done in a far bigger style. Our communication trenches stretch for kilometres, the ground is covered with boardwalk. Each Musketeer has his own secure dugout, a year ago only the officers had them. The advances in armament forced us to dig deeper into the earth. The conflict is slowly turning into an underground war. A sophisticated war full of horrors. Its strange that mobile warfare lacks that kind of sophistication and is far less dangerous. In sophisticated war you sit comfortably, in a well-furnished dugout, but you can be dead from one second to the next. In mobile warfare you sleep on wet ground under an open sky, in all kinds of weather, wet and freezing. Hard to choose what's better. I wonder if I will ever see another year so full of good and bad, of joy and sorrow, of deprivation and indulgence. (Translated by Robin Schaefer)

In transferring to the *Luftstreitkräfte*, the German air service, Röcker was in a position to see for himself the development of the 'underground war', and to ensure that its progress was mapped out thoroughly. But, in common with most pilots of patrol aircraft, he was in constant danger from scouts and, inevitably, Röcker was wounded in aerial combat over the Ypres Salient, at Menin on 28 May 1917. Hospitalised to Germany, like so many others, he died from his wounds in hospital, and was laid to rest at Waldfriedhof in Stuttgart. Already holder of the Iron Cross 2nd Class, he was awarded the Württemberg Military Merit Medal in silver on 21 June 1917. Like so many young aviators, he was the victim of the insatiable need to document and record the evolving battlefield from the air.

Immelmann
Meine Kampfflüge

VERLAG AUGUST SCHERL G·M·B·H BERLIN

8 2

Immelmann, Meine Kampfflüge

MAX IMMELMANN WAS the first German 'fighter ace' of the war. Derived from cards (aces being the best four cards in the pack), the term 'ace' was first given by the French to those pilots who were successful in shooting down at least five enemy aircraft. Immelmann, a quiet, unassuming soldier from Saxony, would become forever associated with the development of acrobatic movements that were essential in order to both take – and preserve – life in the air.

The cult of the fighter ace was popular in the war and was followed by most nations, the heroic exploits of these airmen acting as an antidote to the dull news of the offensives on the ground and the grind of trench warfare. Immelmann was one of the first, but others would follow, with von Richthofen and Werner Voss, Albert Ball, James McCudden and Billy Bishop, Georges Guynemer and Charles Nungesser all receiving positive press. *Immelmann, Meine Kampfflüge* (*My Combat Flights*) was published in 1917, a year after his death, and contained a view of the famous airman as reflected in his letters home. The strong visual imagery of the German eagle flying over the city of Lille in silhouette is typical of German poster design from the war. Immelmann was feted as the 'Eagle of Lille' and was showered with awards and medals before his death. With the interest

Country of origin: Germany

Date of printing: 1917

Location: Private collection

Max Immelmann.

in aces continuing after the war, his letters were republished by his brother, under the title *Max Immelmann, Eagle of Lille*, alluding to Immelmann's earlier book.

His narrative tells the story of his activities as a member of the German aviation service and his rivalry with fellow ace Oswald Boelcke in *Flieger-Abteilung* 10 (and then *Flieger-Abteilung* 62). Immelmann's fortunes turned in the summer of 1915, when Anthony Fokker delivered two of his fighter monoplanes to the squadron. Equipped with an interrupter gear that prevented the forward-facing machine guns from destroying the propeller, this provided the German ace with the opportunity to aim the whole aircraft at its target. He described his first aerial victory, against Lieutenant William Reid of the RFC:

I tried to keep my machine above my opponent's, because no biplane can shoot straight up. After firing 450–500 shots in the course of a flight which lasted 8–10 minutes, I saw the enemy go down in a steep glide. When I saw him land, I went down beside him. I went up to him, I shook hands and said: 'Bon Jour, monsieur.' But he answered in English.

This statement encapsulates a sense of chivalry that allowed the public to escape from the drudgery of the war – and the public lapped it up. Immelmann was responsible for another sixteen combat successes before his death, and the success of the otherwise unimpressive Fokker EIII monoplane in 1915–16 was such that the Germans gained the upper hand. The 'Fokker scourge' was eventually answered by British aircraft with an unrivalled field of view – 'pusher' aircraft such as the de Havilland DH2, which featured a propellor behind the pilot's nacelle. Max Immelmann died on 18 June 1916 while attacking British 'pushers', his Fokker destroyed in the air. Whether it was by artillery, the bullets of his foes – or even from his own, malfunctioning interrupter gear, is difficult to ascertain. His reputation as a proponent of fighter tactics lives on even today through the 'Immelmann turn', a simultaneous loop and roll that allows pilots to both evade and attack pursuing aircraft. But his loss was much more than the death of a pilot. A much decorated soldier of Saxony and Germany, Max Immelmann's passing marked the move away from aerial chivalry to the melée of dog fights and flying circuses.

8₃

Dardanelles forts

Dardanelles forts
Kale-i Sultaniye (top
and Kilitbahir Kalesi
(bottom).

Country of origin:
Ottoman Turkey

**Date of
construction:**
c. 1493

Location: Historic
monuments,
Çannakale and
Kilitbahir, Turkey

WITH THE OTTOMANS committed to the war in
August 1914, some means was sought to ensure that
they would be quickly dispatched. Standing in the
way of the winter supply line to Russia, through the
Dardanelles and Bosphorous, the loss of the Turkish-
led empire to the Central Powers was a significant diplomatic failure, especially as there was now the direct
possibility of Ottoman belligerency towards Allied possessions and protectorates in the Middle East.

Dawning in the minds of the British was the old concept,
exercised since the late nineteenth century, of 'Forcing
the Dardenelles' in order to threaten Constantinople –
especially if the north shore of the Straits, the Gallipoli
Peninsula, could be taken by force by the Greeks, and
if the Russians could be on hand to meet the Allies at
Constantinople. This would surely lead to the surrender of
the Ottomans, and thereby remove the threat to Egypt and
the Suez Canal. In November 1914, at the first meeting
of the War Council set up to advise the Cabinet on directions in the war, First Lord of the Admiralty Sir Winston
Churchill, reignited the Dardanelles question by suggest-
ing the best way to protect Egypt and the Suez Canal was
to 'capture' the Gallipoli Peninsula; on 13 January 1915 he
was to persuade the War Council that this would be possible by purely naval action.

On 3 January 1915, the admiralty signalled to Admiral Carden, commanding the Eastern Mediterranean Squadron, for his views on the forcing of the Dardanelles. As First Lord of the Admiralty, Churchill had hopes that the age-old naval concept of pitting ships' guns against stone fortresses in 'forcing' a passage through the Dardanelles Straits could be achieved. The fortifications were impressive – on paper at least.

For the British, knowing that the Dardanelles were well-defended, Carden was cagey with his political masters, replying: 'I do not consider Dardanelles can be rushed. They might be forced by extended operations with large numbers of ships.' This cautious, politically worded statement was taken as positive by the admiralty, who asked Carden to expand his ideas. His detailed four-stage plan that followed involved the reduction of the forts at Sedd el Bahr and Kum Kale at the mouth to the Dardanelles, destroying the inside defences up to Kephez at the entrance to the Narrows, reducing its forts and, finally, clearing the minefield, reducing the defences above the Narrows and advancing into the Sea

Kilitbahir Kalesi fort.

of Marmara. The plan was careful and cautious, but it caught the imagination of Winston Churchill, who, almost by seeing the plan written down, could imagine it executed. It was Carden's plan that would ignite the flames of the Dardanelles expedition.

Forcing the Dardanelles was attempted in February–March 1915. Testing the outer defences brought heart to the Allies, who could see the possibility of reducing the solid forts to a pile of rubble, after the fort at Sedd el Bahr had been badly damaged in a show of strength there in November 1914. And this may well have been true; but the admirals had not banked on the ability of the Ottomans to defend their shores with mobile howitzers, and by mines. On 18 March 1915, the Allied ships advanced in lines, the lines of mines crossing the channel having been indifferently swept. Tellingly, a line of mines in Erin Keui Bay laid by the Ottoman mine layer *Nusret* in early March had gone undetected. In a matter of hours the *Bouvet*, *Inflexible*, *Irresistible* and *Ocean* had all been mined. The attack was called off. In total, the Allied navies lost nineteen vessels and 700 men in their attempt to force the Dardanelles; the course was set for the military landings a month later – transferring the problem to the military.

In April 1915, the Allied armies would struggle to gain a foothold on the peninsula – and would lose sight of their goal: to remove the mobile defences, clear the mines, and let the ships through. Throughout the five-month campaign, the navy gradually melted away.

With the Dardanelles forts being still strategically sensitive during the later Cold War era, they have been preserved. The stone fort of Kale-i Sultaniye on the Asian side of the Dardanelles is now preserved close to the Turkish naval museum. Equipped with four large artillery pieces, the fort was damaged by the super dreadnought HMS *Queen Elizabeth* in March 1915. It was constructed by Fatih Sultan Mehmet in 1493, designed to face the heart-shaped Kilitbahir Kalesi, its partner on the other side of the Narrows (the name Kilitbahir meaning 'lock of the sea'). Both have served as guardians of the Narrows of the Dardanelles for centuries.

The "Lusitania" (German Medal)

An exact replica of the medal which was designed in Germany and distributed to commemorate the sinking of the "Lusitania".

This indicates the true feeling the War Lords endeavour to stimulate, and is proof positive that such crimes are not merely regarded favourably, but are given every encouragement in the land of Kultur.

The "Lusitania" was sunk by a German submarine on May 7th, 1915. She had on board at the time 1,951 passengers and crew, of whom 1,198 perished.

<u>Please do not destroy this</u>
When you have read it carefully through kindly pass it on to a friend.

A
German Naval Victory

"With joyful pride we contemplate this latest deed of our navy."
Kölnische Volkszeitung, 10th May, 1915.

...medal has been struck in Germany with the object of keeping alive in ...arts the recollection of the glorious achievement of the German Navy ...rarely destroying an unarmed passenger ship, together with 1,198 non-combatants, men, women and children.

On the obverse, under the legend "No contraband" (*Keine Bannware*), there is a representation of the *Lusitania* sinking. The designer has put in guns and aeroplanes, which (as was certified by United States Government officials after inspection) the *Lusitania* did *not* carry; but has conveniently omitted to put in the women and children, which the world knows she *did* carry.

On the reverse, under the legend "Business above all" (*Geschäft über alles*), the figure of Death sits at the booking office of the Cunard Line and gives out tickets to passengers, who refuse to attend to the warning against submarines given by a German. This picture seeks apparently to propound the theory that if a murderer warns his victim of his intention, the guilt of the crime will rest with the victim, not with the murderer.

Replicas of the medal are issued by the Lusitania Souvenir Medal Committee, 32, Duke Street, Manchester Square W. 1.

All profits accruing to this Committee will be handed to St. Dunstan's Blinded Soldiers and Sailors Hostel.

84

Lusitania medal

THE STRENGTH OF the Royal Navy in the North Sea and English Channel was such that it could dictate terms to all shipping in the region. With Germany dependent upon its North Sea ports, the British were in the strongest position possible, and from November 1914 operated a blockade that effectively sterilised the North Sea to any trade with their enemies. First Lord of the Admiralty, Winston Churchill, was also insistent that there should be an aggressive response to any U-boat sightings by merchantmen. Faced with starvation and the suppression of war materiel brought by neutral shipping, the Germans countered with an announcement on 4 February 1915 in the Imperial German gazette, the *Deutscher Reichsanzeiger*:

Country of origin:
United Kingdom

Date of manufacture:
1915

Location: Private collection

All the waters surrounding Great Britain and Ireland, including the whole of the English Channel, are hereby declared to be a war zone. From February 18 onwards every enemy merchant vessel found within this war zone will be destroyed without it always being possible to avoid danger to the crews and passengers.

Neutral ships will also be exposed to danger in the war zone, as, in view of the misuse of neutral flags ordered on January 31 by the British Government, and owing to unforeseen incidents to which naval warfare is liable, it is impossible to avoid attacks being made on neutral ships in mistake for those of the enemy.

The Germans were in a position to back up their threat through the use of their submarine fleet. In 1914, there were just twenty-nine U-boats (*Unterseeboots*), but with the impotence of the German High Seas Fleet came reliance on these sleek vessels as an effective threat to Britain's naval dominance – and an exponential increase to a high of 142 submarines in 1917. Fear of the U-boat had led to a rise in the use of neutral flags by British vessels – but with the German announcement of unrestricted submarine warfare came the probability that such vessels would still be targeted.

The RMS *Lusitania*, one of the largest and most impressive ships on the Cunard transatlantic fleet, had flown a neutral flag on 31 January when faced with reports of German U-boats in the vicinity. The giant liner was stalked again in March in the Western Approaches. But when it sailed from New York to Liverpool in May 1915, the liner's luck had finally run out. Returning from New York on 7 May 1915, while off the coast of Ireland the *Lusitania* was struck by a single torpedo fired from a German U-20. The massive ship sank in eighteen minutes, with the loss of 1,198 lives – of whom 128 were American. The outcry and negative backlash against the Germans was huge.

Sinking of the *Lusitania*.

Our object is a British propaganda medal, manufactured in cast iron and paid for by the American department-store owner, Gordon Selfridge. Some 300,000 of the medals were cast, and were issued with a leaflet that decried the 'German Naval Victory'. The casting is a replica of a bronze medal that was created by the medal maker Karl Goetz. Goetz had already

The medal.

issued bronze medals that had condemned British activities on the high seas; his medallion, bearing the date 5 May 1915, illustrates the figure of death selling tickets for the liner while others look on, reading a newspaper carrying the warning issued by the Imperial German Embassy in New York against sailing across the Atlantic. Above the figure reads *Geschäft über Alles* (business over all). The other side of the medal shows the *Lusitania* foundering in the Atlantic, with the words *keine Bannware* (no contraband) prominent.

Goetz's medal had the wrong date; this was reproduced faithfully by the British, who claimed the date was evidence of a pre-planned action. The leaflet commented bitterly:

> The designer has put in guns and aeroplanes, which (as was certified by United States Government Officials after inspection) the *Lusitania* did not carry, but has conveniently omitted to put in the women and children, which the world knows she did carry.

The sinking was universally condemned on both sides of the Atlantic. The *Lusitania* had been constructed to be a naval auxiliary cruiser if necessary, but no guns were fitted. The hold did contain cargo, which included small arms ammunition, but did not carry larger weaponry. The arguments as to whether the *Lusitania* represented a legitimate target still resonate down the ages. But the great loss of life, and the propaganda victory scored by the British, were a disaster for the Germans. The submarine campaign was scaled back; the Americans were enraged. The sinking of the *Lusitania* would be a *cause célèbre* that would start the United States on a track that would ultimately see them join the war two years later, and with it the promise of greater numbers of men and materiel crossing the Atlantic than could ever have been envisaged at this early stage of the war. It was a costly mistake for the Germans.

85

Albert Ball's grave

CAPTAIN ALBERT BALL, one of the most celebrated of all fighter aces, lies buried in a cemetery that was built by the Germans in the village of Annoeullin. Ball was posted missing after a patrol over enemy lines on 7 May 1917, and the nation held its breath. The interest in the exploits of the daring aviators was such that news of Ball's fall was carried by newspapers across Europe. And it was not until the end of the month that definite news was received from the Germans, who dropped a note over British lines, the text of which read: 'RFC. Captain Ball was brought down in an air fight on May 7th by a pilot who was of the same order as himself. He was buried at Annoeullin.'

Credited with shooting down the officer was Lothar von Richthofen – the brother of Manfred von Richthofen – who claimed he shot down the officer at 8.30 a.m.: 'On May 7th I had a combat with many triplanes. One of them attacked me in a very determined manner. We fired a great deal at each other, and during the combat he came very close. He came down under my fire.'

Yet Albert Ball was flying a SE5a, not a Sopwith Triplane, and though the younger von Richthofen supplied Ball's engine serial number, many experts hold that Ball was killed by gunfire from the ground, and not in aerial combat.

Country of origin:
Germany and
United Kingdom
(in France)

**Date of
construction:**
1919 (replacing
1917 original)

Location:
Annoeullin
German Cemetery,
Annoeullin, France

Albert Ball.

In any case, the Germans buried their enemy with full honours two days later; and in June 1917 a memorial service was held for him in his hometown of Nottingham. In France, his grave was marked with a simple white cross bearing the painted inscription: *Im Luftkampf gefallen für sein Vaterland* [In air combat, fallen for his country] *Engl. Flieger-Hauptmann Albert Ball Royal Flying Corps gef. den 7. 5. 17.*

Ball's grave cross, sitting amongst German soldiers', was replaced with a larger one bearing an English inscription; in 1919, his father, the Mayor of Nottingham, paid for its replacement by a substantial black stone cross that bears the wings of the Royal Flying Corps (he would also buy the field where his son had crashed).

Albert Ball was the epitome of the dashing airman. He was young, handsome and impetuous. Joining the army early in the war in the 2/7 Battalion, Nottingham and Derbyshire Regiment, he took private tuition in order to attain his Royal Aero Club certificate that would allow him to transfer to the Royal Flying Corps. He was granted his 'wings' on 26 January 1916, and on 29 April scored his first combat victory while flying a BE2c; his first victory in a single-seater 'scout' came on 15 May. His final tally was forty-three aircraft and one balloon. He would be awarded the Victoria Cross, its citation, published in the *London Gazette* for 8 June 1917, reading:

> For most conspicuous and consistent bravery from the 25th of April to the 6th of May, 1917, during which period Capt. Ball took part in twenty-six combats in the air and destroyed eleven hostile aeroplanes, drove down two out of control, and forced several others to land.
>
> In these combats Capt. Ball, flying alone, on one occasion fought six hostile machines, twice he fought five and once four. When leading two other British aeroplanes he attacked an enemy formation of eight. On each of these occasions he brought down at least one enemy.
>
> Several times his aeroplane was badly damaged, once so seriously that but for the most delicate handling his machine would have collapsed, as nearly all the control wires had been shot away. On returning with a damaged machine he had always to be restrained from immediately going out on another.
>
> In all, Capt. Ball has destroyed forty-three German aeroplanes and one balloon, and has always displayed most exceptional courage, determination and skill.

As with the very first grave markers, Ball's monument sits quietly alongside those of his former enemies, now in peace.

86 SPAD XIII

THE RISE OF the fighter ace was matched with the need for aircraft that would have a higher rate of climb, greater speed and manoeuvrability, increased resilience and devastating firepower. By the end of the war, technological advances were such that aircraft could fly at a speed undreamt of by their 1914 counterparts, and there was continuous competition to outperform the enemy. There were many aircraft that could claim to be the best fighters of the war – the Sopwith Camel and the Fokker DVII amongst them – but it was the fighter or scout aircraft produced by the *Société anonyme pour l'Aviation et ses Dérivés* (originally the *Société de Production des aeroplanes Deperdussin*), usually simply known as SPAD, which were amongst the most famous aeroplanes produced by the French.

The problem that had plagued the early years of aerial combat had been the ability of the pilot to fire forward-facing machine guns through the propeller arc without destroying the propeller. But it was the development of the interrupter gear, which interrupted the rotation of the

Country of origin:
France

Date of construction:
1918

Location:
Smithsonian Institution, Washington DC, USA

propeller when the machine guns were fired, that really solved the problem. The war in the air became a techno-logical battleground, with the latest technology – affect-ing engines, speed, firepower, turn-rate, height and so on – creating the possibility of gaining the upper hand.

The first SPAD aircraft were not ultimately success-ful. Attempting to fix the problems of forward fire, they were ungainly, with the pilot sitting behind the propel-ler but a machine gunner sitting in a nacelle in front of it. Few of these were produced. But it was the produc-tion of a superior aircraft fitted with a Hispano-Suiza V8 water-cooled, in-line engine that was to make the SPAD marque famous. The SPAD S.VII was designed by Louis Béchereau and was developed from the SPAD V, the first of the line to be engined by the Hispano-Suiza. It was a neat design with a distinctive profile. First appearing in April 1916, the SPAD VII was robust, a little difficult to manoeuvre but definitely fast, and it had an excellent rate of climb. It had a strong gun platform for its single Vickers gun. Some 5,600 of this type were produced in France alone. It served with several fighter units (*escadrilles de chasse*), including Georges Guynemer's *Les Cigognes* – his aircraft, *Vieux Charles*, is preserved in Paris.

But the aircraft illustrated is of a later type, the SPAD XII, equipped with a more powerful 220hp Hispano-Suiza 8, equipped with twin Vickers – making the air-craft a formidable fighting machine. Over 8,400 of this type were constructed, equipping most French fighter units; Guynemer lost his life in one such aircraft. The SPAD XII is notable as being the prime fighter air-craft of the sixteen aero squadrons of the American Expeditionary Force, with 893 aircraft committed to the Americans; over half of these returned to the United States at the end of the war. This particular aircraft – No. 20, *Smith* IV – was flown by Lt A. Raymond Brooks of the 22nd Aero Squadron (2nd Pursuit Group), and is now preserved in the US National Air and Space Museum in Washington DC. Brooks was an ace – cred-ited with six victories – and chose this aircraft to bring back to the United States for evaluation. It is an excep-tional survivor of an exceptional type of aircraft.

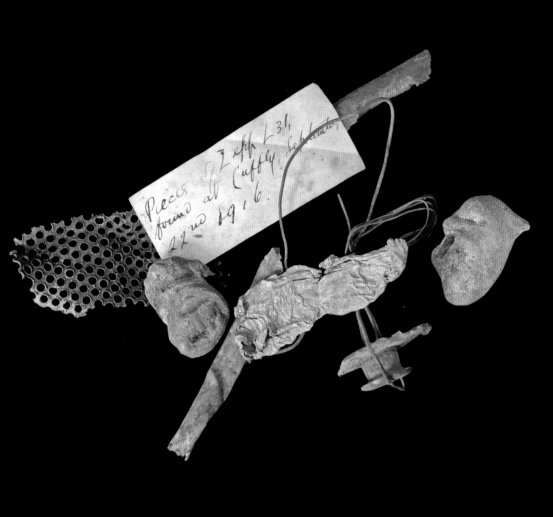

87

Zeppelin fragments

THE FIRST GERMAN assault on British soil came from the sea. At the outset of war, with the British Royal Navy dispersed to tackle its commitments, the more concentrated German Imperial Navy sought opportunities to trap small numbers of British ships and destroy them. With this in mind, Admiral Hipper planned raids on the British coast that he hoped would bring him success. The first of these, at Great Yarmouth on 3 November 1914, was a failure. A more ambitious raid, targeting Scarborough and Hartlepool, was planned for 16 December 1914. At 8 a.m., German ships shelled Scarborough, hitting the Grand Hotel, churches and private properties; the nearby town of Whitby was also hit. Hartlepool was assaulted ten minutes later; over 1,000 shells were hurled at the town, damaging factories, homes and churches. Eighty-six civilians and seven soldiers were killed and 438 were injured. The raids were a propaganda victory for the British – 'Remember Scarborough' now replaced 'Remember Belgium' on recruiting posters.

The assault on Britain was not limited to bombardment from ships, however, and the next phase would be the use of airships – Zeppelins. The first aerial attacks were approved by the kaiser himself in January 1915 – though at first excluding London – with night raids

Country of origin:
Germany

Date of manufacture:
1916

Location: Private collection

Monument to Leefe Robinson, victor over the SL.11.

that were intended to target military installations on the Thames estuary. The raids soon escalated. The first successful one was on the night of 19 January, when two Zeppelins attacked East Anglia with high explosive bombs and incendiaries, killing four and injuring sixteen; it was the shape of things to come. London was admitted as a target in February. Though early attempts were ineffectual, at 11.00 p.m. on 31 May 1915, Captain Linnarz of Zeppelin LZ.38 dropped the first enemy bombs – some 3,000lb of explosives – on the capital. Seven people were killed and thirty-five injured. The response from the ground was non-existent, with no aircraft to meet it, no guns fired at it, no searchlights trained on it.

Raids on Britain would continue into the summer, though the short nights were a problem for the Zeppelins, which depended on the cover of darkness, and the bombing started to get heavier. Anti-aircraft defences were still ineffectual, and though the pencil-like shapes of the airships were often caught in search-lights – the problem was that neither anti-aircraft fire nor aircraft were able to intercept the high-flying air-ships. The Zeppelin raids continued into 1916, with larger numbers of airships targeting London and other cities in the eastern part of the country. The largest raid was on the night of 2 September, which was to prove a turning point in the aerial war as on this night Lt William Leefe Robinson became the first pilot to actively shoot down an airship over Britain, the rigid-bodied Schütte–Lanz SL.11. Robinson fired three drums of ammunition into the airship, which quickly caught fire and was sent to the ground as a fireball, the crew killed outright. His report recorded the event:

> I had hardly finished the drum before I saw the part fired
> at, glow. In a few second the whole rear part was blazing.

This event was to become celebrated, and fragments of the stricken craft were sold to aid the Red Cross; a memo-rial to the event is to be seen at Cuffley in Hertfordshire. The fragments of the SL.11 illustrated were collected by a soldier in the Royal Field Artillery for his officer – an inveterate collector of such artefacts.

Leefe Robinson would be awarded the Victoria Cross for his gallant act – the first of many such acts carried out by RFC airmen in tackling the Zeppelin 'baby kill-ers'. Later, Robinson would be shot down in France by fighters of von Richtofen's *Jasta* 11, to spend the rest of the war in a prison camp – tragically succumbing, on his return home at the end of the war, to the influenza pandemic that killed so many people in 1918–19.

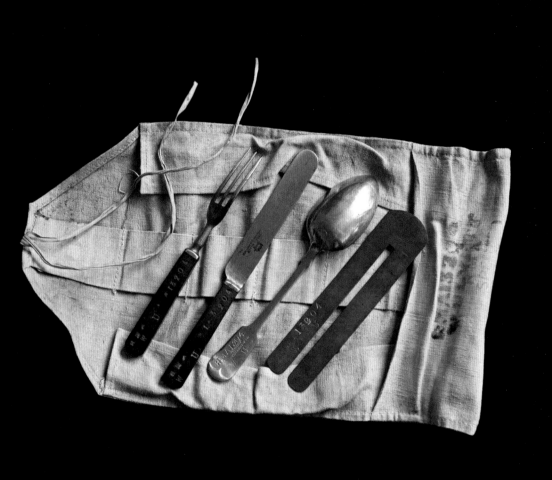

88

Royal Marine 'necessaries'

Country of origin:
United Kingdom

Date of manufacture:
1914–16

Location: Private collection

WHILE NAVAL ENGAGEMENTS were being fought in odd corners of the world, the U-boats were plying their trade. Considered only as a defensive arm at the opening of the war, the public expected much of their dreadnought and battlecruiser fleets. With the dreadnought having thick armour and in-line all-big-gun weaponry, the battlecruiser was favoured by some – especially the British First Sea Lord, Jacky Fisher – as a much faster alternative. With its thinner armour, Fisher believed that speed would be the battlecruiser's answer to the heavier armour of the more lumbering ships. HMS *Lion*, launched in 1910, was one of the best of its type. Created during the British and German naval arms race at the turn of the twentieth century, the *Lion* was a formidable ship, armed with 13½in guns and considerably faster than others in its class, this 'splendid cat' was one of the biggest warships in the world, and was destined to be Admiral Beatty's flagship of the 1st Battlecruiser Squadron, consisting in 1916 of four ships, the *Lion, Princess Royal, Queen Mary* and *Tiger*. All would be severely tested during the Battle of Jutland.

British ships were manned by officers and ratings of the Royal Navy and the Royal Naval Volunteer Reserve, as well as the sea-soldiers of the Royal Marines, then divided into two branches – the Royal Marine Light Infantry and the Royal Marine Artillery. The gunners manned at least one turret on a warship, and all were involved in gunnery control. Marines were equipped as soldiers and were provided with all the 'necessaries' that a soldier would require. The set of equipment illustrated belonged to one man, Bombardier Wilfred Robert Ulyatt of the Royal Marine Artillery. His knife, fork and spoon are all marked with his regimental number; this matches his kit roll, known as a holdall, which also contains his button brass – specifically designed to protect his uniform from staining while he was cleaning his buttons. Bombardier Ulyatt was one of the complement of marines who manned a turret in Beatty's flagship, HMS *Lion*, and who are mute witness to its actions at Jutland.

The Battle of Jutland was the largest fleet battle of the war and provided the opportunity for the British Grand Fleet and the German High Seas Fleet to finally meet in strength on 31 May 1916 in the open waters in the North Sea, north of Denmark and the Jutland peninsula. The German strategy had long been to create a fleet that would threaten the security of Britain simply by its existence. But numerically it was still weaker than that of the British; an all-out battle would inevitably lead to more losses and a further weakening of their position. With this in mind, the Germans created several elaborate ploys intended to lure out the British in sufficient numbers that they could be taken on by submarines, and sunk. Raids on the east coast of England caused outrage – and created opportunities for the British to sit on the moral high ground, claiming that the Germans had set out to murder civilians in the coastal towns. The plan was simply to force a naval reaction – and to gain the chance to destroy the British ships in detail, and submarines were ready to pounce on any unwary ship – as they had done in 1914. This cat-and-mouse campaign created many frustrations and forced the hand of Admiral Scheer, commanding the German High Seas Fleet. In May 1916, Scheer dispatched his battlecruisers under Admiral Hipper to the Skagerrak, on the pretence of threatening merchant shipping. But it was Scheer's hope that Hipper's battlecruisers would be too tempting a target for Jellicoe and, specifically, for Hipper's opposite number, Admiral Beatty and the 1st Battlecruiser Squadron. Scheer expected Beatty to take up the challenge and, with the High Seas Fleet lying in wait, to be able to trap and destroy them. It was unfortunate for the German commander that British intelligence knew of his intention. Suitably warned, the British Grand Fleet moved into position. And at 3.30 p.m. on 31 May 1916, Beatty in HMS *Lion* made contact with his German opposite numbers, who turned to the south in order to lure Beatty's ships into the embrace of the German High Seas Fleet.

At 3.48 p.m., the battlecruisers from both sides opened fire. Within minutes, the first casualty was HMS *Indefatigable*, serving with the 2nd Battlecruiser Squadron. With better gunnery and more effective double-skinned armour, the German ships easily bested the British. Under fire from the SMS *Von Der Tann*, HMS *Indefatigable* was ripped apart, all but two of its crew killed. Fisher's expectation that speed would provide the safety net for his battle-cruisers was clearly inadequate. Beatty's flagship, the *Lion*, was the leading ship and engaged the *Lützow*. With German gunnery proving highly accurate, the *Lion* received several hits – including a direct hit on Q turret with a 305mm shell. The shell penetrated the turret and blew off its armoured roof, killing or wounding its crew; Bombardier Ulyatt was one of those who lost his life. A fire was started that could have threatened the ship – fortunately the RMLI turret commander, Major Francis Harvey, had the foresight to order the shell magazine to be flooded. Harvey later died of his wounds but was awarded the Victoria Cross for his bravery. The *Queen Mary* was next, receiving hits on its magazine from the *Derfflinger*. The ship exploded, again with great loss of life. Beatty's laconic comment was: 'There seems to be something wrong with our bloody ships today.'

Though suffering many grave losses, the remaining battlecruisers were turned away from the battle when the main German fleet was spotted at 4.40 p.m. Beatty hoped to lure the Germans into an open conflict with the Grand Fleet, approaching from the north-west. With both sides conscious of the possibility of defeat, and with Jellicoe fearing submarines, the fleet action that followed was not decisive. By the following day, both fleets remained, and both sides claimed success. The Germans had sunk more ships and killed more sailors than the British. But the German High Seas Fleet never put to sea again. The bravery of men like Wilfred Ulyatt had made sure of that.

AUTHORITY TO WEAR
WAR MEDALS FOR THE MERCANTILE MARINE,
Awarded by H.M. The King
through the Board of Trade

W.M. 2.

William Pittuck

024498) is authorised to

T.B. 3.

Issued by

TORPEDO BADGE AND BAR
for the Mercantile Marine
AWARDED BY
H.M. THE KING
through the Board of Trade

Board of Trade.

(Full Name of Master or Seaman) William Pittuck
is authorised to wear the Torpedo Badge (and one Bar) whi
to him; and he is required to retain this Authorisati

BOARD OF TRADE,
MARINE DEPARTMENT.

Signature of Superintendent who issues the Badge (and
Bars) and this form, with date, and T.B. Stamp

Signature of Master or Seaman

NOTE.—The Authorisation is only for Masters and Skippers, and for
Certificates of Discharge. In all other cases the Authorisation
Superintendent on the Dis. A, Dis. I or Form E.

(x) (8261) Wt. G763 2500 5-18 W B & L

R.S. 2.

BRITISH MERCAN

IDE

SERVIC

Date and

No. 82

TORPEDO BADGE, BAR AND STAR.

Instructions how to wear them
(1) The Torpedo Badge is to be sown of
tened horizontally on the cuff of the left
ve of either arm or above the with high
g, pointing away from the body
The Bar is to be sown or fastened in
ly below the Torpedo, and parallel
and each additional Bar parallel
one, and parallel to the previous one.
(3) The Star is to be sown
high above the Torpedo.
(4) In Regulations for the Distance for
wear or supply a Torpedo, Badge, Bar
Star without Board of Trade authority

BOARD OF TRADE

89

Torpedo badge

IN THE WAKE of the *Lusitania* affair and complaints from the US president, Woodrow Wilson, the German policy of attacking all ships that entered the designated war zone around the United Kingdom was suspended. Wilson had sent three firmly worded notes to the Germans expressing the right of the American ships to sail unmolested on the high seas, and the US president went so far as to warn the Germans that any further deliberate acts of war against American shipping would be seen as 'deliberately unfriendly'. The sinking of another liner off the coast of Ireland on 19 August 1915 – the White Star Line's SS *Arabic* with a cost of forty-four people – did little to allay American fears, and with the Germans becoming increasingly nervous about the reaction of the US government, the U-boats were withdrawn from attacking merchant ships and turned their attention to the Grand Fleet.

But for Admiral von Holtzendorf, chief of the admiralty staff of the German navy and a convert to the doctrine of 'Unrestricted Submarine Warfare', there was a gamble to be taken. With the odds stacked against the Germans on the Western Front, and with the strength of the British Navy rising, von Holtzendorf issued a top-secret memorandum on 22 December 1916, advising the kaiser and the military High Command to resume submarine attacks on all shipping:

Country of origin:
United Kingdom

Date of manufacture:
1918

Location: Private collection

Most Secret!

I have the honour to respectfully submit to your Excellency [...] a memorandum on the necessity for the commencement an unrestricted campaign of submarine warfare at the earliest opportunity.

The war requires a decision before autumn 1917 [...] If we succeed to break England's backbone, the war will immediately be decided in our favour. England's backbone is the merchant tonnage, which delivers essential imports for their survival and for the military industry of the British islands [...]

Based on a monthly rate of destruction of 600,000 tons of shipping through a campaign of unrestricted submarine warfare [...] at least two fifths of the neutral tonnage sailing in the trade with England will be deterred by such a campaign [... and] the current volume English sea borne trade will be reduced by 39% within five months. This would not be bearable for England, neither in view of her future position after the war, nor in view of her ability to continue the war effort. Already, the country is at the verge of a food crisis, which will soon compel it to attempt to undertake the same food rationing measures, which we, as a blockaded country, have been forced to adopt since the outbreak of the war.

Therefore my conclusion is that a campaign of unrestricted submarine warfare [...] has to accept the risk of American belligerence, because we have no other option. In spite of the diplomatic rupture with America, the unrestricted submarine warfare is nevertheless the right means to conclude this war victoriously.

The kaiser took the gamble; he agreed to the new campaign and authorised its start from 1 February. For the merchantmen, the idea of being attacked by submarines, a hidden menace, was terrifying. The torpedo – the self-propelled, submarine-launched weapon – had been effective since the turn of the century and was a means of ensuring that a ship was struck by a significant warhead, with devastating results. For a merchantman, being 'torpedoed' or 'submarined' meant loss of ship and livelihood – and the need to find a new berth.

As a recognition and mark of distinction for those mariners who had been sunk by submarines (or mines), and who had lived to sail again, the Board of Trade granted the right to wear an embroidered torpedo badge on the left sleeve – the torpedo meant to face forwards. The example illustrated was awarded to William Williams Pittuck of Essex who, in his sixties, was a veteran seaman and master, who carefully preserved the honour as a remembrance of a sinking – most likely by submarine, most probably by a torpedo itself.

At first, the British response to the submarine menace was an Admiralty-sponsored scheme of direct attacks on U-boats by merchantmen – a policy that led to the execution of Captain Fryatt, captain of the SS *Brussels*, who had attempted to ram the U-33 on 28 March 1915. With the resumption of unrestricted attacks in 1917, the rate of shipping losses doubled and then tripled; only then, in the early summer of 1917, was the Convoy System introduced, providing safety in numbers and the support of naval ships, which led to a decline in shipping losses.

The Germans had gambled that they could bring Britain to its knees by their policy of submarine attacks – but failed. The stakes were high, for the Americans broke off diplomatic relations with Germany and formally declared war with them on 6 April 1917. At this point, for the Germans the war was, ultimately, lost.

90

HMS *Vindictive*

IN APPRECIATING THE military reasons which directed the [...] blocking of Zeebrugge, it is desirable to recall to mind the general naval situation at the beginning of 1918. Briefly stated, the German High Seas Fleet was contained [...] whilst German submarines were engaged on vast operations, having for their object the stoppage of the trade of Great Britain [...] In the face of such an attack, the aim of Great Britain was either to destroy the enemy submarines, or, failing destruction, to prevent their egress from their bases [...] it was with this military object that plans for the blocking of Zeebrugge were initiated.

Admiral of the Fleet, Earl Beatty, 1921

Country of origin:
United Kingdom

Date of construction:
1897

Location: Ostend Harbour, Ostend, Belgium

The British had tried many ways of ensuring that the German submarines – based too close for comfort to British ports on the coast of Flanders – were kept bottled. The Germans had established their submarine base inland, close to Bruges and connected by canals to the sea at Zeebrugge and Ostend. The Royal Navy had tried to bombard the lock gates without success, and with the submarine war telling heavily upon the British merchant trade, it was necessary to take direct action. That action involved simultaneous attacks on

HMS *Vindictive* at Zeebrugge mole.

the harbours at Zeebrugge and Ostend, attacks that would remove the threat by blocking the channels using old ships that were specially prepared so that they could not easily be removed. This, it was hoped, would ram home the stopper into the bottle, and remove much of the U-boat threat.

Zeebrugge was the larger target – it had a wider channel and was a greater threat. It was also heavily defended, with a garrison of 1,000 men stationed on the huge curving 'mole' that protected the harbour entrance, which was equipped with a battery of guns that posed a direct threat to any attacking force. To take on the harbour, the navy would need to ensure that its blockships were guided into position, while simultaneously assaulting the mole, its battery and its connecting bridges. The attack on Zeebrugge and Ostend was launched on 23 April 1918 – St George's Day.

The bow of HMS *Vindictive* stands close to Ostend harbour. With so many other monuments to the war in

Belgium, until recently the *Vindictive* stood a little out of the limelight, rusting, perhaps not venerated as those battle monuments of the Ypres Salient. Yet the actions this memorial commemorates are every bit as significant; renovated in 2013, it has been given greater prominence.

The *Vindictive* was a light cruiser that was committed to the Zeebrugge raid as a means of taking on the German garrison on the masonry mole. At 29ft high, this was a formidable target. Equipped with howitzers, flame-throwers and specially constructed gangplanks, the *Vindictive* operated with the shallow draught Mersey ferries the *Iris* and the *Daffodil*, both commissioned into naval service. While the *Daffodil* pushed the *Vindictive* against the mole, the *Iris* carried part of the naval landing party. The intention was that 200 Royal Marine Light Infantrymen would storm the gun battery, while two elderly submarines packed with explosives would destroy the bridge that connected the mole with the harbour. And all to let the three blockships – *Thetis, Intrepid* and *Iphigenia* – pass through the harbour entrance to block the channel. The assault was terrifying in its intensity.

All three ships were scuttled, though the *Thetis* sat outside the channel. The submarines did their job – and the action of the *Vindictive* in the storming of the mole was held up as one of the most daring acts of the war. In all, eight Victoria Crosses were awarded for this action. And while the channel was blocked, that at Ostend remained open, for the Germans, using a ruse de guerre, moved the navigation buoys, leaving blockships grounded outside the harbour. With this channel still open, the patched-up *Vindictive* itself was sent to block it in a second raid at Ostend two weeks later. It only partially succeeded – but the noble ship's bows remain today as a memorial to the men who carried out these raids in defence of the coasts of Britain from the U-boat menace.

At Home

91 Iron for gold

THE WAR WAS never going to be a short affair. With rapidly spiralling costs, the burden of paying for it would have to be met by the public. In Britain, for instance, while the cost of the war was estimated at £1 million per day in 1914, by its end, this had increased to around £5.7 million. Taxation could only go so far, so money had to be raised through the issue of War Bonds – *Kriegsanleihe* in Germany and Austria – which required personal investment in the national scheme, with the promise of rewards later. In most cases, and in all countries, War Bonds were portrayed as part of the patriotic duties of the people. In Germany, a total of nine War Bonds were issued between 1914 and 1918 that earned 98 billion Reichsmarks, which covered some 60 per cent of the war costs. And, while most belligerent countries depended on similar schemes, there is one that was typical only of Germany: the concept of freely 'giving gold for iron'.

There was a precedent. On 31 March 1813, during the Napoleonic wars, Princess Marianne of Prussia personally appealed to all Prussian women to hand in gold jewellery for their country in order to finance the campaigns. In exchange they received simple iron jewellery

Country of origin: Germany

Date of manufacture: c. 1914–15

Location: Private collection

marked 'Gold I gave for iron' or 'Gold for defence; iron for honour', and very quickly the wearing of iron rings, earrings and bracelets became fashionable. With a world war in progress, the appeal was repeated in 1914, and with similar success. Though voluntary, there was huge social pressure on people to hand in their gold: watch chains, rings, jewellery of all types. The system was simple: if you wore iron jewellery you were a patriot; if you were still wearing gold, you were a traitor.

The medallion illustrated was handed out by the *Reichsbank* in exchange for not only gold, but also silver and bronze. It depicts a person offering gold '*In eiserner zeit*' (In iron time), and carries the message *gold gab ich zur wehr eisen nahm ich zur ehr* (gold I gave to the military I took iron). The medal was designed by the German artist and sculptor Kurt Hermann Hosaeus (1875–1958). Gold was not only given by individuals but also by institutions such as churches and public offices. Appropriately enough for a city associated with steel, in 1917 the Mayor of Magdeburg donated the city's seventeenth-century golden chain of office in support of the war effort; the iron chain given in exchange is still in the local museum.

For the Germans, iron had a deep meaning, linked directly to Germanic mythology. During the Iron Age the process of melting and forging iron was thought to be a mystical process: few people knew the secrets that made it possible to forge weapons of iron, and with human blood tainted with the smell of iron, so this metal was considered to be the blood – or life force – of the Earth. A popular nationalistic song, *Der Gott der Eisen wachsen ließ* (The God that made the iron grow), written by Ernst Moritz Arndt in 1812, begins with the words: *Der Gott der Eisen wachsen ließ, der wollte keine Knechte. Drum gab er Säbel, Schwert und Spieß dem Mann in seine Rechte* (It was the God who let iron grow and wanted no slaves, who therefore armed the Germans with sabre, sword and spear). Giving gold for iron meant much more to the German public than simply funding the war; it meant the direct defence of the Fatherland.

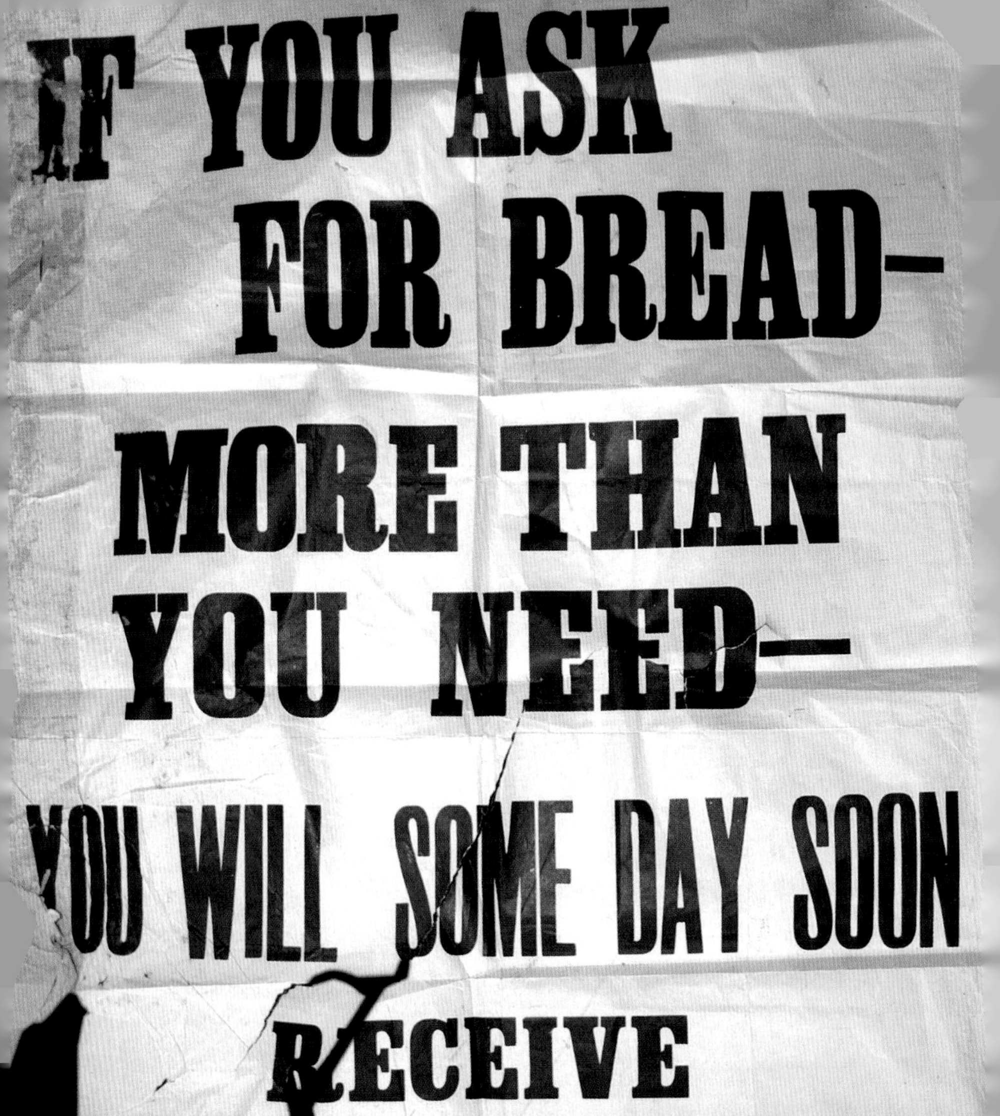
IF YOU ASK
FOR BREAD—
MORE THAN
YOU NEED—
YOU WILL SOME DAY SOON
RECEIVE
LY A STONE!

92

Glasgow food poster

THE QUESTION OF adequate food supply was to become a major issue during the war.

Early on, with its naval dominance, the British established a blockade of the German ports, with British ships patrolling the North Sea and English Channel. The Royal Navy was intent on preventing imports of 'contraband' to Germany, which included foodstuffs. By 1915, imports had fallen by half and feeding the German people became increasingly difficult. The health of the nation declined, and '*erstaz*' substitutes for staples increased, their nutritional levels much reduced. By the end of the war, some 700,000 civilians are known to have died through malnutrition and associated diseases in Germany.

With Britain so hopelessly dependent on imports (up to 60 per cent of its food stocks), it was vulnerable to attacks on its supply system. Yet early on in the Great War, food control was unheard of, and it was not until 1916 that there was a move towards some form of formal restrictions on consumption. At the outbreak of war, concerns over shortages among the middle and upper classes led to widespread hoarding. That other unholy act, 'profiteering', was also a major preoccupation of the newspapers, and the opportunity to make money from decreased supply was perhaps too much to miss for some retailers. Both actions were loudly condemned in

Country of origin: United Kingdom

Date of printing: 1915

Location: Private collection

the press, yet rationing was not to be enacted until 1917. Imperial Germany was intent on starving Britain into submission, with U-boats targeting any ship – neutral included – that might represent a lifeline for Britain in terms of food supply. Around 300,000 tons of shipping was sunk per month; in April 1917 alone, a record 550,000 tons of shipping was lost. This level of destruction meant that some foodstuffs were going to be in short supply.

Food was not the only concern; housing was in crisis too. In Glasgow, with its tradition of tenement houses, families regularly squeezed into apartments with two rooms. With available tenements reduced due to the influx of munitions works, unscrupulous landlords increased rents dramatically. Militant women's groups were raised, and there were rent strikes against profiteering private landlords. On 17 November 1915 the women of Glasgow rose up and marched through the streets to protest about rents, the rising prices and the hoarding of food. On the strength of the march, the Rents and Mortgage Interest (Rent Restriction) Act 1915 was introduced in order to rule out some of the worst practices. But ill-feeling still simmered. Our object is a poster, produced for just this one march by a local printer, which expresses the feeling of frustration by the women of Glasgow. It demands fairness and threatens violent action against those who sought to take more than their fair share – of food, in this case.

Glasgow food poster (restored).

It was not until December 1916 that there was a specific government department – the Ministry of Food – to deal with such issues in Britain. Set up in the wake of concerns over profiteering and hoarding (rather than the bite being taken out of imports by the action of submarines), this body replaced the Cabinet Committee on

Food Supplies that had been created early in the war to ensure that there were adequate supplies of the most important foodstuffs. Exports of food were prohibited, and a raft of subcommittees and commissions were charged with keeping prices down and ensuring supplies were adequate.

Bread was an important food reserve for much of the population – it was processed, already cooked and cheap. Attempts to increase the yield of wheat from British farms were reasonably successful, yet the supply of wheat from overseas meant that baking sufficient bread to meet demand was a challenging task. Appeals were made to 'eat less bread' in order to conserve stocks, with campaigns and propaganda to boot; but poorer families found this self-sacrifice to be a difficult task. In early May 1917 the king issued a royal proclamation: 'We, being persuaded that the abstention from all unnecessary consumption of grain will furnish the surest and most effectual means of defeating the devices of Our enemies [...] We do for this purpose more particularly exhort and charge all heads of households to reduce the consumption of bread in their respective families by at least one-fourth.' For some families, this was easier said than done.

British ration books: rationing was introduced in 1915 in Germany, and 1918 in Britain.

PERSEVERANCE OVERCOMES

DORNOCK

SHELLS AND
MORE SHELLS

Doing her Bit

ON WAR

1916

SERVICE

93

'Munitionette' model

Country of origin:
United Kingdom

Date of manufacture:
c. 1916

Location: Private collection

THE BRITISH MUNITIONS of War Act of August 1915 (that followed the 'Shell scandal' of early 1915) brought all munitions manufacturers under the control of the new Ministry of Munitions. By 1918, it managed directly 250 government factories and supervised 20,000 more. There was a bewildering array of types: National Filling Factories (NFF), National Projectiles Factories (NPF), National Shell Factories (NSF) and a whole host of industrial sites concerned with the myriad aspects of trench warfare. While just 500,000 shells were produced in 1914, in 1917 some 76 million were manufactured. In all, some 2.5 million men would work in munitions factories during the war – but this would be inadequate. New sources of labour would be required, and the government turned to the unions in order to implement what would be termed 'dilution' of the skilled workforce – the use of unskilled male labour, and women.

One of the phenomena of the war was the production of heraldic china mementos in the shape of tanks, ships, weapons, aircraft and a miscellany of other military subjects. Heraldic china was an output of pre-war Staffordshire, and was born from a desire of day-trippers to bring back souvenirs of their visits to the seaside. On the outbreak of war, the representation of military objects

Munitions workers.

in china was a new and lucrative market, and there was no end to the ingenuity of the often fiercely competitive 'crested china' designers. The model illustrated is a representation of a female munitions worker, clad in simple working overalls and headgear, wearing her distinctive triangular badge and offering up an example of her output, with the words: 'Shells and More Shells: Doing her bit.' This model carries the crest of the huge munitions factory situated at Dornock, near Gretna, Scotland – so it may well have been the property of a 'munitionette', or perhaps was purchased for her family. Here, the huge National Filling Factory was constructed late in 1915, and was truly vast, stretching some 9 miles from Dornock to Longtown. The factory complex manufactured cordite – the principal propellent in munitions.

Prior to conscription, men had been encouraged to register as a 'war munitions volunteer', a status that exempted them from military service – at least in the short run – but required them to be mobile. Women war-work volunteers had been sought in March 1915, yet take-up of the volunteers by the factories was slow at first. Viewed with some suspicion by many male workers, agreement had to be reached between employers and unions – the first of which was attained in

November 1914, followed by a variety of others leading up to the adoption of the Munitions of War Act in 1915. With this in place, further negotiations would follow to allow women to take on more and more work in what were traditionally 'closed shops'.

With these moves, and with an increasing number of men being 'combed out' of war work in order to take their place on the front line, women would be called to the munitions factories as 'munitionettes' or as 'Tommy's sister'. With munitions including everything from the filling of shells through to the manufacture of boots, bandages and tents, there was a crying need for labour, and an estimated female workforce of 800,000 would be employed in all aspects of their creation, some 594,600 working under the aegis of the Ministry of Munitions in one role or another. Of these, the largest proportion, almost 250,000, would be engaged in the filling and manufacture of shells; the remainder would help create ordnance pieces, rifles, small arms ammunition; they would work with chemicals and on the myriad devices needed in trench warfare. In many cases, women would come to outnumber men in the factories. At Dornock there were some 11,576 women employed, almost 70 per cent of the workforce making cordite, nitroglycerine and other explosives.

Munitions work would be long and hard, but women were attracted to it for a variety of reasons, whether from patriotic duty or simply a desire to better their lives. They would also be reasonably well paid, typically £2 2s 4d per week; yet this was still half the amount that was paid to men – there would be a long way to go for equal treatment.

94

Hospital mementos

Country of origin:
Canada (in United
Kingdom)

**Date of
production:** 1916

Location: Private
collection

IN THE AFTERMATH of an attack many men would be stranded in no-man's-land, sheltering in shell holes, waiting and hoping for the arrival of stretcher-bearers. Under the Hague Convention, stretcher-bearers were given non-combatant status so long as they wore an appropriate armband to identify them. In all armies, it was the duty of stretcher-bearers to search the battlefield for casualties. Regimental stretcher-bearers' responsibilities usually ended at the regimental aid post; from here men would be dispatched to the rear areas and would be in the care of the army medical services, whose role it was to care for the wounded and to evacuate them efficiently from the front line to hospital and then home: *heimat* or 'Blighty'.

Movement from the front was long, laborious and, for the wounded, painful. The chain was a long one: in the British Army, the first move would be to the regimental aid post, run by a doctor and a small number of orderlies, and which was set up close to the front line; next would be the advanced dressing station, set up at the farthest frontwards limit of wheeled transport, and run by the Field Ambulance, with three such units of men attached to an infantry division; from there the next move would be to the casualty clearing station, the first of the major hospitals and then, ultimately, to the base hospitals. At this point, doctors made the fateful decision whether or not to move the sick and wounded home. Similar chains existed in the other combatant nations.

Across the United Kingdom, as in Germany, war hospitals received soldiers 'from the front'. In addition to military hospitals, many civilian premises were handed over to military use. Soldiers arriving from the continent by hospital trains were then dispatched across the country. They were then set up in large private houses, municipal buildings and other premises in order to satisfy the demand for suitable accommodation, often staffed by volunteer nurses. With the outbreak of war in 1914 there would be floods of volunteers in all combatant countries, not all of the volunteers being suited to medical work, and many of them with little or no experience. In Britain and Russia, the royal families led by example, with Princess Mary and the imperial grand-duchesses of Russia wearing the uniform of nurses.

It was a fashion of the day for nurses to keep albums that were used to record sentiments, poems, drawings and simple signatures penned by their patients. Many are poignant; the soldiers concerned could be patched up and sent back to the front line. Illustrated is a page from

Inside a war hospital.

one nursing sister's album from the Endsleigh Palace Hospital in Bloomsbury, central London. Lt George Ansley Wallace of the 25th Battalion (Nova Scotia Rifles) Canadian Infantry, who served in France, recorded his appreciation: 'They [sic] will ever be fond memories of our thoughtful sister'. The entry was written on 5 July 1916 – together with a Flanders poppy. His fondness went further: as a gift he gave his nurse a maple-leaf frame made from a shell case discarded on the field of battle. In most cases, hospitals in Britain were segregated according to rank. The Endsleigh Palace Hospital is typical. Originally a hotel, it was requisitioned by the War Office in 1915 and turned into a hospital for officers, equipped with 100 beds. Here, male medical orderlies also acted as 'valets' for the officers, with the nurses – a mixture of volunteers and trained staff – tending to their recovery.

Wounded soldier in a British war hospital, recipient of the Military Medal.

Across Britain, some 38,000 Voluntary Aid Detachments (VADs) worked in hospitals – while others would serve overseas. VADs administered some 3,000 military auxiliary hospitals (created in a variety of settings, from grand houses to public buildings) and convalescent homes during the war. Some 10–15 per cent of soldiers mobilised were killed, but many more were wounded or taken prisoner, and it was relatively rare for a front line soldier to survive the war completely unscathed. Wounding was a common experience; most longed for the opportunity of gaining a minor wound that would take them back home. Not everyone would have the opportunity.

95 Telegram

RECEIVING A TELEGRAM from the War Office was dreaded during the war; more often than not it would signify that a loved one had been killed, wounded or taken prisoner. Usually the preserve of the officer, ordinary soldiers would receive instead a standard letter with blanks filled in with the soldier's details. Similar letter were sent by German authorities to their soldiers' families. Sometimes, however, the first inklings of a casualty might be a letter returned home with the brutal and stark message 'Killed in Action' written or stamped as a cachet on its unopened cover; in other cases, letters would be written from the adjutant or chaplain to

Country of origin:
United Kingdom

Date of issue:
1918

Location: Private
collection

soften the blow. More often than not, these letters would profess that the soldier in question had not suffered, and had died instantly; the truth might be harder to bear. For example, in the case of Private Charles Chard of Somerset, serving with the Yorkshire Regiment, the colonel of his battalion was to write: 'Pte Chard was killed in the Arras Sector in August 1917 while out on a daylight patrol "instantaneously", he is buried in the Sunken Road Cemetery in Fampoux.'

Captain Perry of the 9th King's (Liverpool Regiment) was one of the lucky ones. Captured in the German offensives of 1918, he spent the remainder of the war as a prisoner. One can only imagine what his family felt when they received a telegram from the War Office, and the fear that they must have felt as they opened the envelope. His family in Birkenhead was to receive two telegrams: one informing his family that he was missing; the other that he had been wounded but was a prisoner. The telegrams, stark in their brevity, at least brought news that he was safe. So many other telegrams would not.

For the British, some 10–15 per cent of those who joined up were killed, a figure comparable to the German Army. But it was the Scots who would lost twice as many men. The Scots were not the only group to lose heavily; with large numbers of middle-class men joining the colours in the early years, there was a dispro-portionate number who died, again almost one-quarter of them. Many would serve as officers, and officers would lose more in proportion than ordinary soldiers. This would be the 'lost generation' that would be much discussed in post-war years, the flower of British youth. For the next of kin of those who had given their lives in the war there would be a plaque that resembled an over-sized penny – earning it the nickname of the 'death' or 'dead-man's' penny – more than 1 million plaques were produced to commemorate those who died. Many more would be seriously wounded, maimed or psychologi-cally damaged – for these men, re-adjusting to family life after the war would be a struggle.

96 CWGC grave

NOW THE COMMONWEALTH War Graves Commission, then the Imperial War Graves Commission, the CWGC has a history that dates back to the early part of the war, and to one man, Fabian Ware. At the outbreak of war, Ware was rejected for military service, but volunteered to command a mobile unit of the British Red Cross, which supplied motor ambulances to the battle front. With casualties mounting, it was obvious to Ware that the British had no effective means of maintaining a record of the battlefield graves of those soldiers who had died in action – and who had been buried by their comrades. With this important duty largely neglected, Ware set about collecting and marking the position of such burials, and in 1915 he was transferred to army control, leading the newly formed Graves Registration Commission (GRC). The GRC

Country of origin: United Kingdom (in France)

Date of construction: 1916 (replaced 1923)

Location: Gordon Dump Cemetery, Ovilliers, France

soon set about its task: by October 1915 it had recorded 31,000 graves; within eight months, 50,000. And with so many men posted as missing, and so many families wanting to see the graves of their loved ones while the war still raged, Fabian Ware's GRC also acted to send out photographs of graves in an attempt to alleviate some of the suffering – 12,000 had been dispatched by 1917.

But simply recording the graves was not sufficient for Ware. He became increasingly concerned that the graves so recorded should be tended and maintained. With the support of the Prince of Wales, the Imperial War Graves Commission (IWGC) came into being, established by Royal Charter on 21 May 1917. The IWGC faced tough choices: from its outset there would be no repatriation of the dead, there would be no distinction based on rank, and the grave markers would be uniform. There was opposition from some quarters, but the questions were finally settled: the IWGC would ensure that the sacrifice of the men and women who had served would be remembered in perpetuity.

At first, graves were marked with simple wooden crosses. That for Lance Corporal Kettlewell of the 10th Battalion West Riding regiment is typical. Killed in action on the Somme on 28 July 1916, his simple grave marker was placed in Gordon Dump Cemetery, near Ovillers on the Somme. Weather-beaten and worn, the cross was returned to his family when the IWGC commenced their long job of replacing the crosses with headstones. In France and Flanders this was a momentous task; replacing the crosses demanded 4,000 stones per week to be sent from Britain in 1923; just four years later, 500 cemeteries had been completed and 400,000 headstones were in place. Admired the world over as havens of peace and tranquillity, Commonwealth War Graves Commission cemeteries are maintained to the highest standards; fitting tribute to the men and women who lost their lives – and to the vision of one man, Sir Fabian Ware.

97 Prosthetic limb

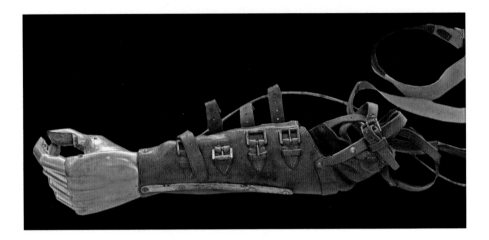

THE VAST MAJORITY of wounds suffered by soldiers in the Great War were caused by artillery fire – some estimates place the figure at 70 per cent. The scale of devastation wrought by the lethal shards of metal from artillery shells is staggering. Protection for the fragile body of the average soldier was limited; the very fact that the war had developed into parallel lines of trenches, with men garrisoned in dugouts that got progressively deeper, demonstrates the need to escape the destructive power of the artillery shell. In 1915–16, the arrival of steel helmets on the battlefield improved protection for the head, but in most cases, helmets were only proof against small fragments such as shrapnel balls and spent bullets. Both the Germans and the Italians produced heavy steel armour to protect their sentries, and some companies entered the marketplace, producing such items as the Dayfield Body Shield. But most cases, soldiers were simply caught unprotected in the 'storm of steel'.

The figures for the wounded are stark. For both the British and German armies, some 31 per cent of those who served were wounded, with the wounds created by the explosion of steel artillery shells being the most traumatic. Amputation was the only option, yet surviving

Country of origin:
France

Date of manufacture:
c. 1918

Location:
Historial de la Grande Guerre, Péronne, France

the operation – in the days before penicillin – depended on the soldier's fitness and a good deal of chance. With shrapnel and shell shards carrying the dirt of the trenches into the soldiers' bodies, the possibility of gangrene was high – particularly when men had to wait for an operation while still in the battle zone. In the British Army alone, some 41,000 men lost a limb: 69 per cent of them a single leg, 28 per cent an arm and the remainder double amputees. For the Germans, there were almost twice as many, some 74,620 amputees; of these, 21 per cent lost one or both arms and 32 per cent one or both legs, while the remaining 47 per cent had partial limb loss.

The provision of prosthetic limbs for disabled soldiers was a task that was not taken lightly. While newspapers and subscriptions to patriotic magazines such as *John Bull* provided insurance schemes for soldiers that would pay out £50 for the loss of a limb, £100 for two, this would be little consolation for men who might not be able to work. Limbs were expensive to make and fit; wooden ones were the cheapest, with lighter aluminium ones being preferred. Images from British war hospitals in 1916 show cheery soldiers trying out their new limbs while still in hospital. Our example is a sophisticated leather-and-aluminium creation that was intended to give functionality and was designed to mimic the missing hand as closely as possible. Yet, despite its sophistication, many men preferred simple hooks – perhaps because they were easier to handle or more robust.

Austrian poster promoting the employment of mutilated men.

Those mutilated were only too evident across Europe; the scar left by the war was deep and its effects lasting. The images of amputees begging in the streets of Europe in the harsh economic climate of the 1920s are enduring in their poignancy.

337

98 Inter-Allied Victory Medal

THE VICTORY MEDAL was one of the many that were issued to all Allied nations. British, French, Belgian, Italian and US versions are illustrated; there are many more. The idea of a common victory medal, similar in design, came about in 1916, when the Allies together discussed the possibilities of victory.

The details of the scheme were drawn up by a committee formed by the British war cabinet, chaired by Sir Frederick Ponsonby, with representatives from every relevant government department in order to consider the question. Their findings were clear:

> In wars in which European countries had been allied together, it has been the practice for the Allies to exchange a certain number of war medals, e.g., the Crimean War and the Boxer Rebellion. This was a comparatively easy matter when the forces were not so numerous, but in the present war, where armies are composed of millions, it

Country of origin: United Kingdom, France, Belgium, Italy, USA

Date of manufacture: 1919

Location: Private collection

would be practically impossible to distribute with any fairness a certain number of war medals from each ally. It would, moreover, be extremely unfair on the troops who had fought in theatres of war outside Europe, since they would probably be excluded from this distribution.

From these deliberations came the formulation of a policy that would help direct Allied thoughts. The Victory Medal was born from these discussions and came about from the meeting of the representatives of all the Allied powers in Paris in March 1919. At this meeting, it was agreed that an Allied war medal would be produced that would be called the 'Victory Medal'. The simple principle behind this was that it was the one name that the countries of the former Central Powers could not claim for a decoration. It was agreed that the medal should be 36mm in diameter and would bear an identical ribbon of watered silk that comprised two rainbows joined by red in the centre. As the committee wished to issue the medal as soon as possible, it was also decided that, with time short, each country should apply its own design. However, central to this should be an allegorical figure of Victory on the obverse, while on the reverse there would be the inscription: 'The Great War for Civilisation.' Victory was to have been represented as a female winged figure; this held true for all excepting Siam and Japan, which adopted figures relevant to their cultural traditions.

In the end, Belgium, Brazil, Cuba, the new nation of Czechoslovakia, France, Greece, Italy, Japan, the newly independent nation of Poland, Portugal, Romania, Siam, the Union of South Africa, the United Kingdom and its Empire and the United States all issued their own medals. The greatest number of medals issued was by Britain: some 6,334,522 medals to men and women from across the empire (though South Africa issued its own, bilingual, version). The United States (2.5 million) and France and Italy (both 2 million) come next, with the other nations issuing the medals in the thousands. An upper estimate of awarded medals might be some 14.6 million.

99 *Borne de la Terre Sacrée*

THE IDEA THAT the soil of France was sacred dates back centuries. With two German invasions within fifty years – during the Franco-Prussian War in 1870 and the Great War in 1914 – France had suffered the marching boots of enemy soldiers all too often.

For one man, the sculptor Gaston Deblaize, the very soil of the battlefields of France, where the *poilus* had lived and died in the defence of their country, had great significance. Deblaize was a former soldier and served for forty months at the front with the 356th Regiment of Infantry. He served at Verdun, in the *Tunnel des Tavannes*, and was awarded both the *Médaille Militaire* and *Croix de Guerre* for his bravery. Gaston as an artist was inspired by the earth itself and by the simplicity of the soil, by the wheat that grew in the rich arable lands of France and by the comradeship of his friends. Drawing on these concepts, Deblaize developed the idea of a ceramic container that would contain the sacred soil

Country of origin: France

Date of manufacture: *c.* 1927

Location: Private collection

taken from the battlefield at Verdun, acting as a monument to his dead comrades. With that ground so heavily fought over, these works had great significance.

The example illustrated is typical. It is based on the way-marker stones (*'borne'*) that Deblaize happened across during his years of marching along the roads of France as a soldier. It is topped with the Adrian helmet, that symbol of the *poilu*; again, this reflected times when the artist had placed his own helmet on the wayside markers. Marked with the dates 1914 and 1918, it carries the immortal name 'Verdun', with the phrase *'Cette borne renferme une parcelle de terre sacrée de Verdun'* (This marker contains a piece of the sacred ground of Verdun). The concept grew and the markers sold: 'In memory of the dead of the Great War – of the Mutilated – of Veterans' under the patronage of *l'Association des Gueules Cassées* (the Association of 'Broken Faces'), remembering those men who had been horribly disfigured by the brutality of the Great War. The first to be made was presented to the president of the republic; it contained soil from the 'trench of the bayonets' from Verdun – a trench that contained the bodies of men permanently entombed by a collapse.

Symbolic of the link between the dead, the mutilated and the earth of France, the project was expanded to other parts of the battlefront: to Alsace, Champagne, the Somme and Yser. Mindful of the sacrifice of the soldiers for the sacred soil of France, Gaston Deblaize went on to extend his project to the construction of seven large-scale *'bornes'*, each containing ceramic containers of the soil of the battlefields. And at each harvest time, the wheat ripened, it is laid at the foot of each one, a remembrance of the capability of the land for rebirth.

IOO
Menin Gate

THERE ARE MANY memorials to the dead. In London, the Cenotaph is the national place of mourning, the impressive stone 'empty tomb' that sits in Whitehall. Raised as a temporary structure for Armistice Day 1919, it was reconstructed in stone for the same day in 1920 and has been the focal point for British mourning ever since, matched by equivalent structures across the British Commonwealth. In France, national commemoration is focused at the Arc de Triomphe, where from 1920 was interred the Unknown Soldier: '*Ici repose un soldat Français mort pour la Patrie 1914–1918*'. Across Britain, France and the other Allied nations, local memorials sprang up that sought to remember the sacrifice of their men and women in war. In Germany, memorialisation was more difficult. While some local memorials did spring up, the last large national monuments were those constructed in the late nineteenth century, particularly the *Kyffhäuserdenkmal* in Thuringia that commemorates the reign of Kaiser Wilhelm I. With no large monuments constructed in the aftermath of the Great War, German veterans sought out these relics of their imperial past as a point of meaning.

On the battlefields of France and Flanders, the war cemeteries remained the ultimate memorial to the 'lost generation'. For France and Germany, smaller

Country of origin: United Kingdom (in Belgium)

Date of construction: 1927

Location: Ypres (Menin Gate) Memorial, Ieper, Belgium

cemeteries were combined to make visually impressive statements of loss; for France, there was the need to cleanse the soil and return it to agriculture. Here, the use of ossuaries and huge 'national cemeteries' was the norm. For the Germans, concentration of their soldiers' graves into large cemeteries was required by their former enemies, there was no debate. For the British, it was different again. Small battlefield cemeteries, immaculately kept, dot the landscape and permit the reconstruction of battle lines on the ground; larger cemeteries were formed to free the soil for cultivation but also to take the bodies of those men recovered from the battlefields after the war.

The Menin Gate is one of many memorials on the Western Front that commemorate the missing, those men who fell and who have no known grave. Designed by Sir Reginald Blomfield, it took four years to build and was constructed on the site of one of the gates in the Vauban fortifications that surround the city of Ypres – and which, in part, protected it during the war. Through the gate passed the British armies on their way to the front, along the straight road that gradually rises from the clay plain of Flanders to the low hills that surround the city. The gate lists the names of 54,389 men of the British and Commonwealth armies who fell in the Ypres Salient during the war. There are other monuments of similar scale in France: the Notre Dame de Lorette, the Douaumont Ossuary and the monumental Thiepval Memorial on the Somme. But there is one thing that makes this memorial unique: here, on every night since its inauguration (excepting the years of Nazi occupation), buglers from the city's fire brigade sound the last post in memory of the soldiers who died in the war – 'At the going down of the sun, and in the morning, we will remember them.'

Acknowledgements

A BOOK OF this scale requires the support of a great deal of people, all of whom have given their time and advice freely. Very many people assisted me by giving me their views on what should be included in my 100 object list. Jo de Vries at The History Press provided the original inspiration for this project. My close friend Chris Foster has been a constant support and has helped me craft the images contained within. Rob Schaefer, an unstinting purveyor of historical wisdom, materially enhanced my views of Imperial Germany, while Paul Reed, generous to a tee, supplied images and advice, as did Alex Churchill, taking time out of her writing schedule. My understanding of the naval war has been greatly enhanced by calm advice provided by Phil Weir, and Commander John Drummond is thanked for his images of HMS *Vindictive*. I am grateful to the many people who have provided images or have allowed me to photograph objects, particularly Richard Archer, Steve Britton, Paul Laidlaw, Laurie Milner and Ted Peacock; special mention must be given to Howard Williamson for access to his superb collection of period weapons and militaria. The Australian War Memorial kindly supplied an image of their Gallipoli trench sign. The support and belief of Julie and James provides the platform for all my endeavours.

Index

THE CLASSIC LIBRARY
OF THE FIRST WORLD WAR

BENEATH FLANDERS FIELDS
THE TUNNELLERS' WAR 1914-18

PETER BARTON, PETER DOYLE and JOHAN VANDEWALLE

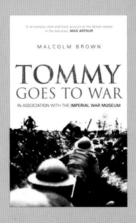

'A remarkably vivid and frank account of the British soldier in the trenches' MAX ARTHUR

MALCOLM BROWN

TOMMY GOES TO WAR
IN ASSOCIATION WITH THE IMPERIAL WAR MUSEUM

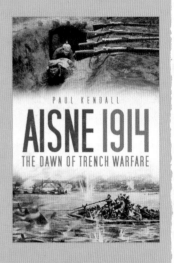

PAUL KENDALL

AISNE 1914
THE DAWN OF TRENCH WARFARE

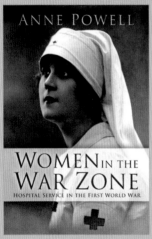

ANNE POWELL

WOMEN IN THE WAR ZONE
HOSPITAL SERVICE IN THE FIRST WORLD WAR

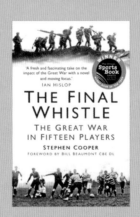

'A fresh and fascinating take on the impact of the Great War with a novel and moving focus.' IAN HISLOP

THE FINAL WHISTLE
THE GREAT WAR IN FIFTEEN PLAYERS
STEPHEN COOPER
FOREWORD BY BILL BEAUMONT CBE DL

MUD, BLOOD AND BULLETS
MEMOIRS OF A MACHINE GUNNER ON THE WESTERN FRONT

EDWARD ROWBOTHAM
EDITED BY JANET TUCKER

To explore these and all our commemorative titles visit:
www.thehistorypress.co.uk

The History Press